PETERSEN'S BASIC CARBURETION AND FUEL SYSTEMS NO.6

INTRODUCTION

COVER PHOTOGRAPHY: PAT BROLLIER

While the total fuel system of the modern automobile is a very complex integration of sophisticated components, its individual parts and pieces are not as formidable as one might think. Open the hood of a late-model automobile and take a look at what Detroit has nightmarishly fashioned: lines, hoses, tubes, wires, rods and all manner of linkages, valves and springs face us. Most, in one way or another, lead to or from the carburetor, and most of them have something to do with air pollution control. Taken one piece at a time, though, all that "mysterious" plumbing is there for a common cause—to help us propel ourselves about in a clean-air environment.

For it is the automobile's induction system that mixes air and fuel in the proper proportions, resulting in self-propulsion with as few harmful tailpipe emissions as possible. The subject of this book, **Basic Carburetion & Fuel Systems No. 6,** is the real "smog" culprit. It is the carburetor and the rest of the fuel system that are giving the bureaucrats fits and causing much midnight oil to be burned in the automakers' engineering labs. Too, it is the fuel system that is using up much of our gasoline supplies and driving crude oil prices ever higher.

Yet for all the hue and cry over fuel consumption, smog and the rest of it, the fuel system is really a simple thing. If you take each link in the chain between the fuel tank and the exhaust pipe, analyze it, understand where it fits into the scheme of things and wind up with a broad perspective on the fuel system overall, then you'll know why a gallon or so of liquid poured into one end of your car can drive that car a good many miles. Each part of the total chain is, by itself, really elementary. Our readers, having grasped these simplified functions, will then be undismayed when they probe their car's induction system components in a self-help quest for better performance, improved fuel economy and a trouble-free auto that will behave as it did when new.

But whether you're a tinkerer, a lover of basic theories, an average car owner who doesn't care a thing about his car as long as it runs, an ecologist intent on keeping our air clean or just a car buff, there's something on these pages to interest and perhaps educate you.

Flip on back as we explore the "mysteries" of the carburetion and fuel systems—and find that they're not so mysterious after all.

SPENCE MURRAY

PETERSEN PUBLISHING COMPANY

R.E. PETERSEN/Chairman of the Board; **F.R. WAINGROW**/President; **ROBERT E. BROWN**/Sr. Vice President, Publisher; **DICK DAY**/Sr. Vice President; **JIM P. WALSH**/Sr. Vice President, National Advertising Director; **ROBERT MacLEOD**/Vice President, Publisher; **THOMAS J. SIATOS**/Vice President, Group Publisher; **PHILIP E. TRIMBACH**/Vice President, Financial Administration; **WILLIAM PORTER**/Vice President, Circulation Director; **JAMES J. KRENEK**/Vice President, Manufacturing; **LEO D. LaREW**/Treasurer; **DICK WATSON**/Controller; **LOU ABBOTT**/Director, Production; **JOHN CARRINGTON**/Director, Book Sales and Marketing; **MARIA COX**/Director, Data Processing; **BOB D'OLIVO**/Director, Photography; **NIGEL P. HEATON**/Director, Circulation Marketing and Administration; **AL ISAACS**/Director, Corporate Art; **CAROL JOHNSON**/Director, Advertising Administration; **DON McGLATHERY**/Director, Advertising Research; **JACK THOMPSON**/Assistant Director, Circulation; **VERN BALL**/Director, Fulfillment Services

PETERSEN AUTOMOTIVE BOOKS

LEE KELLEY/Editorial Director
SPENCE MURRAY/Automotive Editor
DAVID COHEN/Managing Editor
SUSIE VOLKMANN/Art Director
LINNEA HUNT-STEWART/Copy Editor
FERN CASON/Editorial Coordinator

BASIC CARBURETION & FUEL SYSTEMS No. 6

**Library of Congress Catalog Card No. 68-6315
ISBN 0-8227-5013-9**

CARBURETION & FUEL SYSTEMS

CONTENTS

THE EXHAUST EMISSIONS STORY

BY JIM McFARLAND

Aside from the fact that air quality is important to us all, it is clear that the contributions of the automobile to this problem have had some pretty strong political overtones during the last few years. Like almost anything else which involves substantial amounts of money, the design, manufacture, marketing and use of contemporary automobile engines *and parts* have become the object of much conversation, worry, spending and legislative operations. Today the owner of a new vehicle is faced with the reality of much of the technology that has been changed to meet air quality standards that were set down years ago—technology that is constantly subject to change. Of these changes, overall vehicle drivability and fuel economy are probably two of the more significant areas of car owner concern. It is no secret that both of these have suffered with the advent of contemporary emission controls.

This is a book about carburetion (and related areas). But since the owner of any street-driven vehicle today is subject to state and/or federal exhaust emission standards, we felt it would be wise to discuss some of the background of what has happened and is continuing to happen to automobile engines (performance-oriented or otherwise) in terms of the induction system.

This background includes how performance and emissions are related (if they are), what the current standards mean, what the street vehicle enthusiast can expect to face now and during the next few years in terms of available induction system parts and enforced roadside emission tests, where the specialty equipment industry stands today relative to meeting "smog" legislation and what, if any, future can be expected for those of us who enjoy tinkering with engines in general and induction systems in particular.

This portion of the book is intended to be a brief introduction to the subject of exhaust emissions and both how and why the performance engine enthusiast can relate to the business of air quality, energy resources and "his car." It is no longer possible to say, "That emissions stuff just goes on out there in California, where they have all that smog." California's stiff standards will soon spread to the nation as a whole. Also, air quality is critical worldwide now, and *any* contribution to the degradation of the atmosphere is worth concern, even though the automobile may not contribute as much as those who do not want to investigate the amount of industrial air pollution would lead us to believe.

THE ELEMENTS OF CONCERN

Today, new vehicles come equipped with a variety of devices designed to keep exhaust emissions low. Those combustion elements thought to be worthy of minimum standards are unburned hydrocarbons (HC), carbon monoxide (CO)

and oxides of nitrogen (NOx). These are the result of hydrogen, oxygen, nitrogen and carbon that have passed into an engine through the mixing of gasoline and air and have been subjected to combustion under pressure. Because the piston engine as we know it today is relatively inefficient (it has low thermal efficiency), certain elements are present in the residue from combustion (exhaust gas) . . . which leads us right back to the HC, CO and NOx for which there is air quality concern.

Piston engines today (and this seems to include the rotary engine, too) do not promote complete oxidation of gasoline (hydrocarbon fuels). By oxidation we mean the combination of some element with oxygen. For example, the incomplete oxidation of carbon to carbon dioxide (CO_2) produces carbon monoxide (CO). This happens during normal combustion engine operation. Also, a certain amount of unburned hydrocarbon (HC) is produced; more results from relatively low thermal efficiency in the engine. And finally, since nitrogen is part of the air taken into an engine prior to combustion, some nitric oxide is produced during combustion, as a result of the heat and pressure of combustion.

At the risk of oversimplification, these by-products combine to form the elements of HC, CO and NOx present in a given exhaust gas sample. Exactly *how much* of these elements will show up at the tailpipe requires a little more explanation, but the point here is that we can assume that HC, CO and NOx will be produced from any commercially available internal combustion engine using hydrocarbon fuel (gasoline). Here is a little discussion and some examples just so you can see how the carbure-

tor and overall induction system fit into the scheme of things.

INDUCTION SYSTEM VS. EXHAUST EMISSIONS

Let's consider a sample engine. Suppose we have a conventional V-8 piston engine fitted with O.E.M. parts as produced in the early 1960's. We'll build a few examples around this package and then shift our attention to what sort of engines may be in production today, with emphasis on the induction system and what may lie ahead.

At the carburetor, air is mixed with incoming fuel. In the past, we were evidently not as concerned with air quality as we are today, so engine efficiency was important largely in terms of drivability or fuel economy. As a result, the mixing of air and fuel

was very forgiving. If some of the fuel particles were substantially larger than others, it didn't seem to be all that important. Furthermore, engines were permitted to run slightly on the rich side, both to help parts life and to prevent stumbling.

There is a theoretical ideal balance between air and fuel (air/fuel ratio) of about 14.7:1. This is called the stoichiometric mixture. Carburetors were calibrated somewhat richer than this in the idle circuits to avoid stumbling and cover up for any flaws in the design of the intake manifold. However, since it is this idle circuit of a carburetor on which much of today's emissions testing is done, carburetor manufacturers can no longer afford to run very much richer than the stoichiometric mixture in idle calibration.

Also, before emissions concern

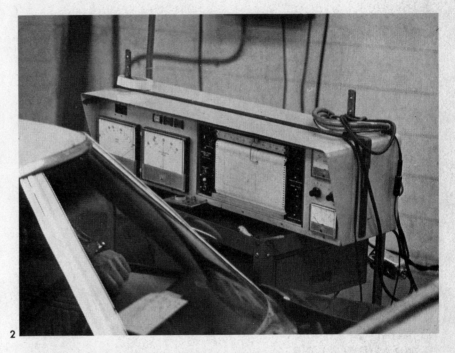

2

3

1. For both 7-mode and California/Federal Constant Volume Sampling (CVS) tests, a specific driving cycle is required. This cycle is designed to be representative of the driving patterns that an average-use vehicle would see: acceleration, deceleration, idle and cruising conditions.

2. With the vehicle loaded against the rolls of a chassis dynamometer, the operator must make the strip chart pen follow the line set down on the chart. Since this chart is moving at a constant rate, the various conditions of acceleration idle, deceleration, and cruising can be performed and repeated from test to test.

3. Typical bank of exhaust emission sampling equipment includes means for reading hydrocarbons (HC), carbon monoxide (CO), oxides of nitrogen (NOx), carbon dioxide (CO_2) and related combustion components. Means for calibration of each gas sampling/measuring circuit are built into the console. Calibration is made against known concentrations of "shelf" gas.

EMISSIONS STORY

reached the point it has today, intake manifold design was not so critical. Low- and mid-range throttle response was important to everyday passenger car operation, so two-plane manifolds were (and are) used at the O.E.M. level. Very little engineering time was devoted to the perfection of intake manifolding that would improve cylinder-to-cylinder mixture distribution and maintain acceptable throttle response.

Early 1960's engines also deviated little, if any, from camshaft design that incorporated lobe displacement angles of 110-112° and relatively short overlap periods. The high-lap, tight-displacement-angle camshafting was left to the specialty equipment industry, except for a periodic urge on the part of certain O.E.M. factions to ''go racing'' and produce high-performance cams for factory engines.

Along these same lines, it does not appear that much consideration was given to the combustion-surface-to-combustion-volume relationship in the pre-emission engines. This is not a criticism of O.E.M. engineering. Only in recent years have those areas that relate to the formation of HC, CO and NOx begun to be tickled at the O.E.M. engineering level. And the fact that the production of HC, CO, and NOx relate directly to combustion efficiency (vehicle performance and fuel economy) makes you wonder if it is not a matter of economics that is generating the rate at which O.E.M. emissions reduction technology is progressing. But we were discussing the matter of combustion surface to combustion volume, weren't we?

If considerable surface area is involved in combustion (combustion surface volume), there is more area on which fuel particles separated from the air/fuel mixture can land and cause cooling of the remaining air/fuel mixture. This reduces the amount of air and fuel involved in combustion. Stated another way, you could say that separated fuel particles do not burn as easily as those suspended in the mixture. This separation tends to cool the combustion flame and increase hydrocarbon formation through incomplete oxidation (burning). As a result, HC increases at the tailpipe.

If you are a proponent of the rotary engine, you might want to give this subject of combustion surface to combustion volume ratio a little thought. The rotary engine has a very high ratio of combustion surface to combustion volume.

In the main, that is the way pre-emission engines were designed. Such things as close cylinder-to-cylin-

der mixture distribution, lean idle mixture circuitry, low compression ratios, vacuum spark disconnects, air reactor pumps and exhaust gas aftertreatment were not matters of concern. As a result, the level of sophistication required in engine package development was completely different from current practice, despite the fact that combustion and thermal efficiency were involved then as they are now in the reduction of exhaust emissions.

Today induction system design is far more demanding. Emission tests have been devised that simulate the

everyday use of a passenger car, while the car is situated on a chassis dynamometer. In most cases, vehicle speed is never greater than 45-50 mph during the course of everyday driving (expressway driving notwithstanding), and with the rear gear ratios in today's cars, this means that engine speed is not likely to exceed 2600-3800 rpm. With the exception of those times when the car is accelerated quickly enough to bring the accelerator pump circuit into play, the engine is operating off the carburetor idle circuit.

Since this is the range in which the emissions tests are run, why not calibrate the carburetor lean enough to be capable of meeting the required levels of HC, CO and NOx? Well, to a certain extent, this is what was initially done. The problem is that when the mixture ratio gets leaner, cylinder-to-cylinder mixture distribution becomes increasingly sensitive, and if there is a problem in the intake manifold (basic distribution) or ignition system that causes an excessively lean condition, misfiring results and raw fuel passes right through the engine, increasing the HC level. In addition, engine efficiency (fuel economy, etc.) is reduced. A too-lean engine also produces less power, and normally the vehicle operator will drive "deeper into the carburetor" to try to regain the lost power—which further passes raw fuel through the engine, which adds more HC to the atmosphere, which lives in the house that Jack built.

What it all seems to boil down to is this: Automakers are faced with meeting certification levels of HC, CO and NOx. To do this, several changes or add-on parts have been devised to hold emissions to a minimum.

"Clean Air" carburetors were introduced; these did not have idle mixture adjustment screws that could upset a basically lean idle circuit cali-

1. Within the specialty equipment industry, research is going on constantly, with many of the companies producing performance aftermarket replacement parts. Here are Edelbrock's Murray Jensen and Holley Carburetor's Bud Elliott clamping on an experimental EGR (Exhaust Gas Recirculation) prototype Tarantula for '73 CVS test.

2. Inertially loaded vehicle (on chassis dynamometer) provides road load conditions for exhaust emissions testing. Amount of preload set into dyno depends upon vehicle weight. Some sort of load conditions are required for all but no-load idle emissions testing.

3. One of several types of emissions testing equipment (of low retail price) now on the market is manufactured by Hawk/Cal Custom. This unit can be plugged into tailpipe and provides both CO (carbon monoxide) and A/F ratios.

4. Simplicity of Hawk unit makes it suitable for use by almost any auto enthusiast. Additional scale is provided for use on engines using LP (liquefied petroleum) gas. Power supply is 12-volt battery, making it possible to use this instrument onboard while driving. Mixture conditions at idle are different from those indicated when car is under way. To best determine on-the-road mixture conditions, meter should be installed in car. Once this is done, several other states of engine tune can be determined (secondary throttle tip-in, decel mixture ratio, cruising ratio and cylinder-to-cylinder mixture status) if you plumb the exhaust system to allow sample gathering at each exhaust port.

EMISSIONS STORY

bration as supplied by the car manufacturer. Idle mixture screws now come with adjustment limit stops to prevent enrichment outside the range specified by the manufacturer. PCV's (Positive Crankcase Vents) were installed to route combustion residue and some vaporized oil back into the induction system on a sort of recycling basis. Air reactor pumps and plumbing were installed to put fresh air into the exhaust gas (at the exhaust port) to further oxidize any HC and CO present after combustion.

Other emissions features, such as slightly retarded spark (also part of the original Chrysler Clean Air Package) and the Ford Thermactor system (a counterpart to the GM air reactor system), were added along the way to help reduce HC and CO.

More recently, equipment was added to return a portion of the exhaust gas directly into the intake manifold, after the air and fuel are mixed but before entry into the combustion chamber. This feature was intended to reduce the level of NOx by a dilution of the incoming air and fuel. This dilution decreases the combustion properties of the fresh air and fuel, causing a cooler burning process and a subsequent reduction in NOx. To a certain extent, NOx formation is a function of heat: more heat, more NOx; less heat, less NOx.

At any rate, this EGR (Exhaust Gas Recirculation) calls for a slight calibration change in the carburetor. If you decide to disconnect the EGR unit (a violation of the law, we might add), mixture enrichment will effectively change toward rich and you will alter the vehicle's emission characteristics. Let us say now that we strongly urge you (as does the emissions committee of the Special Equipment Manufacturers Association) not to tamper with any element of a stock emissions package. As explained below, performance, drivability and fuel economy improvements are all available while maintaining emissions levels well within the law. However, if you tamper with the clean air pieces, these gains may or may not be achievable. Leave the stuff alone; it's there for a reason.

CONTEMPORARY INDUCTION SYSTEM DESIGN

For several years, the two-plane intake manifold has been the choice of Detroit engine designers. This concept calls for two separate air chambers that connect the inlet ports of an engine. Ordinarily, it is the V-type engine that lends itself to this manifold design, although it is theoretically possible to split the manifolding for inline engines into two or more air chambers (or planes). The second most common manifold design is the single-plane design (an air chamber with branches connecting all inlet ports). With the introduction of the so-called spread-bore carburetor (Rochester Quadrajet, Carter Thermo-Quad or Holley spread bore) with its high area ratio of primary to secondary throttle bores, the function of intake manifolding and the behavior of these types of 4-bbl. carburetors on both single- and two-plane manifolds present some problems. Since the basic mixture distribution characteristics of an intake manifold have a major effect on carburetor flow size and fuel calibration, we'll talk a little about inlet manifolds.

We mentioned the two-plane mani-

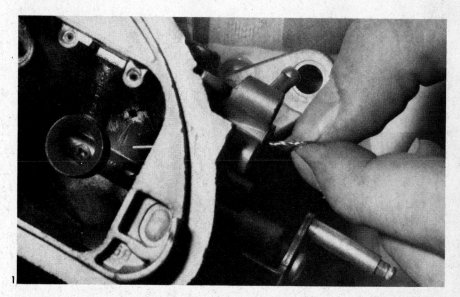

fold first. Consider it as two separate air chambers connecting the throats of a 4-bbl. carburetor with the eight inlet ports of a V-8 engine. Suppose the firing order of a given engine is 1-8-4-3-6-5-7-2. If you join every other cylinder in the order (1-4-6-7) into one of the two air chambers and the remaining four cylinders (8-3-5-2) into the other chamber, you can see that in proper firing order, each successive cylinder will take its air/fuel mixture from first one air chamber and then the other. This alternation between the two chambers (planes) is the conventional 180° firing order you've probably heard about. Two-plane manifolds are characterized by relatively sharp throttle response, since there is smaller volume of air mass to be excited during each inlet

period, and the possibility of poor mixture distribution if sufficient flow bench and engine dynamometer work was not performed in the initial design stages of the manifold. Two-plane manifolds can be made to distribute mixture satisfactorily, but it requires some time and expertise.

1. Secondary throttle tip-in point (or actuation of end carburetors in 3x2 multiple-carb package) can be governed by removal of vacuum diaphragm unit and plugging of idle kill-bleed hole (passage shown). You can use small lead shot for this. With this passage blocked, secondary tip-in is immediate. Then by inserting secondary diaphragm spring stiffer than stock, you have better control of when you want this part of the carburetor (or carburetion package) to operate. Reduction of spring tension (old method for tip-in point changes) is limited in amount of control provided.

2. VW carburetion possibilities today are varied and highly specialized. Use of Weber or Weber copy carburetor with IR (individual runner) manifolding is more raceworthy than suited for the street. Packages like these are available from such manufacturers as SCAT and similar companies specializing in VW's.

3. Here's a view of a Holley 4-bbl. carburetor metering block containing jets (other side) and vital passages. The following are important to functioning of this type of carburetor and should help locate or label spots to work on . . . or avoid: 1) power valve, 2) idle feed restriction that regulates the amount of idle mixture fuel, 3) passageway for transfer of accelerator pump fuel to discharge nozzles, 4) main fuel system wells (and bleeds) that supply air for mixing and delivery to booster venturi and 5) idle mixture adjustment screw.

4. This is the mating surface for the main-body side of the metering block. Passages shown include 1) idle air bleed hole (notice that these openings repeat on the opposite side of the carburetor), 2) main air bleed hole, 3) curb idle discharge, 4) passage to discharge nozzle, 5) accelerator pump discharge passage, 6) power valve vacuum chamber and 7) passage to the idle transfer slot located in the carburetor throttle flange base just below the throttle plates.

From the standpoint of carburetor size selection for two-plane manifolds, it is often possible to use units of higher flow capacity than for single-plane designs. The two-plane tends to move the mixture more rapidly at intermediate engine speeds than the single-plane design.

Single-plane manifolds are one-chamber units with manifold runners (branches) connecting the inlet ports of the engine to a common volume below the carburetor. In this design, airflow is generally slower at low and middle engine rpm. This means a reduction in mixture turbulence and the need to increase accelerator pump output to improve full-throttle response. However, equality of mixture distribution from cylinder to cylinder can be better accomplished with this design. This evenness is of prime importance to overall exhaust emission levels, since multi-cylinder engines should be treated as a collection of single-cylinder engines that ideally operate at peak thermal and combustion efficiency on an individual basis.

As for carburetor type (1-bbl., 2-bbl., 4-bbl., spread-bore, etc.), both the two-plane and single-plane manifolds have certain characteristics worth mentioning. For example, let's consider the spread-bore carburetor and how it performs on a two-plane manifold. At wide-open throttle, this carburetor displays two different pressure differentials (drops), one across the small primary throats and a second across the larger secondary throats. On a two-plane manifold, one side (one primary and one secondary) of the spread-bore feeds one of the air chambers and the other side of the carburetor feeds the other air chamber. For all practical purposes, to the manifold this 4-bbl. spread-bore carburetor is a 2-bbl.

On the other hand, if we put the same spread-bore carburetor on a single-plane manifold at wide-open throttle, the air chamber just below

the carburetor experiences two substantially different flow pressure conditions, one across the primary and a second across the secondary.

One other significant intake manifold feature is reversion (reverse pressure toward the carburetor). This condition is a result of scavenging or backflow through the cylinder and into the intake manifold during the valve overlap period. (Overlap is the time when the inlet valve is just opening and the exhaust valve has almost shut.) Some energy is also released toward the carburetor at the time the intake valve shuts, immediately following cylinder filling, but the overlap flow situation seems to be of particular significance.

In two-plane manifolds, this pulsing has a chance to dissipate itself in one air chamber while the other air chamber is supplying air/fuel mixture to another cylinder. Single-plane manifolds do not offer this opportunity. Instead, the reversion energy has a chance to disrupt clean inlet flow during cylinder filling. Some intake manifold manufacturers are beginning to contain this unwanted pressure condition, but it remains one of the design headaches of single-plane manifolds. You may be familiar with this situation under the name of carburetor fuel "standoff."

But regardless of the manifold type now supplied at the O.E.M. level or on the aftermarket, exhaust emissions requirements are changing the nature of traditional designs. For example, performance equipment manifold designers have recently said that the single-plane concept would be one of the better ways to achieve uniform cylinder-to-cylinder mixture distribution and help lower emission levels. These same people have repeatedly proved that this notion was fact. Fuel economy gains and performance benefits have also been shown. Now, it seems, there will be a gradual shift at the O.E.M. level toward single-

EMISSIONS STORY

plane manifolding for new cars, particularly in the interest of improving emission levels.

Manifold heat has also come into play in emissions manifolding. An SAE (Society of Automotive Engineers) paper of a few years ago dealt with a grille-like device placed in the floor of the plenum chamber of a single-plane manifold for the purpose of supplying early exhaust heat to the manifold for quicker evaporization of fuel. The grille also helped maintain the suspension of the fuel in air after being mixed by the carburetor. It's a matter of trying to aid fuel mixing during cold-start engine conditions, when fuel separation within the manifold can lead to high HC and CO levels at the tailpipe through improper carbon and oxygen oxidation.

Carburetors (thought we'd never mention 'em again, right?) have also been undergoing some changes in the last few years. One of the most recognizable changes has been the use of small primary and large secondary throttle areas. Small primaries allow high mixture velocity, with accompanying quick throttle response, air/fuel homogeneity, etc., and low- to mid-rpm drivability of a vehicle, while the large secondary openings permit good air/fuel flow at high rpm, when the mixture demand increases. Also, most spread-bore carburetors are fitted with air valve secondary throttle functions; that is, the secondary opens on demand or as a result of manifold vacuum. This further enhances the rate at which air and fuel can enter the engine. At least in theory, spread-bore carburetors are an ideal way to carburete a piston engine.

Viewing what may happen to the conventional carburetor during the next few years, we might expect to see some rather significant changes. Ford has already begun using a variable-venturi carburetor, starting on some '77 models. (See page 68.) This carburetor offers such features as no mechanical throttle opening at all. Air and fuel are mixed and delivered solely on the basis of engine rpm, manifold vacuum, etc. We might see something in the mixing valve category that does a better job of atomizing fuel prior to air mixing. We include a description of one such system for your examination in this story.

First of all, it appears now that conventional carburetors are not capable of atomizing liquid fuel into particles of 7-12 micron size, nor can they keep the particle sizes relatively uniform. Some fuel droplets may be in the 14-18 micron range, for exam-

ple, and some might be down around 12. Theory (and some pretty good backup data) suggests that these larger fuel particles create a comparatively rich condition in their boundary layers. So for all practical purposes, these fuel droplets act rich. The smaller particles show leaner boundary layer ratios and give an overall leaner appearance. When these different-sized droplets are mixed with air and burned, it seems there is a tendency for the larger droplets to be too rich for combustion. They pass right out the tailpipe and register as high HC levels. At the risk of oversimplification, we might say that combustion is supported by the smaller, leaner fuel particles, while the larger ones become exempt from combustion.

If we could devise a method of liquid fuel atomization that provided both smaller-than-carburetor-mixed particles and uniform particle sizes throughout a given air/fuel blend just before combustion, we would stand a better chance of burning a higher percentage of fuel. As it turns out, the Autotronics system approaches this ideal through the use of sonics and an attendant system designed to measure airflow and meter fuel for whatever air/fuel ratio is preset in the included computer unit.

What we come away with is both profound and simple: If liquid fuel can be broken down into small enough particles of relatively uniform size throughout a given air/fuel mixture, a high percentage of mixture will burn

and leave less in the exhaust system as a contribution to air contamination. If you're wondering whether automakers are still investigating systems of this sort, we can tell you that they are—thoroughly.

Sonic systems have great potential for meeting future emission and fuel economy requirements. Why? Because in the classical relationship of HC, CO and NOx, NOx levels increase (while HC and CO decrease) as you increase mixture leanness beyond stoichiometric. Now, as leanness increases, there comes a point at which NOx begins to decrease, so that all three pollutants begin to diminish. In terms of air/fuel ratio, this begins to happen somewhere around 17:1 to 19:1. Admittedly, you cannot expect the same sort of performance (acceleration, drivability, etc.) characteristics from air/fuel ratios on the order of 19:1 that you could of 12:1. With small, uniform-size fuel particles (among other engine design features), however, these ratios are providing acceptable performance, higher-than-present fuel economy and substantially reduced exhaust emission levels.

CURRENT TEST PROCEDURES

At the O.E.M. level, current tests are of the Constant Volume Sampling (CVS) variety. For government certification of new vehicles, these are cold-start tests and require the 18-cycle, 22-minute Environmental Protection Agency (EPA) driving cycle on

a preloaded chassis dynamometer. During the test, exhaust gas samples are taken into suspended bags. Then measurements of the concentrations of HC, CO and NOx (among other elements sampled) are made. This test is supposed to simulate an average 7.5-mile trip in a vehicle that has not been run for a period of about 12 hours.

Another test, the 7-mode cycle, was used to certify cars for California sale until 1972, at which time it was replaced by the EPA test. The 7-mode cycle pattern was concerned with seven different driving conditions: 1) idle mode for 20 secs., 2) 0-30 mph acceleration in 14 secs., 3) 30-mph constant speed for 15 secs., 4) 30-15 mph deceleration in 11 secs., 5) 15-mph cruise for 15 secs., 6) 15-30 mph acceleration in 29 secs. and 7) 50-0 mph deceleration (the total 7-mode cycle time = 137 secs.). This test could be performed using only the idle circuit of the carburetor. This was one reason why lean idle misfiring, rough idle and off-idle stumble were features of many new cars during the late '60's and early '70's. Manufacturers were working to meet emission levels with that portion of the carburetor that was involved. Furthermore, since these were cold-soak tests, it became important as to how efficiently carburetor chokes came off during engine warm-up. Long delay or sticking chokes contributed to high levels of HC at the tailpipe.

Yet another test is the Clayton "Key Mode" test. Designed and perfected by the Clayton Chassis Dynamometer Co., this sequence involves samples taken during "key" modes of engine operation: low cruise, high cruise and idle. Although Clayton personnel have advanced this test approach to include other engine conditions, they still believe this to be an economical and quick method for determining basic emission levels (including state of engine tune).

Finally, we come to the method by which most in-service vehicles are now being tested: the no-load idle test for HC and CO levels. This is the so-called "sniffer" test, in which a probe is placed in the tailpipe of a vehicle whose engine is at idle and a CO and HC reading is taken. It's quick, simple, repeatable, requires instrumentation of relatively inexpensive

1. You are looking at a system that may revolutionize automotive engine induction design. This package consists of an air inlet point 1) at which intake air is "straightened" and measured, a mixing chamber 2) where a sonic discharge nozzle admits fuel into the airstream, a fuel pump 3) that meters fuel volume based on the amount of air sensed at the inlet point 1) and a "brain box" 4) that figures out how other engine condition variables affect what is needed for fuel volume to meet a preselected air/fuel ratio.

2. Air travels into the cylindrical mixing chamber on a tangent and swirls into the manifold plenum chamber by way of an exit in the floor of the mixing chamber. One captivating feature of the system shown (a laboratory-use model for fuel emissions study) is that you can look into the mixing chamber and see what you've always wondered about in an intake manifold (mixing, liquid separation, reversion pulsing, etc.).

3. With the mixing chamber lid removed, you get a look at the sonic device that sticks down inside the chamber. Fuel is released out of this tube after being disturbed (and therefore broken down into less than 10-micron particle sizes) by high-frequency energy. Decomposition of fuel by this method generates a veritable "cloud" of fuel in the plenum chamber. By reducing fuel particles to such small sizes and establishing relatively uniform particle size throughout the air/fuel mix, combustion efficiency increases, more of the available fuel is burned, emission levels are reduced and fuel economy increases. Think about it.

4. Brain box used in Autotronics system permits setting of desired air/fuel ratio before engine is started . . . or after it is running! Optimum power or lowest emission levels can be achieved with simple setting. One interesting feature of this system is that it permits use of leaded fuels and relatively high compression ratios (above 10:1) while delivering fuel economy above 20 mpg! Address all inquiries to Autotronic Controls Corp., 6908 Commerce St., El Paso, TX 79915.(915) 772-7431.

EMISSIONS STORY

origin, demands almost no operator training and indicates other parameters of engine condition: mixture, plug misfiring, leaky valves, leaky intake manifolding, ignition advance, etc.

It is this particular test for which some fairly inexpensive test equipment is now on the market. These instruments are not necessarily of laboratory quality, but would certainly be of value in ordinary tune jobs concerned with air quality degradation or meeting the idle emission levels now being adopted by some states. For example, California already has idle emission standards for domestic and foreign vehicles. A chart of the current standards for these groups of vehicles accompanies this story. Generally a vehicle in a proper state of tune can pass these standards and still show satisfactory (if not downright good) drivability.

Roadside inspection stations, encouraged by many states, are often equipped with instruments of this type, called non-dispersive infrared (NDIR) units. Actually, the NDIR instruments are used to measure CO levels in the EPA/CVS test procedure, while flame ionization detection and chemilluminiscence are used to detect levels of NOx.

WHERE ALL THIS HITS THE STREET ENTHUSIAST

Let's assume you already have a car and are concerned about 1) what emission standards are presently facing you, 2) what equipment can be used on the engine and still be acceptable and 3) what modifications to stock parts are legal within your particular state.

As a vehicle owner, the only emission standards for which you are currently responsible are the no-load idle levels, if your state has specified them. If your car falls outside these standards, it becomes your responsibility to have it corrected. This assumes that you have not altered the manufacturer's emissions package, if the vehicle was originally equipped with such pieces. You need not be concerned about the EPA test procedures. These were the basis on which

the new car manufacturer received certification and was able to sell the car in the first place.

If *you* decide to sell the vehicle, an idle emissions check may be specified by your state's motor vehicles department prior to transfer of title from one owner to the other, but as in the case of the roadside check station, idle testing is all that is currently being required.

Probably you have heard various comments about the use of specialty aftermarket items (mufflers, engine parts, etc.). It is in this area that special committees in SEMA (Specialty Equipment Manufacturers Association) have been working with state and federal agencies to show that technology has been and continues to be developed by the performance parts industry that is equal to or better than O.E.M. in air quality and environmental controls. At this writing, substantial progress had been made in demonstrating the value of special engine/chassis parts, and there is every reason to believe that a future exists for the industry that produces these special pieces. Emissions data continues to be gathered that shows how correctly designed performance engine parts can provide drivability improvements in the face of exhaust

emissions reductions. You may have seen ads indicating these accomplishments . . . and you'll have the opportunity to see more soon.

We advise consulting the Consumer Protection Agency (CPA) and/or highway department of your particular state for specifics on emissions testing (roadside in particular), what the standards are and how to keep your vehicle adjusted within the legal limits. If you have any trouble in finding this information or encounter any objection to the use of special engine pieces, contact the SEMA group at 11001 E. Valley Mall, El Monte, CA

91734 for assistance. This organization is vitally concerned with the future of this industry, and any assistance you can render will be assistance you've rendered to yourself.

It would be foolish to suggest that many questions do not remain about the future of piston engines and the performance enthusiast. Obviously, we have witnessed many changes already and can suspect that others will follow. Judging by current trends, however, further progress in exhaust emissions technology is virtually certain to be a part of our automotive future. ♛

1. Inlet air for Autotronics system passes through air-straightening ducting for purposes of measurement. Fuel pump (shown next to air duct) has a variable speed range so that the amount of fuel it delivers depends upon its shaft rpm. This depends upon a command given to it by the brain box as engine load speed requirements change during different driving conditions.

2. These are three types of mixing tubes and a "spinner" which is located in the center of the mixing chamber and around the mixing tube. Its slots and internal "threads" help maintain mixed fuel suspension before entry into intake manifolding.

3. These are the standards facing new car manufacturers and new vehicle certification. Whether the test type is 7-mode or CVS, all data is based on cold-soak tests (see text). If you do not already know how standards dropped for the years 1975 and 1976, you might take a moment to look at the numbers.

4. With the spinner and mixing tube removed, you can see how air enters the mixing chamber tangentially before being passed through spinner and into inlet manifold. At this point in its development, Autotronics system is of the high-dollar variety, but O.E.M. interest could cut bottom out of pricing. Even so, system is available now and has definite performance engine potential, especially with provision for air/fuel ratio variation from within the car and during vehicle operation. (Credit Petersen's Specialty Publications Division for bringing this to you first, because it is a first!)

EXHAUST EMISSION STANDARDS

EMISSION	Pre-1966	1966[1] Cal.	1970 Cal.	–Fed.	1971 Cal.	–Fed.	1972[2] Cal.	–Fed.
HC—gm/mile	11	3.5	2.2	2.2	4.0	2.2	3.2	3.4
CO—gm/mile	80	36	23	23	23	23	39	39
NOx—gm/mile	4-6	NR	NR	NR	NR	NR	3.2	NR
Evap.—gm/mile	50	NR	6	NR	6	6	2	2

EXHAUST EMISSION STANDARDS

1973 Cal.	–Fed.	1974 Cal.	–Fed.	1975 Cal.	–Fed.	1976 Cal.	–Fed.	1977 Cal.	–Fed.	1978 Cal.	–Fed.
3.2	3.4	3.2	3.4	0.9	1.5	0.9	1.5	.41	1.5	.41	N/A
39	39	39	39	9.0	15.0	9.0	15.0	9.0	15.0	9.0	N/A
3.0	3.0	2.0	3.0	2.0	3.1	2.0	3.1	1.5	2.0	1.5	N/A
2	2	2	2	2	2	2	2	2	2	6.0[3]	N/A

1. 1966 California requirements are the same as 1968 Federal requirements.
2. Standards are based on constant volume sampling technique.
3. Beginning in 1978 the Evap.-gm/mile readings were computed by a new method termed SHED; hence the apparent discrepancy between this and the preceding years.
N/A Not available at press time (4/77).
NR No requirement.
For 1972:
The auto manufacturers have the option of using the 7 mode/7 cycle California test or a CVS followed by two hot California cycles for California. Should 7 mode/7 cycle California tests be used, the standards are: HC: 1.5 gm/mile; CO: 23 gm/mile and NOx: 3.0 gm/mile.

FUEL SYSTEM FUNDAMENTALS

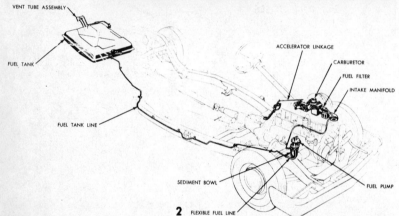

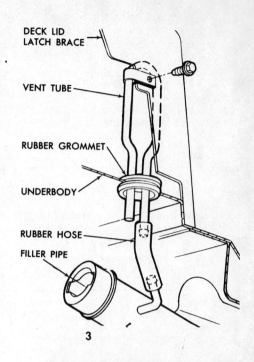

VENT TUBE ASSEMBLY

FUEL TANK

ACCELERATOR LINKAGE

CARBURETOR

FUEL FILTER

INTAKE MANIFOLD

FUEL TANK LINE

SEDIMENT BOWL

FUEL PUMP

2 FLEXIBLE FUEL LINE

1. Get the book out! With a good shop manual or carburetor specification manual, you can fix any carburetor.

2. Typical fuel system — before smog. Fuel lines sometimes run on the bottom of frame members, where they can be squashed shut, causing mysterious fuel starvation problems.

3. Considerable ingenuity has been used to provide a vent but keep the fuel from sloshing out. Vents such as these will soon be antiques. Smog controls don't allow them.

To be a successful hot rodder you don't have to know the automotive fuel system well enough to go to work as a design engineer, but you should have a pretty good idea of how the whole thing works. If you understand the stock fuel system, then when the time comes to run that street job through the quarter you will have a little bit of an edge over the guy who makes changes in his car without knowing why he makes them. Maybe you work on cars for fun or profit. Knowing the fuel system will save time when something goes wrong — and you have to find out why. If you are not a racer or mechanic, but merely curious about your car, then here is the fuel system, and how it works.

Let's start with the gasoline tank, probably the most ignored part of the whole stock fuel system. In the long-gone days when the tank was in the cowl, the driver was at least aware that the car had a tank because he could hear the gas sloshing around. Now that the tank is

"way back there somewhere" nobody pays much attention to it. The manufacturers evidently realize this. They used to put a drain plug in gas tanks so the accumulated water from condensation could be drained. But nobody ever drained the tank, so now most cars are equipped with gas tanks that have no drain plug. This is actually a good thing, because now when the tank needs cleaning, it will be removed and *really* cleaned.

When gas is pumped out of the tank, air must be allowed to enter. If not, the walls of the tank might collapse because of the vacuum formed in the tank. The air enters through a vent, which used to be in the cap. Instead of a plain hole in the cap, most manufacturers formed some kind of intricate passageway which would pass air but would discourage bugs and dirt from getting into the gas.

The problem was that a vent which allowed free passage of air, would also let gas dribble out if the car was parked on a slant. So they put a nipple on the top side of the tank. When the tank was installed, this

nipple was connected to a hose which looped up several inches higher than the tank. It worked, with no leakage on hills, so the tank was fitted with a sealed cap and the problem was solved.

American Motors has even gone so far as to use a nylon surge tank attached to the end of the vent pipe, so that if the tank is full when the car goes through a fast corner, the surge tank captures all the spillage, which then drains back into the main tank after the car gets through the corner.

Once in a while someone puts a sealed cap on a tank that has no vent. The fuel pump really works hard in this case, up to the point where the walls of the gas tank won't collapse any more, whereupon the engine just plain runs out of gas. Pull the tank cap off in this situation and there will be a big "WHOOSH" as air rushes into the tank. Install the correct cap, that is vented, and no more troubles. If you make your own fuel tank, or use a surplus aircraft tank, you might run out of gas halfway down the strip if you forget to provide a vent in the tank.

Some manufacturers have gotten even trickier than using sealed caps. They use a cap that will allow air to enter the tank, but under certain conditions, not to leave the tank. It's called an anti-surge cap. The result is that when the gasoline expands rapidly from the heat of the sun the tank becomes slightly pressurized, which gives the fuel pump a helping hand and prevents vapor lock.

Late-model cars with evaporative control systems have a nonvented cap, sometimes with a positive seal to prevent fuel from coming out even when the car is on a steep hill. Putting a vented cap on those tanks

(by mistake) will not affect engine performance, but will definitely render the evaporative control system ineffective, and may get you a failing grade at your next state inspection.

In most stock systems when the gas leaves the tank, it goes uphill. The gasoline pickup tube hangs from the top or side of the tank and the open end is suspended without touching the tank bottom. If there is any foreign matter on the bottom of the tank it will stay there, whereas if the pickup tube was lying on the tank bottom it would act like a vacuum cleaner. Some pickup tubes have filters on the end, but the filter only stops the big pieces.

Gas filters may be found almost anywhere in the system. Most cars

now have a filter on the pickup tube Some trucks have a filter on the frame rail halfway between the tank and the engine. There are screens in the fuel pump, filters in the line between the pump and carburetor, and even bronze filters in the carburetor inlet fitting. The filters and screens are designed to catch dirt, and they do it so well that almost any one of them can stop an engine if they are not cleaned or replaced at the recommended mileage.

Fuel lines may be steel, gasoline-resistant rubber hose, or flex line. Gas lines used to run from the tank to a point on the car frame near the fuel pump, and then a short flex line with permanently attached fittings would bridge the gap. Now there are

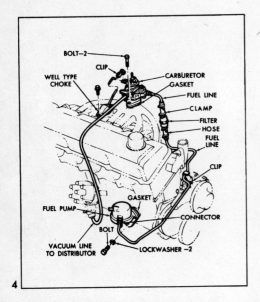

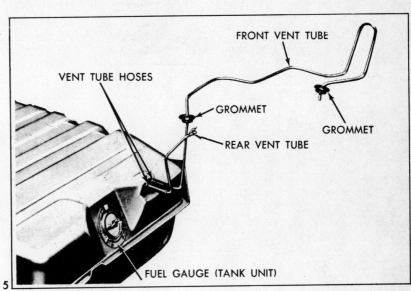

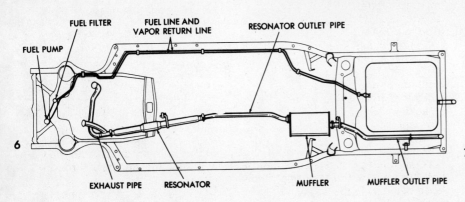

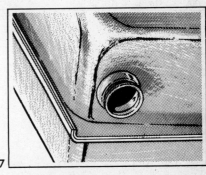

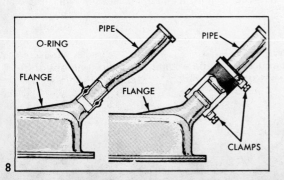

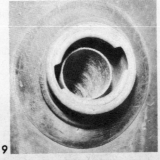

4. This is a typical fuel system as found on a Chrysler slant 6.

5. Vent tubes must be kept open in order to prevent air locks.

6. Fuel lines are usually located on the opposite side from the exhaust.

7. Tanks are seam welded. They will give very little trouble ordinarily.

8. Some tank necks use an O-ring, others will use a hose and clamps.

9. Inner tube in filler neck is to prevent airlock and resulting gas spilling when filling the tank.

FUNDAMENTALS

many manufacturers that have done away with the flex line. They fasten the steel gas line directly into the pump, and then let the line go through open space for about three feet before it reaches the first tie point on the frame. It works very well, and has no adverse effect on either the line or the pump. Many modern fuel systems use rubber hose with removable hose clamps.

All fuel lines and the pump should be situated on the car so they stay as cool as possible. If the pump, or any part of the line between the pump and the tank, should become overheated enough to vaporize the gasoline at a rate faster than the pump can create suction, then we have a condition known as vapor

lock. The pump is still pumping, but it's only pumping vapor, which goes into the carburetor, out through the bowl vent, and the engine doesn't get any gasoline.

Vapor lock happens most often on an extremely hot day in traffic, usually when the car is going uphill. The only remedy is to cool off the fuel pump, and the easiest way to do this is with a stream of water, or even a wet rag. Excessive heat on the line between the fuel pump and the carburetor or on the carburetor bowl, will not cause vapor lock. It will cause percolation and other problems we will take up later.

Almost all stock fuel pumps are mechanical, operated by an eccentric on the engine camshaft. The pump makes suction to get the fuel from the tank, and then pumps the fuel under pressure to the carburetor.

The carburetor mixes the gasoline with air, and then uses this mixture to control the speed and power of the engine. If a carburetor is supplying the engine with an excess supply of fuel and not enough air, it is described as running "rich." If the condition continues long enough your supply of money will have to be very "rich" to buy the gasoline for such an engine.

If you have ever seen an engine give off black, sooty smoke from the tail pipe, you were looking at a rich running engine. It takes a little bit of practice to realize what you are seeing, however. Blue smoke, caused by oil burning in the combustion chamber, can easily be confused with the smoke caused by a rich mixture.

When an engine is getting too much air, and not enough gas, we

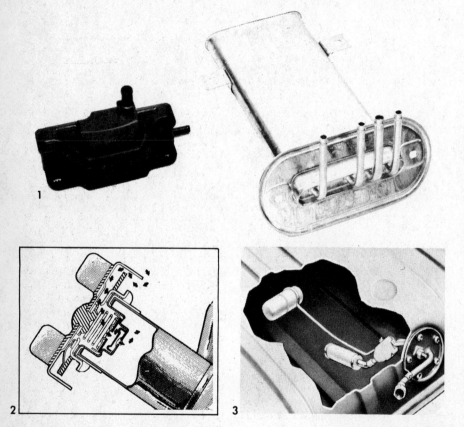

1. Part of vapor control system is a gadget to keep the liquid fuel in the tank, but allow the vapors to go up toward the front of the car to the vapor storage. Plastic liquid-vapor separator at left was used in 1970 Oldsmobiles. They have switched to the metal standpipe for 1971.

2. This vented cap has a surge valve. It allows air in, but will not allow any fuel to slosh or surge out. Under high temperature conditions, pressure will build up and hold the valve closed. If it builds up too high, the spring will relieve the pressure before the tank blows up.

3. On this car the tank gauge unit can be removed without taking the tank out of the car. When the unit is on top of the tank, you have to remove the whole tank to get to the unit.

4. Tank units can be calibrated by bending the arm on the float.

5. Cars with vapor control systems have vacuum-pressure tank caps. The cap relieves pressure at about 1 pound, and allows air to enter the tank whenever a slight vacuum occurs. In most operation, the cap remains sealed. Pressure-vacuum relief is for insurance, if normal venting through vapor control system should become clogged.

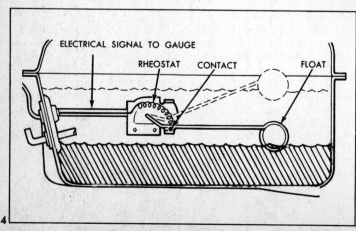

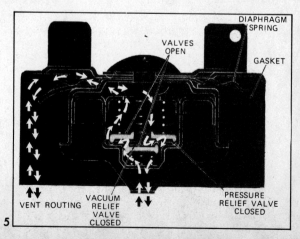

6

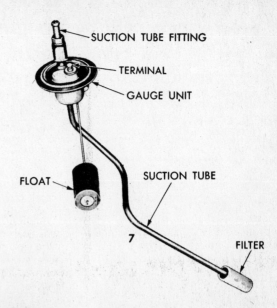

SUCTION TUBE FITTING

TERMINAL

GAUGE UNIT

FLOAT

SUCTION TUBE

7

FILTER

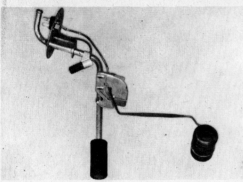

8

9

6. Special wrenches are available to get tank units out, but two screwdrivers will work if you are careful.

7. The filter on the pickup tube can plug up if water hits it.

8. A fuel gauge tank unit is only a small resistance device. This one has an additional fuel-activated switch that lights a low fuel warning signal on the instrument panel.

9. Locking rings are varied, each requiring its own wrench.

say it is running "lean." An engine running on the lean side will get better gas mileage and have less power than an engine running on the rich side. But this is only a general rule. There are some engines that will put out more power if the carburetor is leaned a little, and some engines will get better gas mileage if the carburetor is made to run rich. This is not said to be confusing. It only points out that theories don't always work. The only way to be sure of a theory is to try it on a particular engine and see if it does the job.

The carburetor's fuel mixing actions are all automatic. The air that flows through the carburetor does all the work of mixing and metering the fuel to the engine. When the driver puts his foot down on the gas pedal, the main thing he is doing is opening the throttle valve, which opens up a hole under the carburetor. If he shoves his foot all the way to the floor, then the throttle valve will be wide open, the carburetor will add fuel to the air as it goes into the engine, and the engine will run as fast as it can go for the load it is pulling. If the gas pedal is released, then the throttle valve, which is in the base of the carburetor, will

close down to idle position, and the carburetor will meter the right amount of fuel for that condition.

In order to use one gallon of gasoline, an engine gulps 8000 gallons of air. If all that air wasn't filtered, the engine would wear itself out from the abrasive dust in the air. So the designers put an air filter on top of the carburetor. It is supposed to let the air into the carburetor without restricting the flow, which means that the modern large displacement engines which swallow air at a faster rate must have enormous air cleaners.

If an engine is modified so that it breathes better, than the stock air cleaner might not be capable of passing the added air. In an all-out dragging job, the air cleaner will be sacrificed. Who cares about a little wear if the car goes faster? But on a street job, some kind of an air cleaner should be used, even if it's only a screen to keep out the low-flying birds.

All this air and fuel that goes into the engine should go in a perfectly straight line through the air cleaner, the carburetor, the intake manifold, the intake valve, and into the combustion chamber. Then, after pushing the piston down on the combustion stroke, it should continue that same straight line through

the exhaust valve, into the exhaust manifold or header, and out through the exhaust pipe.

The problem is that nobody has ever been able to design an engine with an induction and exhaust system that is all in a straight line. The system has to have curves and bends in it. Curves and bends may be nice to look at, but every time another curve is designed into an induction or exhaust system it slows down the flow.

A gasoline engine is really not much different from an air compressor. The more air/fuel mixture it takes in, the more power it will develop. This is called "breathing." If an engine can breathe efficiently, then it will be faster and more powerful. Almost all the modification work that is done on induction and exhaust systems is done to allow the engine to breathe easier. If you don't believe this has any effect, close your mouth tightly, pinch off your nose until you only get a little air at a time and then try to run a foot race with somebody.

In the chapters that follow we will describe the stock fuel and induction system in easily understood language so that you will have a pretty good idea of how it works. ♛

HOW A CARBURETOR WORKS

Mixing gasoline with air to form a combustible mixture is a fairly simple process. However, the job for an automobile engine takes on considerable complication because of the great variety of crankshaft speeds and load conditions under which such an engine operates. But those complicated automobile carburetors work on the same basic theory as a simple lawnmower carb. If you understand basic carburetor theory, you can apply this to any carburetor.

To make a carburetor easy to understand we divide it into "systems." Most carburetors have six systems. They are the float system, cruising or high speed system, idle or low speed system, accelerating pump system, power system, and choke system.

Each system or control in a carburetor must function correctly if the engine served by the carburetor is to deliver the performance and fuel mileage it should, and the adjustments required by each of them must be correct. Making these adjustments is an important part of tuning, whether the engine is used for normal driving or some sort of competition. Making them correctly is simplified if the fellow doing the job understands why each system and control is necessary and has a working knowledge of its function.

So let's start "building" a carburetor. We will start with the elementary parts and keep adding until we get a carburetor that will work. We begin with the float system.

FLOAT SYSTEM

When fuel reaches the carburetor it flows through the inlet fitting and through a seat. From the seat it flows past the end of a needle and into the float bowl. As the float bowl fills up, the float in the middle of the bowl rises with the fuel, pushes the needle into the seat and shuts off the fuel. If the engine uses some of the fuel from the float bowl, then the float will drop, which lets the needle off the seat and the fuel will flow into the bowl.

The float usually has a mechanical advantage in the way it is hooked up to the needle so that it exerts enough pressure to firmly seat the needle. Thus the float is constantly moving up and down, letting fuel in and shutting fuel off, but the fuel level stays fairly constant because the needle only opens a few thousands of an inch for all normal running. At wide open throttle it's a different

1

story. Then the fuel level falls, the float drops, and the fuel pump has to work like mad to keep enough fuel in the bowl. Sometimes the poor, old, neglected fuel pump just can't put out, and we have an engine that runs out of fuel at wide open throttle.

Fuel level is adjustable by bending the arm on the float or by bending a little tab that is attached to the arm and pushes on the needle. The "float level" specification is a measurement from some part of the carburetor casting to the float, with the float resting on a closed needle. If the float is attached to the bowl cover then the measurement is taken between float and cover with the cover inverted. Some floats must be adjusted at both heel and toe, and the alignment of the floats from side to side must be checked to be sure they don't rub the sides of the bowl. On some Holley 2- and 4-barrel carburetors, the float is adjusted by moving the seat in or out with an adjusting nut and lockscrew arrangement.

If the float is attached to the bowl instead of the bowl cover, then the whole carburetor is inverted for setting float level so that the float rests on a closed needle, and the measurement is taken from the top edge of the bowl to the float. In this case the measurement can also be taken by leaving the carburetor in the normal position and filling the bowl with fuel until the float rises against the closed needle. It is dan-

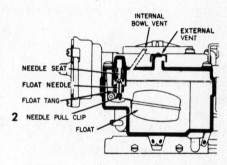

2

INTERNAL BOWL VENT
EXTERNAL VENT
NEEDLE SEAT
FLOAT NEEDLE
FLOAT TANG
NEEDLE PULL CLIP
FLOAT

gerous at any time to push the float into the closed position against the needle with finger pressure. Pressure applied in this manner may bend the float or ruin the tip of the needle, or the seat.

Some specification sheets also give a "fuel level" measurement. This is a measurement from the top of the bowl or some part of the carburetor to the actual level of the fuel if the bowl were filled under normal pressure from the fuel pump. Sight holes are sometimes provided in the side of the float bowl for checking fuel level. To check, remove a pipe plug and look in. If fuel runs out, the level is too high. In most cases, the bottom of the hole should be just barely wet by the fuel. The *fuel* level specification in most cases is not an adjustment specification, but is provided as a double check to be sure the *float* level setting was done correctly.

"Float drop" is a measurement of the amount that the float can drop when it opens the needle. It is con-

1. Topside of the double-pumper Holley. Choke is mechanical. Note the center inlet bowls, with sight plugs in the end for checking fuel level, and adjustable needles and seats.

2. Some float systems use a combination of internal and external vents. It's all designed to control the amount of fuel through the main nozzle.

3. When the level of fuel drops, the float drops too, letting the needle come off the seat so that fuel can enter. Actual amount of float and needle movement is very slight.

4. Pushing on the needle for any reason is verboten. Rubber tip of the needle can be easily compressed out of shape.

5. Note that the level of fuel in the float bowl is below the outlet of the main nozzle in the center of the venturi If the fuel level is too high, fuel will drip from the end of the nozzle, and you will get poor gas mileage and a car that won't idle right.

6. Float system with a horizontal needle. A vertical needle works better. The tube at upper left is an internal bowl vent which raises pressure above the fuel when the engine is running fast.

trolled by a little tab that is bent to get the correct measurement. On some carburetors the float can drop too far and bind the needle so that it sticks in the open position. Of course, if the float doesn't drop far enough it won't allow enough gasoline to flow through the seat at wide open throttle.

This float system works as long as the fuel pump can supply the fuel bowl with enough fuel to keep it full. If the fuel pump doesn't keep up with engine demands the fuel level will drop, causing the fuel mixture to lean out. If the wrong pump is installed, so that the fuel pressure is too high, it is possible for the needle to be forced off the seat, which will flood the engine with fuel, result in an extremely rich mixture, and the engine will have difficulties about the same as a person trying to breathe under water.

The needle and seat is one of the biggest sources of trouble in the carburetor. A small flake of rust or

dirt between the needle and its seat will let fuel in fast enough to flood the engine. The Stromberg 97 carburetor on early Fords was famous for "sticking" needles. Actually, the needle was not sticking, but small particles of foreign matter from the fuel tank were sticking between the needle and seat, causing flooding. The 97 did this because it had a horizontal needle, which is not self-cleaning. If the needle is designed to sit vertically in the carburetor, any dirt in the fuel will have a tendency to fall past the needle instead of getting trapped. Most modern carburetors have vertical needles.

All kinds of ideas have been tried on needles and seats to keep them from flooding the engine. Some needles have rubber tips, or a steel tip with a rubber seat. Some carburetors even have a flat rubber disc instead of a needle. This is all necessary because of the foreign matter that comes into the carburetor with the gas. But it's not the fault of the

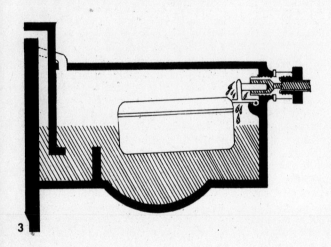

3

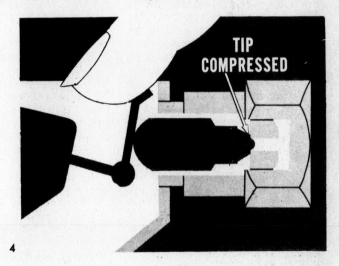

TIP COMPRESSED

4

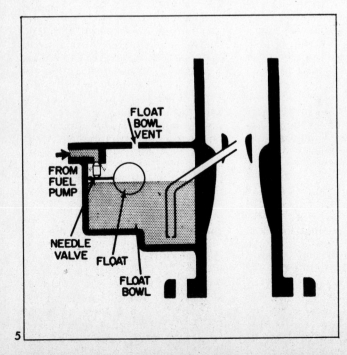

FLOAT BOWL VENT

FROM FUEL PUMP

NEEDLE VALVE

FLOAT

FLOAT BOWL

5

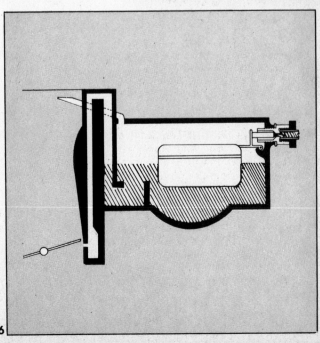

6

HOW CARBS WORK

gasoline manufacturers. Most of the foreign matter is rust from the vehicle's gasoline tank, or dirt that gets into the tank when the cap is removed. If we can keep the fuel clean and under pressure, then the fuel level will stay where it is supposed to. And keeping that fuel at the right level in the bowl is important. We will see why when we go to the high-speed system.

CRUISING OR HIGH-SPEED SYSTEM

When the driver sticks his foot in it, he opens up the throttle valve in the base of the carburetor. The suction created by the intake stroke of the pistons draws air into the air cleaner and through the carburetor where the air picks up fuel, and goes into the engine.

As the air passes through the bore of the carburetor, it goes through a section that is slightly narrower than the rest of the carburetor bore. At this point there is a pressure drop, or partial vacuum, which increases according to how fast the air is rushing through. Now if we take a hollow tube and run it in a straight line from inside the fuel bowl to that low pressure area, the suction of that partial vacuum will draw fuel out of the bowl. This is known as the venturi principle. It was discovered by a scientist named Venturi, and the narrow part of the carburetor bore where the suction is created is known as the venturi. Most carbs now use triple venturis that multiply the suction.

The tube from the float bowl to the venturi is called the main nozzle. After the fuel is sucked up from the float bowl through the main nozzle and into the venturi, it is carried by the airstream into the engine. The amount of fuel that goes into the engine is determined by the main jet. It is a calibrated orifice that is screwed into the bottom of the float bowl. Between the main jet and the lower end of the main nozzle is a chamber known as the main well. It is here that air bleeds and little baffles are located which break up the fuel for better distribution into the engine.

Some carburetors place that jet with its orifice in a vertical position and put a metering rod in the jet. As the throttle is opened, the metering rod, which is mechanically linked to the throttle, lifts out of the jet and allows more fuel to flow into the nozzle.

Some carburetors use vacuum-operated rods in the jets. It's easy

CHANGE FLOAT LEVEL TO CORRECT

to see how this works. If you are sucking on a straw and someone pinches the straw, a high vacuum will be created in your mouth, just as closing the throttle creates high vacuum in an engine. The metering rod is hooked to a vacuum piston so that when there is a high vacuum within the engine the rod is pulled down into the jet, cutting down on the amount of fuel.

If someone pulls the straw out of your mouth, you will get a lot of air and very little vacuum, which is exactly what happens when the engine throttle is opened. When the vacuum falls off, a small spring under the vacuum piston pushes the rod out of the jet. This means that at low vacuum the engine gets a lot of fuel, and at high vacuum the engine gets less fuel. Is this what we want? Sure. We only have low vacuum when the throttle is opened. That's when the engine needs lots of fuel. When the throttle is closed we have high vacuum and we don't need as much fuel so we use the high vacuum to pull the rod down into the jet. Some metering rods are controlled by a combination of vacuum and mechanical linkage. As the throttle is opened, the linkage lifts the rod out of the jet. If this system is used, the linkage can be adjusted to lift the rod sooner or later. On a pure vacuum-controlled metering rod, the only control is the strength of the spring, and this is not adjustable.

The metering rods and jets are just metering devices. The only thing that makes the fuel flow is the low pressure area in the venturi at the tip of the main nozzle. Actually there is no such thing as suction drawing the fuel out of the carburetor. Any time a partial vacuum is

created, there is a pressure from outside the vacuum which attempts to fill the space. Therefore, fuel is not drawn or sucked out of the main nozzle by the vacuum, but in reality if pushed up out of the nozzle by the atmospheric pressure on the fuel in the bowl. But as we said in the beginning, it isn't necessary for hot rodders to be design engineers, so we will discuss the flowing of fuel in terms of suction, which makes it easier to understand for everybody.

If the fuel level in the bowl is correct, then fuel will be just below the tip of the main nozzle, ready to be sucked into the venturi. But if the fuel level in the bowl is low, then the fuel will be down inside the main nozzle. It won't come into the venturi as easily and the engine will run lean or have a flat spot when you step on the throttle.

If the fuel level is too high, then fuel will actually drip out of the end of the nozzle, even when the engine is shut off. This can result in an engine that gets about one mile to the gallon and has an oil pan full of gasoline.

Other refinements have been added to the cruising system through the years. Air is now bled into the main nozzle for better mixture control, and the nozzles have been set at various angles for better pickup. Some carbs have even done away with removable jets. A hole is drilled in the carburetor casting and becomes the jet.

In the early days all carburetors had only one throat. When large 6's and V8's came into the picture, it was discovered that the fuel was distributed better if the carburetor was made with two throats, or barrels. The parts in the second throat

1. We have never seen anyone use one of these gauges, but the picture proves that they have existed. If a Holley float bowl does not have sight plugs, this is what you have to use to check actual wet fuel level on the car.

2. In this representation of a carburetor, the restriction at the bottom of the main nozzle represents the main jet. The size of the main jet regulates the mixture above idle. Note the external bowl vent at the top of the bowl.

3. In this representation of the main metering system there are several basic but interesting points. Notice the double venturi to increase suction and the air bleeds in the nozzle to help atomize the fuel.

4. We talk about suction, but it's pressure that does the job. Reduced pressure in the venturi allows atmospheric pressure in the bowl to push fuel through the main nozzle.

5. Here's a closeup of the main nozzle, or main discharge tube. Take note of the small holes in the tube which are air bleeds to atomize the fuel.

are exactly the same as in the first. Each throat uses its own main nozzle and main jet, and each has its own idle system. One float system supplies both barrels with fuel.

The cruising or high speed system works fine, as long as the throttle is open wide enough to let a good, fast air stream through so the low pressure will be created at the venturi. But if the engine is throttled back, the airstream will slow down to the point where no vacuum is created at the venturi, and fuel will stop being drawn out of the bowl. So we need another system to make the engine run at slow speeds. That is the idle and low speed system, coming right up.

IDLE & LOW SPEED SYSTEM

When the throttle is open just enough to allow the engine to idle, there will be a high vacuum on the engine side of the throttle plate. This high vacuum is used to draw fuel into the engine. This could not be done during cruising or high speed because as the throttle is opened the vacuum falls off. At wide open throttle the vacuum will be zero or almost zero, but the airflow is fast so the venturi principle works fine.

Since there is such a high vacuum at idle, we use this vacuum to draw the fuel for idle through various passageways with drilled holes or air bleeds. This is necessary because at idle the air moving into the engine is going very slowly, and any fuel dumped into this slow moving air has a tendency to settle out onto the walls of the manifold and ports. The air bleeds vaporize the fuel before it leaves the carburetor.

Idle fuel is taken from the float bowl through a tube and then up through a passageway which is

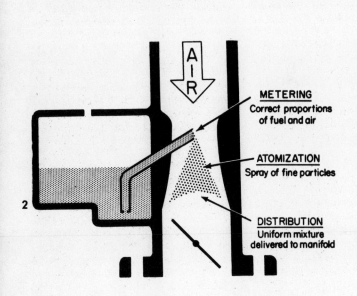

METERING
Correct proportions of fuel and air

ATOMIZATION
Spray of fine particles

DISTRIBUTION
Uniform mixture delivered to manifold

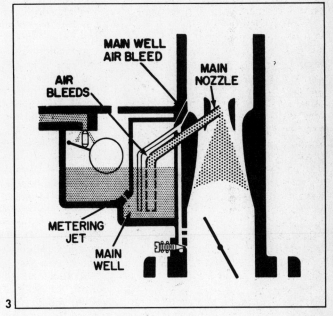

MAIN WELL AIR BLEED

AIR BLEEDS

MAIN NOZZLE

METERING JET

MAIN WELL

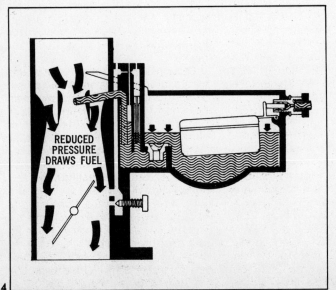

REDUCED PRESSURE DRAWS FUEL

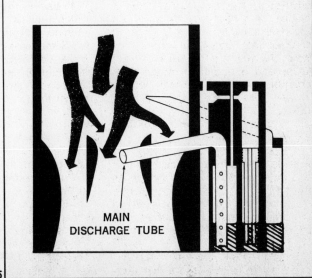

MAIN DISCHARGE TUBE

HOW CARBS WORK

higher than the level of fuel in the bowl. Air is introduced through air bleed holes, and then the idle mixture is routed through passageways down to the vacuum side of the throttle plate. The tube which picks up idle fuel from the bowl is usually removable, and one end of it has a calibrated hole. This tube is the idle jet. Usually, the idle jet picks up the idle fuel after the fuel has passed through the main jet, but since the main jet is considerably larger than the idle jet, it doesn't affect the calibration.

Before the idle mixture goes into the engine underneath the throttle plate, it goes past a needle and seat which are adjustable from outside the carburetor. If the needle is screwed in, it allows less mixture to pass. If it is screwed out, it allows more mixture to pass. When this mixture is combined with the air that is flowing around the partially open throttle plate, it results in a total mixture that allows the engine to idle.

One mixture screw is supplied for each primary bore in the carburetor. Turning the mixture screws in leans the mixture. Turning them out richens the mixture. The mixture screws have very little effect on the engine idle speed. This is controlled by the amount that the throttle plate is open, regulated by a throttle stopscrew acting on the shaft.

Some carburetors allow the throttle to close completely at idle. These carburetors have a large air screw, which performs the same function as the throttle stopscrew; that is, it allows air to enter the engine.

So now we have an engine idling on air entering around the throttle plate or through an air screw, combined with mixture entering past an adjustable mixture screw in each throat. The problem now is to get a smooth transition from curb idle to cruising speed, and this is another area where carburetion engineers have spent a lot of time.

As the throttle opens, the vacuum will fall off, so of course less fuel will be drawn into the engine from the idle port below the throttle plate. In order to compensate for this, a second port, called the idle transfer port, is drilled further up the bore so that it is uncovered as the throttle opens. Above idle the engine is running on fuel mixture coming from the idle port and the idle transfer port.

As the throttle continues to open, the vacuum gets less and less, which means that less fuel is drawn out of the idle ports, but by this time there is enough airflow through the venturi

that fuel is beginning to flow out of the main nozzle. If the carburetor is properly designed, the transition between idle and cruising will be smooth and unnoticeable.

On some carburetors the idle system quits completely when the cruising system takes over, but on most modern carbs the idle system never stops. It still feeds slight amounts of fuel into the engine even when going down the highway at 70 mph. In fact, some problems of lean mixtures at high speed are cured by installing richer idle jets.

To make use of a basic carburetor metering system as a method of reducing cold engine stalling—instead of relying on the choke—Chrysler Corp. devised a special idle enrichment system to be incorporated in the carburetors fitted to '75 cars equipped with an automatic transmission. Known as the Coolant Control Idle Enrichment (CCIE) system, this new design richens the mixture in an off-idle area while the engine is warming up; this is done by closing off the idle air bleeds in the carburetor. Carburetors using an idle enrichment system have one or two air inlet ports located on the air horn at a point near the enrichment valve. These ports let air pressure into a cavity around the enrichment valve, where it is either allowed to pass on or is stopped from entering the idle air bleed circuitry.

There are two different methods of activating this system. In one, a thermal switch passes a vacuum signal to a small diaphragm mounted near the top of the carburetor. As vacuum is applied to this enrichment valve, idle system air is cut down and the resulting air loss within the idle system intensifies the vacuum signal, causing a fuel flow increase. This means more fuel and less air in the mixture, making it richer.

As engine coolant warms up, the thermal switch senses the temperature change and closes, eliminating the vacuum signal. As vacuum to the diaphragm decreases, the idle air bleeds open once more and the mixture returns to its normal lean state. The total length of this enrichment is governed by an electric delay timer—which also controls the EGR solenoid action—and is approximately 35 secs. in duration after starting the cold engine. If the engine is restarted while it's warm, the thermal switch will prevent idle system enrichment; but whenever the coolant temperature drops below 138° F. (an approximate temperature), the switch opens to permit another 35-sec. enrichment cycle upon restarting the engine. The other method of activating the CCIE system is almost identical, except that

the electric delay timer is not used and the thermal switch controlling the vacuum signal opens at 86° F. In either system, the switch closes when the coolant temperature rises 12° F. above the opening temperature.

With a float system, cruising system, and idle system, our carburetor will now work fine—until we step on the gas, and then it will fall flat on its face. So we will have to add an accelerator pump system.

ACCELERATOR PUMP SYSTEM

When we open the throttle, either from idle or from a constant speed to a higher speed, there is an immediate rush of additional air through the carburetor. The fuel coming out of the main nozzle does not react as quickly as the air. It takes just a fraction of a second for the fuel to get moving with that added rush of air. While the fuel is taking it's time about getting going, the engine has received about a yard of lean mixture, causing a stumble or flat spot. This flat spot is overcome with an accelerator pump.

At one side of the float bowl is a vertical cylinder containing a piston. When the throttle is mashed, the piston is forced down mechanically by the throttle linkage and a stream of fuel shoots out into the carburetor bore. Somewhere in the passageways, usually just before the fuel reaches the carburetor bore, is a calibrated orifice that determines the size of the stream. If the orifice is too small, it will not allow enough fuel to squirt into the engine to overcome the flat spot. If the orifice is too large, it will create its own flat spot by momentarily flooding the engine with excess fuel.

Sometimes it is very difficult to tell if a flat spot on acceleration is caused by not enough pump action or too much pump action. Disconnecting the pump may not help, either, because it's almost certain a flat spot will appear then. Trial and error is usually the best way to figure this one out.

When the throttle is allowed to return to idle, the accelerator pump rises in its cylinder. This sucks fuel from the bowl through the pump intake ball check and the pump is ready to give another shot of fuel. When the pump is forced down by the linkage, fuel passes through an outlet ball check and into the carburetor bore. Sometimes needles are used instead of ball checks, but they both have the same function. If the outlet check is missing, the pump will suck air back from the bore on the return stroke. If the inlet check is missing, the fuel will squirt out into the bowl instead of into the bore, on the down stroke.

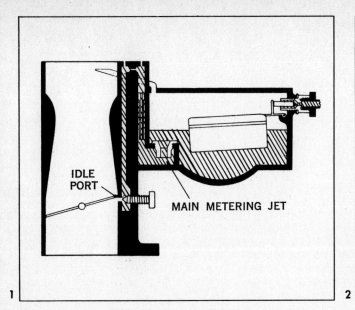

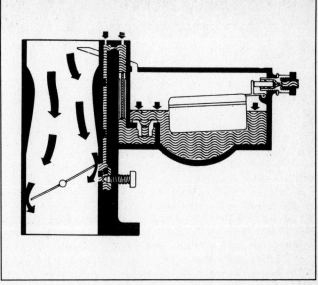

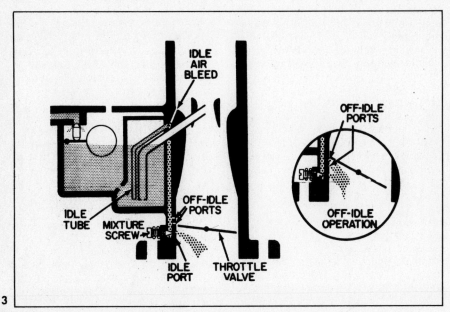

Some pumps have the inlet check in the body of the pump, and others have a vapor vent in the pump so gasoline vapor won't collect under the pump piston. On other designs the accelerator pump is a diaphragm instead of a piston, and on some the pump is operated by a spring so that the rate of pump action is always the same.

On some carburetors the accelerator pump arm can be put in different positions or bent as necessary to vary the length of the stroke. A few designs have winter and summer positions for the arm: long stroke for winter, and short stroke for summer. It's all necessary to get away from that annoying flat spot when you step on the throttle.

So now we have a carburetor with a float system, cruising system, idle system, and pump system. It will work pretty good, until you want to go flat out. For that, we're going to need a power system.

THE POWER SYSTEM

At idle a good stock engine will read 18 to 20 ins. of vacuum. When the driver steps on the throttle the induction system opens up to the whole wide world and the vacuum drops according to how much the throttle is opened. At wide open throttle the vacuum will be zero or almost zero. Anytime the throttle is opened so that the vacuum drops to about 10 ins. or less, the engine needs more fuel than is being admitted by the main jet. This added fuel is supplied by the power system.

Most modern power systems are vacuum-operated. A passageway from below the throttle plate leads to a piston and spring, or a diaphragm and spring. The high vacuum at idle and cruising keeps the power valve closed against the pressure of the spring. When the throttle is opened enough so that the vacuum drops, the spring is then released and pushes the power valve open, allowing more fuel to enter the main discharge tube and go into the engine.

Some carburetors use a mechanically operated power system. As the throttle is opened to a certain point, the linkage pushes on a valve and allows more fuel to enter. And there are some carburetors that don't use a separate power system. In these, more fuel is allowed to enter through the main jet when a metering rod or step-up rod is lifted out of the jet as the throttle is opened.

Now, as far as major design features are concerned, our carburetor will work very well, but it won't start and keep idling, particularly on a cold day. To accomplish that, we have to have a choke.

THE CHOKE SYSTEM

The choke plate and its connecting linkage is usually the first thing most hot rodders get rid of on their carburetors, probably because they reason that racing carbs do not have chokes, so the choke has to go. This thinking is okay, if all they are going to do is go racing; but if they have to drive the car anywhere, the lack of a choke will cause extremely difficult operation until the engine is warm.

When the throttle plate on a carburetor is almost closed, there is a high vacuum below the plate. This

HOW CARBS WORK

high vacuum works on the idle fuel mixture outlet below the plate and draws idle mixture into the engine, as well as drawing air around the partially open throttle plate. If we place another plate in the bore of the carburetor, but put it way up at the top, above the main nozzle, then we will be choking off the air that is passing into the engine. This plate is called the choke plate. When it is closed, a partial vacuum exists underneath it, although not as much as is underneath the throttle plate. But there is enough vacuum under the choke plate to cause increased fuel flow through the main jet and main nozzle into the engine.

This added fuel is necessary because a cold engine does not burn fuel efficiently. Until the engine gets warm, a lot of fuel will condense out of the mixture onto the cold cylinder walls and intake manifold passages. Once the engine is up to operating temperature, then the choke is no longer needed.

Chokes can be manual, in which case the driver needs enough know-how so that he chokes the engine the right amount to get it started, but not so much that he floods it. He also has to remember to turn off the choke as the engine warms up or the gasoline mileage will be so bad he will have to stop at every other gas station he comes to.

Modern chokes do all this automatically. The closing of the choke is accomplished by a thermostatic spring. As the engine warms up, engine vacuum is used to draw heated air from a "stove" on the exhaust manifold into the choke housing, causing the spring to relax and allowing the choke to open. Most choke plates have an offset shaft, so that the choke will open by its own weight if there is no spring pressure holding it closed.

The thermostatic spring is adjustable, either by rotating a housing or resetting an arm, to line up with marks. The factory supplies a normal setting, but most chokes should be tailored to the automobile so that they do a good job on that particular car

1. If idle air is supplied through a by-pass, the throttle plates can be allowed to close almost completely at idle. This helps prevent carbon formation in the throttle bores, causing erratic idling.

2. In this idle system, the idle jet is the little pinched end of the tube that screws into the carburetor underneath the idle passage plug. Note how fuel that comes through the idle jet must first come through the main jet. Some late-model carbs designed for emissions control have the idle jet outside the main well.

3. Idle tube is another name for the idle jet. The calibrated restriction is at the lower end of the tube where it appears pinched together.

4. In 1968, Oldsmobile used a Quadrajet that cracked the throttle plate for idle air. In 1969, they allowed the throttle plate to close completely and idle air came through an adjustable bypass.

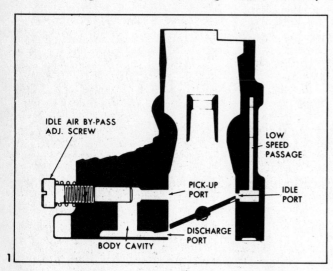

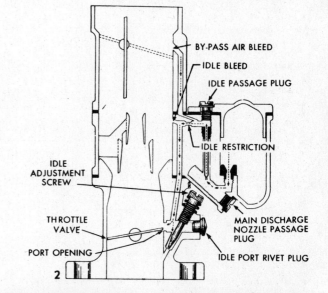

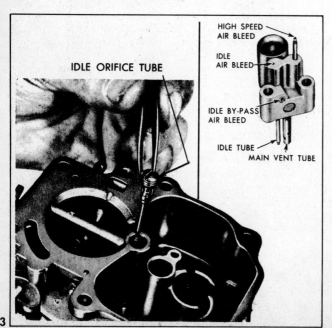

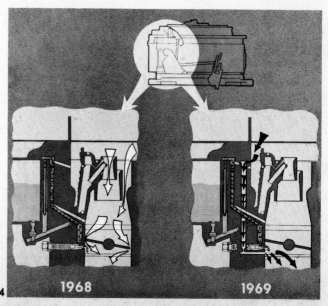

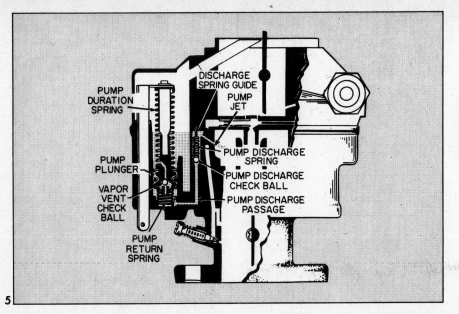

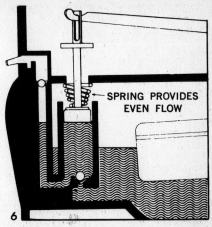

5. *When this Rochester model B pump rod works, it compresses pump duration spring; then the spring pushes the plunger down, resulting in a pump discharge that can continue after the pump rod has stopped moving.*

6. *In this type of spring-operated accelerator pump, it doesn't matter how fast you step on the gas—the spring itself is what pushes the pump plunger down.*

The thermostatic spring is mounted on the intake or exhaust manifold in some cases, completely separate from the carburetor and connected to the choke plate by linkage. Some chokes require several linkage adjustments that must be done in a definite sequence.

While the engine is starting, the thermostatic spring holds the choke plate tightly closed, to provide the rich mixture needed for starting, but as soon as the engine starts, the choke plate must be opened enough to let some air in so the engine can run. This is done with a vacuum piston or diaphragm, which is connected to engine vacuum and pulls the choke plate to a partially open position as soon as the engine starts. In some carburetors this vacuum piston is internal, part of the choke housing or carburetor casting.

Over the years, that vacuum piston has caused more than its share of problems. If the piston didn't gum up and stick by itself, the housing would distort from engine heat, causing the piston to hang up; or the welch plug at the bottom or in the end of the housing would fall out. And when problems such as these arose, you had to pull the carburetor, tear down the housing and free the piston. If the housing had warped, its bore had to be reamed in order to let the piston operate freely. Either way, it was a lot of trouble to go through to get the piston working properly again.

Late-model carburetors have gotten away from that infernal piston by going to an external bolt-on vacuum diaphragm unit that connects to the intake manifold by a hose. The diaphragm may leak or rupture, but not as often as the older piston design would stick—and replacing a diaphragm is child's play compared to freeing one of those stuck pistons.

In order to utilize the rich mixture that is necessary for starting a cold engine, it is necessary to make the engine run at a fast idle. This is done by the fast idle cam and linkage. Before a cold engine is started, the throttle must be pressed all the way to the floor and released. This allows the choke to close and position the fast idle cam so the throttle is held partially open. A few years ago Cadillac had a system that would open the throttle whenever the engine was shut off. This made it unnecessary for the driver to remember to press the throttle to the floor. The system was dropped, and now the Cadillac driver has to press his throttle to the floor just like everybody else.

Suppose the driver absentmindedly pumps the throttle a few times before starting a cold engine? If he pumps it enough, the engine will be flooded. The choke is still closed on this cold engine, which makes the chances of getting it started about as likely as a stock car outrunning a dragster.

But all is not lost. If the throttle is pushed all the way to the floor, a little tang on the linkage called the "unloader" will push the choke open so that some fresh air can get into the engine to cancel out the flooding. The unloader is adjustable by bending, so that it will open the choke the right amount.

Holding choke duration to the absolute minimum required has become important because of emissions levels; to do so, engine heat has been put to use. Early applications used a water-heated cap choke design, in which a heater hose was routed directly against the choke cap; another way was to run the heated coolant directly through the cap. For years, we've been told to "Live Better Electrically," and the auto manufacturers finally caught up with the times, ex-

changing the water-heated choke for one with an electric assist.

Cap-type chokes use a ceramic heating element hooked to the choke coil and to a bimetallic temperature switch which draws power from the alternator on a constant basis. At a temperature of less than 60° F. (all temperature specs are approximate), the switch stays open, preventing current from reaching the ceramic heating element, and allowing normal choking action to take place using the thermostatic coil. But as the temperature climbs above this cutoff point, the sensor switch closes to let current pass to the heating element, causing the choke coil spring to pull the choke plates open within 90 secs.

Remote, or well-type, chokes with an electric assist operate in a similar manner, but the heating element is separate from the choke and is wired to an external control switch, which is connected to the ignition switch. Turning the key to the "on" position activates the sensor, which passes current at about 60° F. but cuts it off at 110° F.

External vacuum break diaphragms have been added in the past few years. When the engine is started, air from the heat tube routed through the intake manifold's exhaust chamber is drawn through the choke housing by vacuum to warm up the thermostatic coil. A primary vacuum break unit modifies choke action in that it opens the choke slightly to let in enough air as the engine starts. A secondary vacuum break diaphragm operates from a thermal vacuum valve which senses the temperature of the heated

HOW CARBS WORK

carburetor air. During cold weather starts, the choke opens fully before the thermal valve reaches its operating temperature, thus the secondary vacuum break has no effect on choke action. But for warm weather starts, the thermal valve opens to actuate the secondary break, which then opens the choke a bit more. This secondary breaking action is delayed a few seconds by a built-in bleed, giving the engine sufficient time (usually between 8 and 20 secs.) to stabilize its operation before the choke opens a second time.

At this point we have a carburetor that will do the job. But engineers are never satisfied, because new problems keep coming up. And to solve those problems there are a lot of gadgets hung on a carburetor, some having to do with carburetion and some used in connection with various accessories. The most important of these carburetor extras are described below.

ANTI-PERCOLATION VENTS

On a hot day in traffic the engine compartment of a car can easily run a temperature of 200° F. The carburetor will get even hotter, resulting in the fuel boiling in the float bowl. If the bubbles of vapor that come off the floor of the float bowl happen to rise into the main nozzle, they will force fuel out the main nozzle and into the engine. This is prevented by a passage in the main well, just before the beginning of the main nozzle. At idle, a poppet valve connected mechanically to the throttle opens the passage and allows the bubbles to vent to the atmosphere before they can push fuel out of the nozzle. Above idle, the poppet valve closes so that the section at the end of the main nozzle can draw fuel into the engine. Most modern carburetors do not use anti-percolation vents. The main well and main nozzle have been designed so that the bubbles break up before they have a chance to do any damage.

BOWL VENTS

Sometimes external bowl vents with a poppet valve are called anti-percolation vents. The only difference is that a poppet valve type bowl vent lets hot fuel vapors out of the float bowl instead of out of the main well. If hot fuel vapors were not vented from the bowl through an external vent, they would go through the internal vent and into the engine, which would cause hard starting. External bowl vents with a poppet valve are open at idle through mechanical linkage. When the throttle is above idle, the external bowl vent closes to allow the internal bowl vent to work properly.

An internal bowl vent is a tube that looks something like a main nozzle, except that it is larger and is located up high near the choke plate. The internal bowl vent is placed in the airstream through the carburetor at an angle so that air is forced into the float bowl above the fuel level. This slightly pressurizes the fuel in the bowl and helps to push the fuel out the main nozzle.

CARBURETOR HEAT

If gasoline vaporized completely as it came out of the main discharge nozzle and stayed vaporized on its way to the cylinders, carburetor heat would not be necessary. Droplets of fuel are constantly collecting along the walls of the manifold and condensing out of the mixture wherever there is a comparatively cool spot. This causes acceleration lag and generally poor running while an engine is cold.

Droplets of unvaporized fuel are considerably heavier than the mixture with which they are traveling. This means that they have greater inertia, which causes them to want to continue in the direction they are moving when the mixture makes a turn to follow a passage or to enter another passage. If possible, the heavy particles will continue straight ahead until they reach a dead end rather than make the turn. This is the reason the end cylinders in many engines run richer than the middle cylinders. The end cylinders get most of the unvaporized fuel, in addition to the vaporized fuel they induct, and the middle cylinders get only vaporized fuel. Better mixture distribution is one of the arguments in favor of special multiple-carburetor intake manifolds.

Good mixture distribution is important to smooth engine operation, brisk throttle response, and reasonable fuel mileage. With present carburetor and manifold design, about the only way to improve mixture distribution is by heating the mixture after it leaves the carburetor so the fuel in it will be more completely vaporized. This is done by routing exhaust gases so they heat the intake manifold. The gases are controlled by a manifold heat valve or "heat riser" valve, operated by a thermostatic spring.

When the engine is cold, exhaust gas from some of the cylinders is routed to heat the intake manifold. On a V-8 with dual pipes, the valve shuts off one pipe and forces the exhaust gas through the intake manifold heat passage and out the other side. This is why a V-8 with dual pipes idles out of one pipe when cold.

1. When manifold vacuum is high, and during closed or partially closed throttle, the power valve piston is held up off valve.

2. As the throttle is opened, vacuum drops and the spring opens the power valve in order to allow extra fuel into main well.

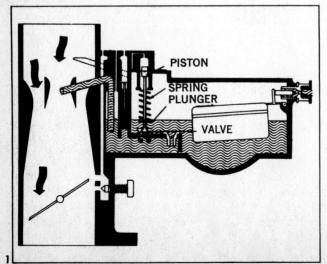

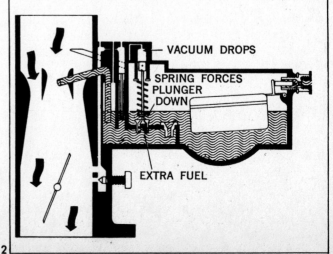

As the engine warms up, the valve slowly opens, until at operating temperature all the exhaust gas leaves the engine in the normal manner through the exhaust manifolds. But a considerable amount of heat still goes through the open heat riser passage even though the valve is not forcing the gases through the passage.

The area of the manifold that is heated is directly below the carburetor. This causes the mixture to pass through a high-temperature area immediately after leaving the carburetor. If the temperature is high enough, most of the fuel will stay vaporized on its way to the cylinders.

Carter AFB carburetors have an open chamber built into the manifold on some applications. When installing the carburetor, a stainless steel plate is first placed over the mounting studs to cover the chamber. Then the carburetor is installed. If the plate is left off by accident, the engine will not idle because fresh air is rushing into the engine without going through the carburetor. This can be embarrassing or funny, depending on who left out the plate.

Some designs use radiator water to heat the mixture with a water passage in the intake manifold. Others use a temperature control air cleaner, without any intake manifold heat at all, and no heat riser valve.

3. The choke system is a balancing of forces. The offset choke valve, the vacuum piston and the heat from the stove all tend to open the choke, while the thermostatic coil spring is attempting to close it.

4. Well-type chokes do have an adjustment, but it is usually only a setting made at the factory.

5. This may not look like part of carburetion, but it is. If the heat control valve is stuck shut, forcing too much heat up under the carburetor, it can cause uneven running.

Heated intake manifolds definitely improve the running of a car around town, but they don't do the power output any good. At wide open throttle an engine will develop more power if the mixture is cooled rather than heated. A cool mixture is more dense than a warm mixture, which means that if the mixture is cool we can pack more gasoline and air into the combustion chamber than with a mixture thinned out by heat. We might figure from this that a cold engine would put out more horsepower than a warm engine. It just isn't so. For maximum horsepower, the engine must be warm and the mixture must be cool. If the engine is cold, the mixture will condense onto the combustion chamber and cylinder walls without burning, requiring an overrich mixture to even keep the engine running. This is solved by using a choke, as we've already seen.

ACCELERATOR PUMP VENTS

When you look down into a carburetor you see, on some models, a little hole above the accelerator pump nozzle. If this hole is inspected more thoroughly, it will be found to connect to the pump discharge passage very close to the end of the nozzle.

This little hole is the accelerator pump vent. It allows air to enter the pump discharge nozzle so that the suction in the bore of the carburetor will not draw fuel out of the nozzle. A relief chamber is provided under the hole so that the pump stream will not squirt up through the hole instead of down through the nozzle. If the accelerator pump vent should be clogged, then there is a chance that fuel would bleed off through the pump nozzle at high speeds, resulting in a mixture much richer than the engine needs.

If your car has an automatic transmission and you start across an intersection with a good healthy boot on the throttle and then suddenly change your mind because of the sudden appearance of an 18-wheel truck, your

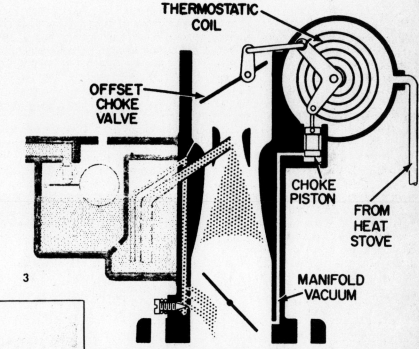

3

MARKS FOR FACTORY SETTING

4

MANIFOLD HEAT CONTROL VALVE

5

HOW CARBS WORK

engine will die—unless you have a correctly adjusted anti-stall dashpot. On a manual transmission car this won't happen. You will quickly de-clutch, the engine will rev up a little and all will be well. But the automatic transmission does not disengage when your foot is lifted off the gas, it pulls the engine down to a normal idle immediately. This causes the en-gine to die because of the big charge of gas mixture that is still on the way to the cylinders. In effect, the com-bustion chambers are flooded with gas. The anti-stall dashpot solves this problem by letting the engine down slowly to a normal idle, thus giving the combustion chambers time to burn off that extra-rich mixture.

Some dashpots are a bolt-on item. It may be on the carburetor or mounted on the firewall. It is easily recognized because it has a plunger that bears against the throttle linkage. All it consists of is a diaphragm, spring, and chamber. When the throt-tle pushes against the plunger, the diaphragm tries to force air out of the chamber, but the only exit is through a small hole, which lets the plunger in slowly. The spring returns the plunger for the next stroke.

Other carburetors have the dashpot built in. Instead of using an air cham-ber, they use a chamber full of fuel. The principle is the same. A dia-phragm or plunger lets the throttle close slowly because the fuel trapped in the chamber can only escape through a small hole. A return spring pushes the diaphragm back to refill the chamber with fuel on the return stroke.

All dashpots are adjustable, usually by varying the length of the plunger with a screw. The dashpot should let

the throttle return slowly enough so that the engine does not die, but not so slowly that the car wants to drive all the way across the intersection. Dashpots have been on most cars with automatic transmissions for years, but have not appeared on manual transmission cars until recent-ly. American Motors is using dash-pots on some manual transmission models to prevent excessive driveline whip, caused by allowing the throttle to snap back to idle.

HOT IDLE COMPENSATORS

A cold engine needs an over-rich mixture because the gasoline will not vaporize around all that cold metal. In order to get enough gasoline vapo-rized so that a cold engine will run, we choke the carburetor to provide a rich mixture. Logically, we might fig-ure that if a cold engine needs more fuel, then an extremely hot engine needs less fuel. This is true. When an engine is idling in traffic on a hot day the underhood temperatures can get hot enough to barbecue a side of beef. Engines start to run rough at idle when hot because the increased temperature gives increased vaporiza-tion of fuel, resulting in a mixture that is just rich enough to upset the idle.

The hot idle compensator is a little air valve that allows fresh air to enter the manifold and lean the mixture when the engine is hot. Some com-pensators are mounted inside the carburetor air horn, some are on the outside of the carburetor, and some are in a vacuum line in the engine compartment. The compensator on a Carter AFB will open and admit air to the intake manifold any time the air temperature at the compensator is approximately 120° F. or more. The compensator could conceivably open at any time, but usually it will only open at idle. At any speed above idle

there should be enough airflow past the compensator to cool it off so it will close.

Hot idle compensators are not ad-justable. If one is found open on a cold engine, it must be replaced. Care must be taken when handling a compensator so that the bimetal spring is not bent or distorted. If it is, the calibration of the compensator will be changed, which could result in a lot of air going into the engine at the wrong time.

ALTITUDE COMPENSATORS

When you're driving in a thinner-than-normal atmosphere, the air/fuel mixture tends to richen, in-creasing emissions levels. Some 4-bbl. carburetors are now equipped with a built-in altitude compensator which maintains the correct air/fuel ratio whether you're driving at the seashore or high in the mountains. Thus far, altitude compensation has taken two forms: One uses an altitude-sensitive bellows and valve which controls a set of passages connected to both the primary and secondary main air bleeds with a cali-brated opening. As the air/fuel mix-ture begins to richen, the bellows starts to open, letting additional air enter the main air bleeds to correct the ratio. When the outside, or atmo-spheric, pressure returns to "nor-mal," the bellows contracts. This closes off the auxiliary air passages and shuts off the system. This circuit works only at cruising speeds.

The other approach uses a bellows called an "aneroid." This barometric pressure-sensitive device is an inte-gral part of the adjustable part-throt-tle metering rod assembly. When it senses any change in air pressure, it automatically expands or contracts to lower or raise the metering rod in the fixed jet. In this way, its response to

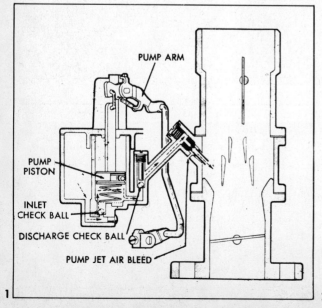

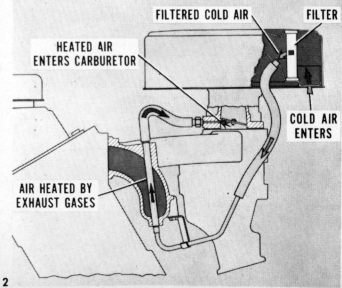

a change in air pressure maintains control of the air/fuel ratio during part-throttle conditions.

SPARK CONTROLS

Vacuum-controlled spark advance is necessary on a stock engine for maximum fuel economy. We won't go into ignition theory here, but we will point out that there are several gadgets on a carburetor that are designed to control the vacuum supply to· the distributor vacuum advance diaphragm. The vacuum line from the distributor goes to the carburetor bore either immediately above or below the throttle plate. The hole where the line enters the throttle bore is known as the spark port. If the engine was designed to have full vacuum advance at idle, the spark port will be below the throttle plate when it is in the closed position. As the throttle is opened, manifold vacuum will decrease and the ignition will go to retard, depending upon how much the throttle is opened.

If the spark port is above the throttle plate, then there will be no vacuum advance at idle. As the throttle is opened, the spark port will be uncovered, the same as the idle transfer port, and the ignition will advance. But as the throttle continues to open there will be less vacuum at the port, so the ignition will retard according to the throttle opening. As the throttle closes, the ignition will advance, until the throttle plate passes the spark port, when the ignition will go to the retard position. In most cases the spark port is slightly above the throttle plate, because putting the port below the throttle plate would give manifold vacuum and there is no need to have a hole in the carburetor for that; manifold vacuum can be taken off the intake manifold itself from a fitting in the manifold casting.

Some Ford and Holley distributors use a fully vacuum-controlled distributor. In this system the spark port is above the throttle plate, but there is also another passage connecting the distributor vacuum line to an additional spark port in the venturi. This type of distributor is controlled by the balanced action of the vacuum in the throttle body and the venturi, working together. Some of these carburetors for fully vacuum-controlled distributors use a spark valve screwed into the side of the carburetor. This valve controls the balance between venturi and throttle body vacuum.

For many years there were only two major systems of vacuum spark advance: the ported spark method, used with a centrifugal advance distributor, and the Ford venturi-vacuum method, which did not have any centrifugal advance. Then came smog. There are so many different systems of spark control now that it's bewildering. The systems that are important to carburetion are covered in our chapter on smog control setups.

The thing to remember is that these carburetor-mounted spark controls are active during part-throttle operation only. If you are concentrating on mileage, then you'd better be sure they are working right, but if you are going racing, then vacuum spark controls are not needed. However, if you remove the spark control and lines and plug up the holes in the carburetor, be sure you have traced the passageways with a wire, or you may plug up the wrong port.

ANTI-DIESELING SOLENOIDS

If you have ever turned the key off and had an engine keep running in a kind of a jerky, jumpy way, then you know what run-on, or dieseling, is.

Problems from dieseling were rare until smog controls came out. With the lean mixtures and high idle speeds required to keep our engines from putting us all in an early grave, it's common to turn the key off and have the engine keep running, especially when it's really hot. The engine does this mainly because the throttle is open so far. So to cure it the engineers designed a gadget to let the throttle close when you shut the key off. It's called an anti-dieseling solenoid. Anytime the key is on, the solenoid is energized and the plunger on the end of it holds the throttle open at the normal curb idle. The idle speed is adjusted either by moving the solenoid in its bracket or adjusting the threaded plunger in the end of it. While the plunger is energized, the conventional idle-speed screw is held off its seat. Turning the key off kills the solenoid, allows the plunger to retract, and lets the throttle drop back so that the idle-speed screw goes against its seat on the carburetor. Thus, there are two adjustments on solenoid-equipped carburetors. The curb idle is set at the solenoid. The key-off idle, or the solenoid de-energized idle speed is set with the usual idle-speed screw. To operate properly, the solenoid must be wired so that it goes off with the ignition switch. If it is mistakenly wired so that it is hot all the time, then it won't drop back when the key is turned off, and the chance of dieseling will be much greater.

What appears to be an anti-dieseling solenoid on '75 Chrysler Corp. carburetors really isn't (with one ex-

1. Here's an accelerator pump that's 100% lever operated. There is no override spring. The spring underneath the pump piston is merely to help linkage return the piston to the top of the stroke and to keep the slack out of the linkage.

2. Some cars have trouble with throttle plate icing, which causes the engine to die or results in extremely rough running. This system on a Chrysler Slant-6 channels heated air to underside of throttle plate, and prevents icing.

3. Vacuum storage tank on a Cadillac is connected to the slow-closing throttle diaphragm. It keeps the throttle open a little longer when decelerating.

4. This is the way a solenoid throttle works to avoid dieseling. Solenoid is necessary on many late-model cars.

3

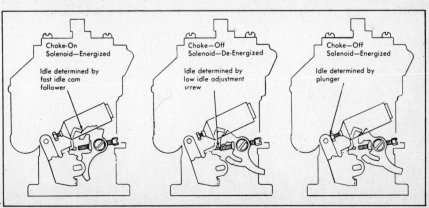

4

HOW CARBS WORK

ception), it's a throttle position solenoid that functions as part of the system designed to protect the catalytic converter from overheating damage.

DECELERATION CONTROLS

The best example of a deceleration control is the Combination Emission Control (CEC) valve on the '71 Chevys. It looks like an anti-dieseling solenoid, but it isn't. If you use the stem of the CEC valve to set curb idle speed, you will get in all kinds of trouble. The CEC valve can be recognized by the vacuum hose connected to it. An anti-dieseling solenoid has no vacuum hose.

Curb idle on carburetors with a CEC valve is set in the old-fashioned way with a throttle-cracking screw. The CEC valve is there only to hold the throttle open a little during deceleration so that the engine doesn't suck a lot of raw fuel into the cylinders and out through the exhaust. The CEC valve plunger is strictly an

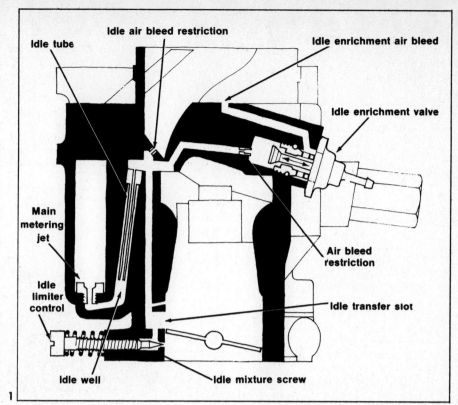

1

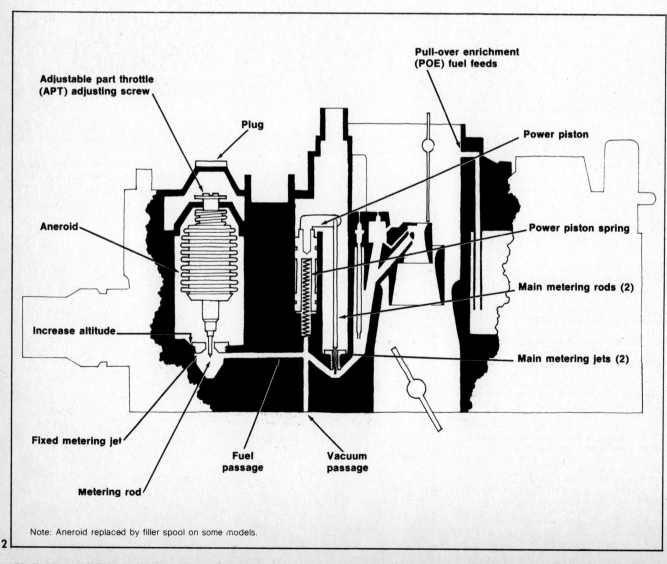

Note: Aneroid replaced by filler spool on some models.

2

emissions control. It has nothing to do with engine performance, so there's no need to change its setting. The plunger in the CEC valve is adjustable, but it is adjusted only after carburetor overhaul, or when the original setting has been disturbed. Adjustment procedure involves energizing the valve to extend the plunger, then turning the stem to get the correct engine rpm.

If the CEC valve is unscrewed far enough to set engine idle, it will open the throttle too far when it is energized during deceleration. It might even open the throttle far enough so that the car doesn't slow down when you take your foot off the gas, which is not only disturbing, but dangerous.

The control circuit for the CEC valve is a maze of wiring, switches, and relays. One of the switches is a transmission switch that turns the CEC valve on in the higher gears. In the lower gears the valve is off, which means that the vacuum supply to the distributor advance diaphragm is shut off, because the vacuum is controlled by the valve.

A peculiarity of the system is a time-delay switch that turns the valve on (extending the plunger) for 15 secs. after the ignition switch is turned on. If conditions are just right, meaning the temperature must be above 82° F., the engine will idle faster than normal during the 15 secs. Don't try to correct that if it happens, because it's normal operation. Below 82°, a temperature switch energizes the CEC valve—but extension of the plunger at that time will not affect idle, because the engine is probably cold enough to be on the choke and fast idle anyway.

By this time you should have a pretty good idea of how a carburetor works. And you should be ready to go on to some of the more complicated 4-bbl. installations. ♛

1. In carburetors equipped with idle enrichment system, the complete idle system is enriched during that part of engine operation carried out under cold or semi-cold conditions.

2. An idle enrichment system consists of an enrichment diaphragm operated by vacuum, and enrichment air bleeds.

3. This diagram shows operation of one type of atmospheric compensator. This device is used primarily on carburetors fitted to California cars; same carburetor casting is used for non-California cars, but the aneroid is replaced by a filler spool when compensation setup is non-functional.

4: Quick-disconnect terminal on this electric assist cap choke is wired directly to the alternator, receiving current whenever engine is running. Bimetallic switch controls current passage to ceramic heating element, depending upon temperature.

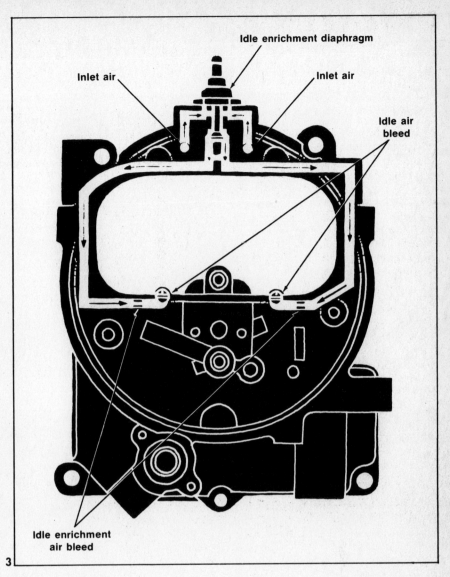

3

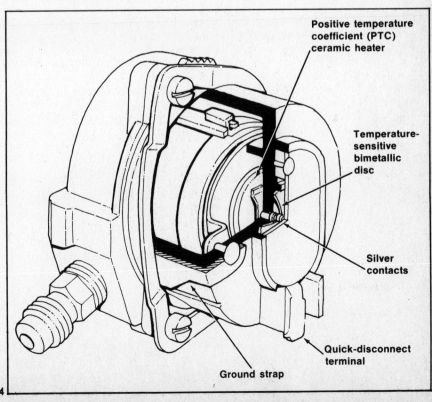

4

AIR CLEANERS

If you drive a car far enough to use up one gallon of gasoline, your engine will have gulped 8000 gals. of air. If you had to carry that air with you, it would take 146 drums, each holding 55 gals. That's a lot of air—but that's only the amount used with a single gallon of gas. Start figuring out how much air you use on an ordinary trip and you'll need a computer to add it all up. The problem with using all this air is simply that it isn't clean. Sure, we breathe it all day long, so it shouldn't be too bad—but remember that we have a built-in air filter in our nose. Our engines deserve an air filter too.

There are all kinds of particles in the air that we can't see. These particles can cause wear at any point in the engine where two surfaces move against each other. The main problem they cause is excessive piston ring wear, but they aren't through when they finish that dirty job. From there, the particles go down the cylinder walls into the oil pan and are circulated throughout the engine until they get caught in the oil filter . . . and by that time it's too late.

FILTER TYPES

Five types of air filtering devices have been used on passenger cars. Classified according to the filtering medium used, they are: dry paper, oil-wetted paper, oil bath, oil-wetted mesh and oil-wetted polyurethane. Production cars today generally use the dry paper filter element, but older cars and some foreign makes, as well as hot rod applications, will be equipped with one of the other types.

Dry paper elements are made with the paper in pleats to provide as much filtering area as possible. The paper is supported by metal mesh

and both paper and mesh are usually molded into a rubber or plastic gasket on both ends of the filter element. When the element is inserted into the filter body, the two gaskets must make an absolutely leakproof seal on both ends of the filter element. If it leaks, the filter won't be able to do its job properly.

All kinds of machines have been devised for testing dry paper elements. If you want to be that scientific about it, okay, but the simplest (and best) test of a dry paper element is to look at it while holding a light close to the other side. A new filter will look bright and clean but on a dirty one the light won't even come through. Dry paper elements can be tapped gently to loosen dirt and then blown carefully with an air hose. A good rule of thumb to follow is that if the filter element is dirty enough to require cleaning, it should be replaced—cleaning by tapping and blowing really isn't all that effective.

Oil-wetted paper elements are used mainly by General Motors. They look identical to the dry paper type, but they require one procedure that must be followed strictly: Oil-wetted paper elements must never be oiled, washed, tapped or blown. Service is limited to testing and replacement. These cautions are necessary because the oil-wetted paper is fragile.

Oil bath cleaners have been around for a long time, and will probably remain in use for some time to come. When air enters the cleaner, it goes down toward the surface of a pool of oil, then makes a U-turn and goes up into a filtering medium—which can be steel wool, copper gauze, loosely packed fibers or even curled animal hair As the air makes the U-turn, centrifugal force throws out some of

the dust, which is trapped in the pool of oil. If the engine is swallowing enough air, some of the oil will be picked up and splashed on the filtering medium. As the air reaches the top of the cleaner, it makes another U-turn and rams into a silencing pad; then it finally goes into the carburetor. Because the spaces between the fibers in the filtering medium are variable, some dust is going to get through. Also, two U-turns cause a lot of restriction in the airflow. The oil bath cleaner will continue to be used for a long time because it does a more than adequate filtering job, and replacing a little oil is a lot cheaper than buying new filter elements.

Oil-wetted mesh is probably the least effective of any filtering medium other than a window screen. But oil-wetted mesh has the advantage of taking up very little space. Some oil-wetted mesh cleaners are made with large chambers for silencing purposes. If noise is not a factor, they can be designed into a very small

1. A low-restriction air cleaner unit will be available for AC Spark Plug Division of General Motors in the firm's new Performance Line. Versatile chrome-plated housing accommodates various air pump and crankcase ventilation systems by means of three removable rubber plugs in the base plate and a selection of four breather tubes packed with the unit. Assembly is designed to fit most popular brand 4-bbl. carburetors with 5-in. diameter air horns.

2. Typical air cleaner used on General Motors cars. The gasket at the bottom goes between the cleaner and the carburetor, to prevent dirty air from getting in. In some cases, the bottom gasket is permanently held onto the air cleaner by metal tabs. Many air cleaners have additional filters inside the can to trap oil that may come in through breather hoses. Don't forget to clean them, too.

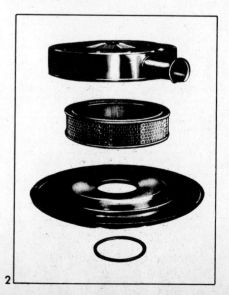

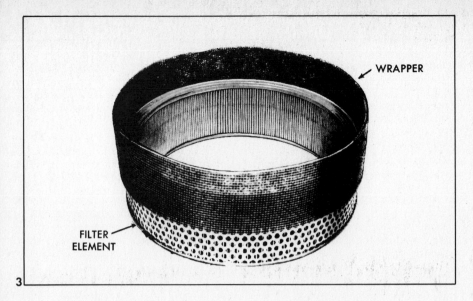

WRAPPER

FILTER ELEMENT

3

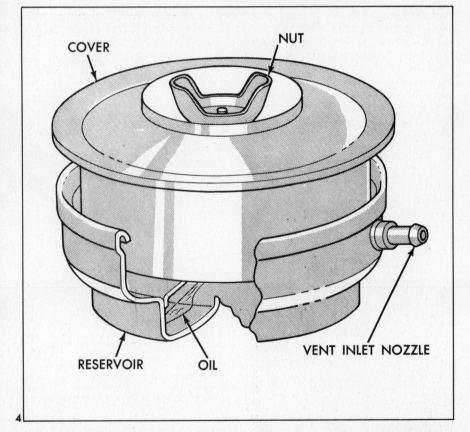

COVER

NUT

VENT INLET NOZZLE

RESERVOIR

OIL

4

ELEMENT & SUPPORT ASSY.

5

3. Some dry-type elements are encased in an outside wrapper, usually made of a screened material. This wrapper is designed to keep the oil fumes from ruining the relatively fragile dry paper element. When removed from around the inner element, the outer wrapper may be washed, dried and replaced. One should never attempt to wash a paper element, however.

4. This type of oil-bath air cleaner was the best design available until the paper- and foam-element filters came on the scene.

5. Foam-type elements must have a metal mesh to hold them in place. Lips of the foam must be over the edges of the mesh for proper sealing.

space. Both oil bath and oil-wetted mesh filters are serviced by washing the filtering medium in solvent. The oil-wetted mesh should be reoiled with a few drops of oil. The oil bath sump should be cleaned and fresh oil of the proper weight installed to the measured line. Never under any circumstances submerge the silencing chamber of any air cleaner in solvent. The chamber will fill, but the solvent cannot be poured out. It takes about 6 months of evaporation off the car or about a week of extremely rich running on the car for the solvent to finally work itself out.

Oil-wetted polyurethane elements are usually interchangeable with dry paper elements. One evidently does as good a job as the other, because cars have come through from the same factory with both kinds of element installed. The polyurethane element must be supported by a steel mesh so it will seal at top and bottom. If this mesh is left out, the filter will sag. When servicing polyurethane elements, use caution. Rough handling may rip the element or cause it to come apart at the joint. It should be washed in solvent and gently squeezed dry, then dipped in oil and the excess oil squeezed out. On some engines, very little oil is required—excess oil will restrict the passages and cause the engine to ·un rich.

If an engine is run under conditions in which it must operate at zero or very low intake manifold vacuum, and if the engine has closed crankcase ventilation, then the polyurethane element may be better than the dry paper. Closed crankcase ventilation utilizes a hose from the air cleaner to the valve cover. Under conditions of low vacuum, oil vapor from the valve cover will go through the hose and into the air cleaner. It's designed this way to keep those vapors from getting out where people can breathe them, so don't remove the hose. If those vapors are ruining your dry paper element, change to a polyurethane one—the oil won't hurt it.

Some dry paper types come with an additional mesh slipped over the outside of the element. This mesh is designed to catch the oil vapors and can be removed, cleaned and reinstalled dry as many times as are necessary to keep the dry paper element from getting oily. Today's filtering devices are much more effective than those of the past, but the original problem which the filter was designed to combat has yet to show any real improvement. The air is just as dirty, if not more so, and nothing makes an engine run richer than a clogged or restricted air cleaner.

AIR CLEANERS

EMISSIONS CONSIDERATIONS

But design engineers have quietly changed the purpose of the air cleaner from an afterthought hung atop the carburetor to an integral part of the underhood emissions package, and, as a result, its purpose is considerably more than simply filtering dirty air on its way to the carburetor. If you expect your engine to perform at top efficiency with maximum economy, you must look at the air cleaner in a somewhat different light.

Quite a number of years ago, the engineers at Lincoln did just that, and in 1957 they brought forth a device to control intake air temperature. By controlling the temperature of the air entering the carburetor, they reasoned that the choke would cut out faster and the air/fuel mixture would not vary according to extremes in outside air temperature. At the time, the advantage was considered primarily to be a safeguard against carburetor icing that would make Lincolns easier to drive in cold climates. Many people have driven all their lives and never had a carburetor ice up on them. For this to occur, the humidity has to be high and the air temperature low. When conditions are just right, ice forms in the carburetor barrels and around the throttle plates so that the engine will hardly run. In some cases, the entire throttle open-ing can become completely blocked by a solid plug of ice.

There isn't much you can do about icing—it's caused by the cooling effect of the expanding air after it leaves the venturi. The same thing happens when you let the air out of a tire by removing the valve stem. If conditions are right, ice will form on the outside of the valve. Mixtures slightly on the lean side help to cut down on carburetor icing, because any excess fuel has a cooling effect that leads to icing. The best way to control the problem however, is with a temperature-controlled air cleaner. But this wasn't fully appreciated until the auto manufacturers mounted their drive against emissions about 10 years later. The approach they took toward cleaner combustion was that of leaning carburetor operation under conditions of idle and partial throttle, as well as leaning the choke calibration. When it became necessary to go toward still leaner calibrations of both carburetor and choke, they took a second look at the mixture control advantages offered by regulating intake air temperature. It was found that such regulation allowed still leaner operation without sacrificing engine response and drivability. As a result, engines that have been modified or specifically designed for exhaust emissions control are now equipped with carburetor-air preheating systems contained within the air cleaner.

All domestic (and many foreign) systems operate in pretty much the same manner these days. Air for the carburetor intake is introduced directly from the exhaust manifold through a system of tubing or ducts and a baffle or shroud called a heat stove or heat shield. When this air heats up to a specified temperature, a thermostat in the air cleaner snorkel opens a heat control valve, or door, letting in cooler air from the engine compartment while closing off the hot air from the heat stove/shield. By varying the degree of heat control valve opening, the thermostat maintains the temperature of the air entering the carburetor at whatever the system requires for proper operation.

System design temperature varies according to the manufacturer's requirements, and can even differ from model year to model year within the same car line, but the temperature range usually falls between 90° F. and 115° F. Whenever the air in the engine compartment exceeds the design's temperature level, the air cleaner will cut off manifold heat completely and draw its intake air from the engine compartment. This means that the carburetor will always be receiving warm air—with the exception of the first few minutes of operation when the cold exhaust manifolds are in the process of heating

This mechanically operated system worked quite well, but as emissions specifications became more stringent, the system design necessarily became considerably more sophisticated. To provide the carburetor with the

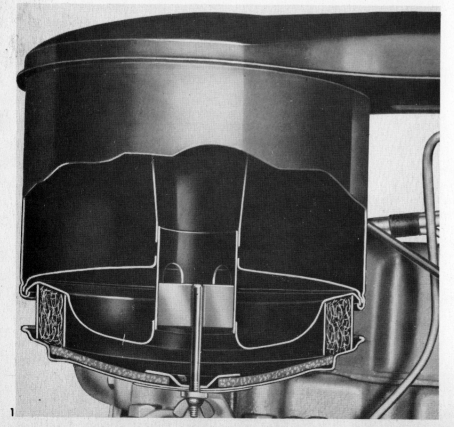

1. This one is almost an antique. It's a Chevy 6, before smog controls —a long time before smog controls. The filter element is excelsior, usually called horsehair. Large chamber is for silencing, as is the little pad at the bottom. This is not an efficient cleaner. Oil bath would be better, and modern paper or foam is better yet.

2. This is a carburetor hot-air system installation on a Chevy 307-cu.-in. engine. The "stove" shielding around the exhaust manifold is intended to preheat the air being fed to the carburetor during cold-engine starting. At the point where the "stovepipe" rises to enter the air cleaner snorkel, a vane selects the airflow from around the "stove" until the engine has warmed up sufficiently.

3. Modern air cleaners are a far cry from the old filter container concept. This exploded drawing of '75 Ford system used on 351 V-8 gives you an idea of their complexity.

4. Some manufacturers no longer recommend cleaning filter element; replace it when necessary after wiping inside of air cleaner with a cloth dampened in solvent to remove accumulated dirt and sludge.

5. Oil-wetted mesh dates back to the early days of the automobile. It is not as efficient as an air cleaner, but it does keep out the low-flying birds.

2

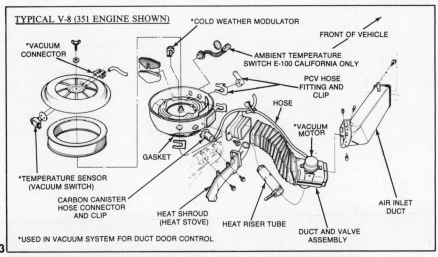

TYPICAL V-8 (351 ENGINE SHOWN)

*VACUUM CONNECTOR

*COLD WEATHER MODULATOR

FRONT OF VEHICLE

AMBIENT TEMPERATURE SWITCH E-100 CALIFORNIA ONLY

PCV HOSE FITTING AND CLIP

HOSE

*VACUUM MOTOR

GASKET

*TEMPERATURE SENSOR (VACUUM SWITCH)

CARBON CANISTER HOSE CONNECTOR AND CLIP

HEAT SHROUD (HEAT STOVE)

HEAT RISER TUBE

DUCT AND VALVE ASSEMBLY

AIR INLET DUCT

*USED IN VACUUM SYSTEM FOR DUCT DOOR CONTROL

3

4

additional air required during cold acceleration conditions, and to keep the air/fuel mixture from becoming too rich (giving off a higher level of emissions), the use of engine vacuum was introduced as a control device. In this type of air cleaner, operation of the heat control door is by a diaphragm-type vacuum motor and spring connected to a bimetallic temperature sensor located inside the air cleaner housing. The diaphragm spring holds the door wide open on a cold engine at rest. Once the engine is started and manifold vacuum builds up to 9 ins. or more, the vacuum motor begins to override the spring, compressing it and closing the heat control door to shut off air intake from the engine compartment.

The bimetallic temperature sensor acts as a modulator to mix the hot and cold air correctly by controlling the position of the door. As air cleaner temperature rises above the system design temperature, the sensor bleeds additional air into the vacuum line by opening a valve. If air cleaner temperature falls below the specified level, the air bleed will close to allow more manifold vacuum to reach the vacuum motor. What this does, then, is to close off the engine compartment air during high vacuum conditions, such as idle, cruise or deceleration, and to introduce it for maximum air flow during low vacuum or acceleration periods.

Should the system fail, the heat control door usually stays open, letting only engine compartment air enter. While this won't bother engine operation during warm weather, you'll notice hesitation, sagging, surge or stalling whenever the mercury dips. Such symptoms in cool weather operation indicate that something is wrong with the air cleaner's operation; check that before you decide that the carburetor is set too lean and needs adjustment.

NEW ADVANCES

Increasing sophistication of the air cleaner's function has brought other uses for its ability to control temperature. GM's secondary choke vacuum break feature, added to its 1975 models, uses a thermal vacuum valve which senses heated carburetor air temperature to control its action. When air cleaner temperature is below the calibration level, the thermal vacuum valve is closed; as the tem-

MESH TYPE AIR CLEANER ELEMENT

5

AIR CLEANERS

perature rises above the calibration level, the valve opens to let vacuum reach the diaphragm and open the choke a little more, letting engine operation stabilize properly.

Ford has added a second bimetallic sensor switch as part of its catalyst protection system. The bimetal contact operates within the 49°-55° F. range to activate the electric circuit to the solenoid vacuum valve. Two types of switches are in use—one that's normally open and one that's normally closed. Regardless of type, the sensor switch causes the the solenoid vacuum valve to block vacuum from a differential valve and, in turn, causes the bypass valve to dump the air pump output when a cold engine is started. Once the engine warms up, the air cleaner sensor switch reverses itself; this results in air pump output flowing through the bypass valve to the manifold.

Incidentally, recent Ford and GM air cleaners are equipped with a separate, small crankcase ventilation filter pack. This acts to trap oil and other contaminants whenever blowby gases reverse their direction under heavy engine load and enter the PCV valve inlet hose and then the air cleaner. As the filter packs are not too durable, cleaning and reuse is out of the question—they should be replaced whenever they become overly dirty. AMC uses a mesh type filter on some models. This unit can be pulled out and cleaned in solvent but, once again, replacement is far more effective than cleaning. This particular filter should not be ignored, as a dirty one will reduce the effectiveness of the PCV system.

TROUBLESHOOTING

As you can well imagine, troubleshooting present-day air cleaners is considerably more complex than in the past. In the days when it was merely a can containing a filter to reduce or eliminate the amount of garbage in the air before it reached the carburetor, all you had to do was remove the top, clean out the inside and replace the filter—simple enough. But with the variety of functions that modern air cleaners perform, you should be able to tell when the systems are functioning as they are supposed to and when they aren't. Blaming the carburetor for poor running conditions and trying to adjust it to correct the problem is a typical response—but a quick look at the air cleaner is in order before you touch the carburetor.

If your car uses one of the mechanically operated temperature control systems, its operation can be checked in much the same way that you'd check a cooling system thermostat. Before pulling the air cleaner off the carburetor, note the position of the heat control door in the snorkel—it should be closed to air from the engine compartment. Dunk the end of the air intake snorkel into a bucket of hot water (100° F.) far enough to cover the thermostat completely, then wait a couple of minutes before checking the door's position, which should still be closed. Increasing the water's temperature to approximately 135° F. should fully open the door. If it doesn't, there's either a mechanical interference in the operation of the door or the thermostat is malfunctioning and should consequently be replaced.

Troubleshooting a vacuum-operated air cleaner system is a little more complex, but if you have reason to believe that yours is not working properly, first check to make sure that all vacuum lines to the cleaner housing are connected properly and that none are pinched—a cracked or pinched hose can play havoc with air cleaner operation. After removing the air cleaner from the carburetor, connect a hand-operated vacuum pump to the vacuum diaphragm unit and apply about 10 ins. of vacuum. This should be sufficient to close the heat control door completely. Then pinch the hose or clamp it off to trap the vacuum in the line. If the door moves from its position, there's a leak in the diaphragm and it should be replaced. If the diaphragm tests out okay, you should check the sensor unit by removing it from the air cleaner and dunking it in hot water—just as you'd test a thermostat; then watch the bleed valve to see if it unseats properly. While this will tell you if the sensor is working properly, it won't tell you if the temperature operating range is correct. And, as with the mechanically operated system, don't rule out the possibility that the linkage which controls the heat door's operation is binding or sticking.

Many fumble-fingers drop their air cleaners occasionally when

1. Newest addition to air cleaner function is the crankcase ventilation filter pack, which prevents oil and sludge from blowing back into the air cleaner, fouling air filter element and possibly seeping into carburetor. It's a good idea to change both the filter element and filter pack at the same time.

2. AMC crankcase ventilation filter is wire mesh; while it can be removed and cleaned in solvent, replacement is a much better idea.

3. Hand vacuum pump is used to check operation of the vacuum diaphragm unit as shown.

4. If you find it necessary to replace temperature sensor, be sure to install the new switch in the same position as the old one. Don't press down on the center of new sensor when installing it or you'll damage the switch inside.

5. The '74 Mustang II uses a zip tube between the vacuum diaphragm unit and air cleaner. A hole in zip tube can cause faulty operation in cold weather, as fresh air that's not supposed to be in the system would influence temperature sensor in air cleaner.

removing/replacing them. You wouldn't really expect that to affect the operation, but dropping it can damage the diaphragm assembly, the temperature sensor(s) or even the linkage connecting the diaphragm and the heat control door. Oftentimes, the temperature sensor is perfectly okay, but the use of an excessively dirty filter element will affect its operation, as the sensor is placed inside the filter's circumference and air reaching it must pass through the filter element.

ZIP TUBES

There's one other thing that bears watching on some of the newer air cleaners. Until recently, everybody in the auto business used an all-metal cleaner unit with one or two open-ended snorkels that drew in air from the engine compartment. But some cars (especially Fords) are now fitted with a flexible connector—called a zip tube—between the air cleaner and a fresh air inlet, to draw in air from outside the engine compartment. Using a zip tube has several advantages, one of which is the ability to pre-filter air entering the system. This prevents rapidly accumulating engine compartment debris and contaminants from gumming up the heat control door and linkage. But zip tubes are far from perfect; made of flexible plastic with a plastic wraparound connector, they have a tendency to crack and tear, especially with rough handling in cold-weather climates.

A damaged zip tube may have no effect on the operation of the heat control door, or it may have an adverse effect, depending upon the overall design of the system. If the vacuum diaphragm is placed between the zip tube and the bimetallic sensor, a tear in the tube won't do much, but many designs place both the diaphragm and the heat door in the fresh air inlet where the zip tube connects, instead of in the fresh air inlet itself. This placement serves to prevent accidental damage if the air cleaner is dropped, but a tear in the tube will let engine compartment air enter the system when fresh air is supposed to be flowing in, leading to a difference in temperature under certain conditions.

As you can see, modern air cleaners have a far more important job than ever before in determining how well an engine will perform, and it's likely that they'll become even more sophisticated with the stringent emissions levels due in the years ahead. But there's one other area where filters are important—the fuel line. Somewhere between the tank and the carburetor, dirt in the fuel has to be trapped and held. We'll find out how in the pages to come ☙

FUEL FILTERS

In the days before most of us were born, gasoline was bought at the general store and strained through a chamois as it was poured into the tank. The chamois would strain out any dirt and, hopefully, would retain any water mixed in with the gas. Nowadays we don't think much about dirt and water in the gas until the car quits, but it's still there.

The gasoline manufacturers put out a clean product, and it is still clean and free of water until it is put into your car's gas tank. From that point on, the gasoline picks up water from the condensation in the tank, and foreign matter through the vent or from scale and rust sloughing off the sides of the tank. In areas where there is heavy rain, some service stations have had their tanks contaminated with water, which then went into their customers' gas tanks, but this seldom happens. The most common cause of water contamination is condensation, resulting from leaving tanks only partially full. The water reacts with the sides of the tank and we get rust and scale. This can happen not only in a service station's tanks, but in your own car's gas tank, as well. Less contamination will result if gas tanks are kept as full as possible at all times.

Car manufacturers have recognized the gasoline contamination problem. The automobile today has more fuel filters than it has ever had. The first filter is on the end of the pickup tube in the gas tank. It can be a fine screen of special metal alloy, but usually it is made of a flexible material that feels like fiberglass. This screen has the unusual property of being able to stop water. In fact, it stops water so well, that it stops the car also. This can be a nuisance, but it was designed this way on purpose. It's a lot cheaper to remove the gas tank and clean it than it is to buy a new carburetor.

If water should get through to the carburetor, it reacts with the metal of the carb and forms a whitish yellow scale that seems to grow almost like moss. Only a few days of running with water in the carburetor means the end of the carburetor. Ordinary carburetor cleaners will not remove the scale. Some mechanics use hydrocholoric acid, but even that won't do any good if the reaction has gone on too long.

The filter in the tank is supposed to stop all this. Water builds up on the .outside of the filter like jelly. Sooner or later no gasoline can get through and the car will be stopped. It's a good system, and it saves a lot of carburetors.

The next filtration point on some cars is the fuel pump, where the filter is inside a glass or metal sediment bowl. This filter can be folded paper or ceramic. If it is ceramic, usually all that is necessary for servicing is to clean the bowl and filter, and replace with a new bowl gasket. If the filter is folded paper it should definitely be replaced. This type of filter can plug up from dirt. It may look good, but could be plugged up so bad it won't pass enough gas to run a go kart, much less an automobile.

After the filter bowl, the fuel may pass through one or two screens in the fuel pump, and then into a "can" or inline-type filter. Many cars today do not use any filtration in the pump itself because the inline filters work so well.

The inline filter cannot be cleaned. It should be replaced on a mileage basis, or if the mileage is not definitely known it should be replaced for safety's sake.

Inline filters on air-conditioned cars do a double job. They filter the gas and act as a vapor separator. The upper section of the can is a

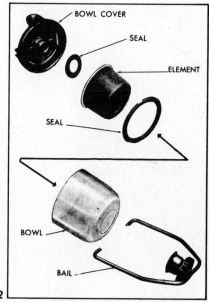

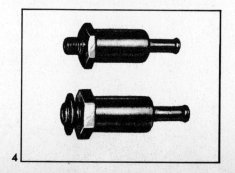

1. You won't find this on any stocker. It's big, with lots of filtering area.

2. Clogged filters — even though they may be the clear bowl-type — aren't readily apparent to the eye, and can cause an engine to run out of gas.

3. Everybody's getting into the filter business. This Varicam model has a single replaceable element, with over 500 square inches of filtering area.

4. Disposable filters like these are found screwed into the inlet side of Autolite carburetors on many new Fords.

vapor trap. A line from the trap runs all the way back to the gas tank, thus carrying any vapors back where they belong. Of course, the line also takes quite a bit of fuel back to the tank, which means that the fuel pump is pumping a lot of fuel in a circle. This means that even when the engine is idling, using a small amount of fuel, there is still fuel coming through the main line and back through the vapor line. This helps keep the lines cool and prevent vapor lock. The pump has to work pretty hard to keep all that fuel moving, but modern pumps have been designed with the extra capacity they need.

Some cars may use a glass bowl filter with a folded paper element instead of the inline filter. These pa-

per elements are also subject to clogging and should be changed.

The last filter in the system, and the one that most people don't know about, is the little bronze one in the carburetor fuel inlet. On some installations the only filtration in the system may be the filter in the tank and the bronze filter in the carburetor. The bronze filter is spring-loaded and seats against a small gasket.

In order to get as much filtering area as possible, the bronze filter is made in a kind of folded design. It's too bad they didn't fold it a few more times, because it can plug up and cause mechanics more grief than a wrench dropped on a big toe.

A dirty filter, no matter where it is in the system, can cause an en-

gine to run out of fuel. Clogged fuel filters have probably been responsible for more un-needed work being done on fuel pumps than any other part on a car. If the gasoline is not reaching the carburetor, a simple test will determine if the trouble is the fuel pump or not. Attach a hose to the fuel pump inlet and drop the end of the hose into a can of gasoline. Hook up another hose to the fuel pump outlet and let it end in an open can. Idle the engine and measure the gas pumped into the open can. A good fuel pump should pump a pint in half a minute or less. If it does, the trouble is probably somewhere else in the system. A complete fuel pump test includes a pressure test, also. That, we will take up in the next chapter. ♛

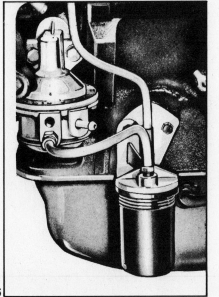

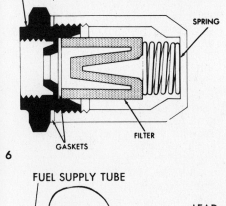

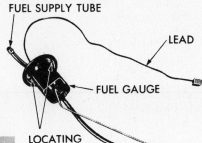

5. Some models of Ford had these filters separate, and some were part of the fuel pump housing.

6. A bronze filter — at the carb's inlet side — is usually a spring-loaded device that seats the W-shaped filter against a small gasket. When plugged, however, it can cause agony.

7. Modern fuel tank package houses a combination fuel pickup, filter and gas gauge sending unit.

8. Fuel filters come in all shapes and sizes and in all levels of efficiency. They should be changed on a regular basis before they plug up and stop you out in the middle of nowhere.

9. Carter's high capacity bowl filter has four ceramic elements inside, with a total of 36 square inches of filtering area, for less fuel restriction.

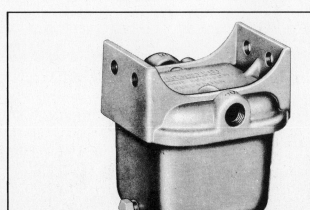

FUEL PUMPS

The mechanical fuel pump that is standard equipment on American automobiles is operated by an eccentric or "lobe" on the camshaft. On some engines the fuel pump linkage operates directly off the cam eccentric. On others, the eccentric operates a pushrod, and the pushrod acts on the fuel pump linkage. When checking for insufficient fuel pressure or volume on a pushrod-operated pump, the pushrod must always be checked for wear and replaced if necessary. Worn pushrods will not give a full stroke at the pump.

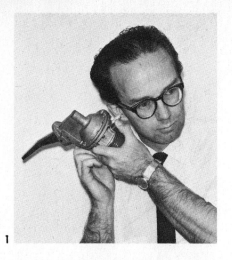

MECHANICAL FUEL PUMP

1

The fuel pump works by creating suction about the same as a person drinking water through a straw. The pump sucks up fuel through its inlet valve, then pushes the fuel through its outlet valve to the carburetor. Inside the pump is a flexible diaphragm that is forced in one direction by the linkage to create suction. At the same time a spring is compressed under the diaphragm. When the camshaft eccentric goes to the low side and the pump linkage relaxes, the spring pushes the diaphragm in the opposite direction and the fuel is pushed out of the pump.

Fuel pressure is determined by the strength of the spring, and pressure can be increased or decreased simply by changing the spring — if you are lucky enough to have a pump that can be taken apart. Changing pressure is rarely done in a stock pump because it is only needed in special situations. Late-model stock pumps have a crimped edge with no screws. If one of these pumps wears out, or develops trouble, it must be discarded and of course, nothing can be done about changing the pressure.

An early-type fuel pump only pumps when it is needed. The linkage is operating anytime the engine is running, but the spring only pushes fuel out of the pump when the carburetor needle valve is open. When the needle valve is closed the spring is pushing, but no fuel is moving, so the spring stays in the compressed position and the linkage idles up and down without actually doing anything. To keep the linkage from being noisy, a small spring in the pump holds the linkage in contact with the eccentric so it won't rattle around.

When the engine is shut off, the pressure spring in the pump maintains pressure in the line between the pump and the carburetor. Everything would be OK if the pressure stayed within specifications, but it doesn't. Whenever an engine is shut off, the heat that would have been dissipated by the radiator comes out into the engine compartment because the coolant has stopped circulating.

Within a few minutes after the engine has stopped, the engine compartment gets like an oven. The heat expands the gas in the line between the fuel pump and the carburetor. When the expanding gasoline tries to get back into the fuel pump, it is blocked by the outlet valve, so the pressure keeps building up. Finally, the pressure builds up so much that the gasoline pushes the needle valve open. This fills the float bowl to overflowing, whereupon the gas goes out the main nozzle and into the engine.

When the driver returns to his car, his engine is flooded, and he has to sit there while the starter cranks away, trying to clean out the engine so it will start. This will not happen on a car with factory-installed air conditioning, because there is a vapor return line that comes off the fuel filter. The second the engine is shut down, fuel pressure drops to zero, and there can be no buildup because of heat.

Something similar was needed on a car that didn't have air conditioning, but without the added expense of that vapor return line that goes clear back to the tank. What the manufacturers have done is put a small hole in the pump that bleeds off the pressure. The hole may be in each pump valve, or in the pump casting. Pumps with these bleed holes will drop to zero pressure immediately when the engine is shut off.

On both systems, the vapor return-line-type and the bleed-hole-type,

2

1. Many late-model pumps have a built-in bleed that prevents a pressure buildup between the pump and the carburetor after the engine is shut off. If you hold your finger over the outlet and work the pump lever by hand, you can easily hear air rushing through the bleed hole.

2. If your fuel pump comes apart, and if you can buy a repair kit, a pump is not hard to repair. If the valves are staked in place, leave them alone. You'll do more damage trying to install the new valves than leaving the old in.

3. A large housing on a pump is mostly for vapor control, not high performance. The pump with the large housing may put out more, but not as a result of having the big housing.

4. The spring under the diaphragm is the source of the fuel pressure. A heavier spring will produce more pressure, if needed.

5. This typical diaphragm-type AC fuel pump uses vacuum — as in an internal combustion engine — to alternately pull gas from the tank, then push it into the carburetor. The vacuum-producing motion of the diaphragm is provided by an eccentric attached to and driven off the camshaft.

6. Old-time dual-diaphragm-type pumps, used on cars with vacuum wipers, had a wiper booster on bottom half of housing.

the pump has to work harder because gasoline is constantly being bled off the pressure side of the pump and routed back to the suction side. This type of pump never stops working. Modern pumps have enough capacity to handle the bleed down system and still keep the engine supplied with sufficient fuel.

A mechanic can really get into trouble with one of these bleed-down pumps. For years it has been accepted practice to put a pressure gauge in the line between the pump and the carburetor. If the pump will put out the specified pressure, usually 3 to 6 pounds at the idle, then it is OK on pressure test. That part of the test is still valid, but it was also accepted practice to shut the engine off and watch the gauge to see if the pump would hold the pressure. Of course a pump with bleed holes is not designed to hold pres-

sure with the engine off. A mechanic is going to be replacing pumps until his arm wears out, if he doesn't know about the bleed-down feature.

Most cars nowadays have electric windshield wipers. Back in the days when wipers were vacuum-operated, a vacuum pump was sometimes built onto the fuel pump so that the wipers would work while the engine was at low vacuum. Low vacuum occurs at wide open throttle, just about the time you have passed another car and are desperately trying to find a hole so you can get back on your own side of the road. It's a little disconcerting to have the wipers quit or slow down at that moment, so the vacuum pump was a pretty important item.

The vacuum pump was part of the fuel pump casting, and it operated off the same linkage, but this was just for convenience. Other than

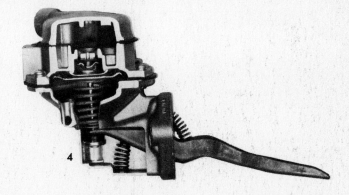

4

3

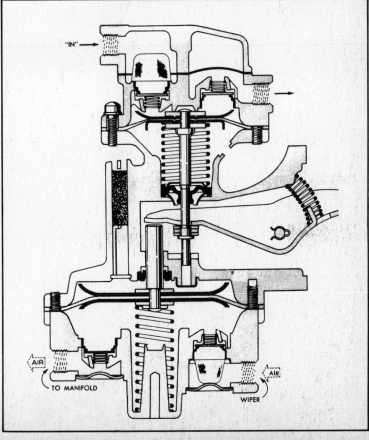

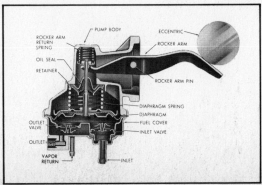

5

6

FUEL PUMPS

that, the two pumps are independent. The disadvantage is that if the vacuum half or the fuel half of the pump goes bad, the whole pump has to be replaced. Repair kits are available for both fuel and vacuum pumps, but the job is so time-consuming and rebuilt or new pumps are so easily available that few mechanics put kits in fuel pumps any more. On late pumps, repairs are not possible because the pumps can't be disassembled. Some of the pumps that will come apart are not rebuildable either, because the valves cannot be removed from the casting without breaking everything up.

The volume of fuel a pump can put out is much more important than the pressure. If a pump is suspected

of not doing its job, it should be tested for output by attaching a hose to the inlet side, with the end of the hose in a bucket of gasoline or solvent. Attach another hose to the outlet side and idle the engine on the gas that is in the float bowl. If the pump will fill a pint can in half a minute or less, it can be considered a good pump. For a complete test, insert a pressure gauge in the outlet hose and see if the pump will maintain specified pressure for that particular engine.

There is nothing that can be done to increase the volume of a pump except putting on a larger pump. Carter, Holley, and some car makers have high-performance mechanical pumps that are a low-cost solution to many fuel starvation problems in race cars. They work well on circle

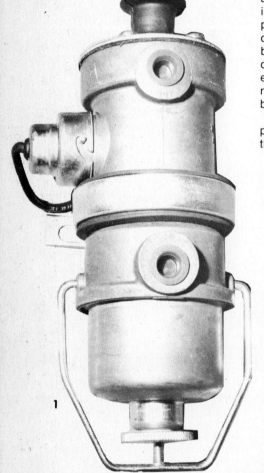

1

2

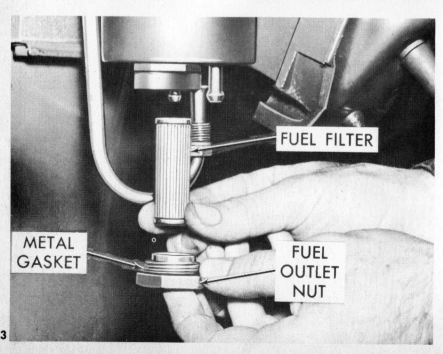

FUEL FILTER

METAL GASKET

FUEL OUTLET NUT

3

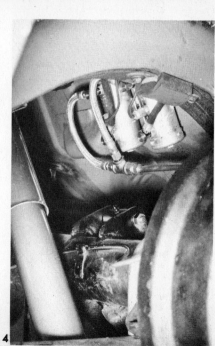

4

5

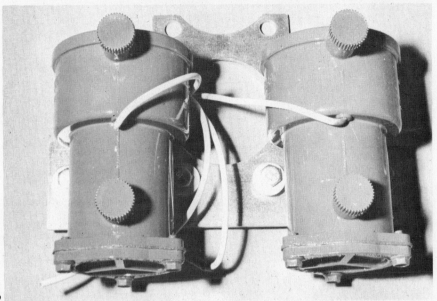

6

track racers that don't have any battery to run an electric pump.

In drag racing, you need a pump back at the tank to overcome the gravity effect of the long column of fuel inside the line from the tank up to the engine. A fuel line with a horizontal length of 10 feet between tank and carburetor will result in a pressure loss of about 3 pounds per g of acceleration. The only answer for drag racing is to put an electric pump back at the tank, so the pump can push the fuel up to the carburetor. Most pumps, whether mechanical or electric, are more efficient at pushing than sucking.

ELECTRIC FUEL PUMP

Electric pumps come in four types — plunger, diaphragm, bellows, and impeller. They can be mounted anywhere in the line between the gas tank and the carburetor, but their main advantage is eliminated if they are not placed as close to the tank as possible.

The advantage of an electric fuel pump is elimination of vapor lock. With the pump mounted at the tank, the whole fuel line between tank and carburetor is pressurized. With the fuel under pressure, it is extremely difficult for vapor bubbles to form, even if the fuel line gets hot. It's a pretty safe bet that anytime a fuel pump is mounted at the tank that vapor lock will be eliminated. Also, it's much cooler back there, so the pump is not likely to become overheated.

The disadvantage of electric pumps is in educating the driver to use them. Electric pumps are ordinarily hooked up to the ignition switch. Any time the switch is on, the pump is maintaining pressure in the fuel line. This is fine, until the switch is left on accidentally and the carburetor happens to have a needle valve that leaks a little. In such an unfortunate combination of circumstances, the complete contents of the gas tank will be pumped into the float bowl, filling the engine and overflowing onto the ground.

The plunger is without any rings or seal. Fuel constantly leaks between it and the cylinder wall, so that even when the engine is not running, the pump will slowly tick away, maintaining pressure in the line. With age, the pump will operate faster because of wear between the piston and cylinder wall.

The advantage of this pump is its reliability. There is no diaphragm to rupture, and the piston and valves can easily be removed in case they get loaded with dirt. A strainer and sediment chamber can be cleaned by removing the bottom cap.

1. One of the earliest of the high capacity pumps is the still popular Stewart-Warner model 240. This pump can deliver up to 8 psi but has an average setting from the factory of 4 psi. Pressure is adjustable.

2. Volume is much more important than pressure. The old standard of a pint in 30 seconds is inadequate for today's engines. Some original equipment pumps will put out a pint in less than 10 seconds. A high-performance pump will put out enough to water your lawn.

3. The fuel filter on a '69 Cadillac is an intergral part of the fuel pump — mounted on the left front of the engine — and should be changed every 12,000 miles or 12 months.

4. Two Bendix pumps mounted at the tank. An electric pump belongs back there where it can push the fuel forward.

5. Dual Stewart-Warner fuel pumps are needed to keep the line flow high enough to feed Dick Landy's hungry 16-plug elephant. Flow — not line pressure — is important factor here.

6. Dual Conelec pumps are used for racing where high volume is necessary.

7. Conelec pump comes in single and dual models. It is waterproof, in case you want to drive under water.

8. Cutaway of Conelec pump shows central plunger, the only moving part.

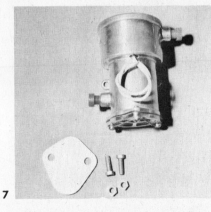

7

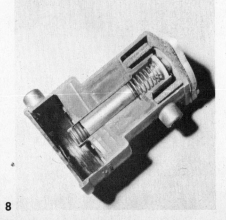

8

FUEL PUMPS

Stewart-Warner also makes a piston-type pump for racing and other high-output applications. It has one definite advantage over other pumps in that the pressure is adjustable between 3 and 8 pounds, without disconnecting or dismantling the pump.

Conelec makes an ''electronic'' pump. It is a plunger type, but differs from other pumps in that is has no contact points to wear out. The electromagnet that moves the plunger up and down is controlled by an electronic switching device with no moving parts. Because of its electronic design, this pump has very low current draw. It is available in single and dual models.

DIAPHRAGM PUMPS

Only one diaphragm pump, made by AC, remains on the market. It is motor-driven, and is considered a heavy-duty design, but in all the years we have been looking under frame rails to find out what kind of pump was installed, we have never discovered one of the AC motor-driven diaphragm pumps. AC also makes some motor-driven in-tank models, but they are an impeller design rather than a diaphragm, and are primarily used on trucks. The long-available Stewart-Warner diaphragm pump, the 220-A, has at last been discontinued. It was a low-output pump, so we're not sorry to see it go.

BELLOWS PUMP

Bellows pumps are made by Dupree, who appear to have inherited the design from the old Autopulse Co. There are several single models, a dual, and a triple, all with different capacities. Check the latest specs before you buy, to be sure you are getting a pump that is big enough to handle the job.

AC also puts out a bellows pump based on the old Autopulse design. In fact, the AC bellows pump appears to be a slightly modified Dupree. The difference is that the Dupree can be had as a single, dual, or triple, while the AC comes as a dual only. Included in the AC package is an oil pressure switch that turns off the pump when the oil pressure drops below 2 pounds. It's a good safety feature, and should be installed with any electric pump.

IMPELLER FUEL PUMP

Impeller pumps are made by Carter and Holley. Impeller pumps work

1

2

3

1. Dupree puts out this single model, and several others, including a triple that should take care of anything. Dupree design is based on the old Autopulse pump.

2. AC — makers of several original equipment in-tank models — also puts out these fuel pumps for universal electric applications. The one with the bracket is the heavy-duty unit for high output for use in racing engines.

3. AC puts out this high capacity duplex pump, which is similar to the Dupree. The pump is supplied with a safety switch to cut off the pump when oil pressure drops below 2 pounds.

4. Holley's GPH-110 comes in this racing model with a pressure regulator. It's also available in a lower-pressure model for the street — at a lower price, too.

5. This Carter electric is not upside down. Carter found out the top (bottom) bearing will last longer if the pump is run with the terminals down.

6. Cutaway of Carter electric shows motor cavity that fills with fuel to make bearings last longer. Carter sells this pump in an Electromech package, which includes a mechanical pump to go on the engine in place of the stock pump.

7. Cross-sectional view of the old Autopulse shows the basic workings of the unit where many of the moving parts — such as the short pump assembly — were replaceable items.

8. It's a pump, pickup tube, filter, and gauge unit for the inside of the Vega fuel tank. It's made by AC Division of GM.

the same way a fan blows air. The impeller creates suction to bring fuel into the pump and push it out through the line to the carburetor. Impeller pumps have no valves. The fuel is delivered in a steady flow, without any of the pulsating that hammers needles and seats to death. Most electric pumps are more efficient when they are pushing the fuel. They should be mounted below or at least level with the tank so they receive the fuel by gravity. You might be able to get away with a mounting position in the engine compartment or halfway between the tank and the carburetor on a bellows, piston, or diaphragm pump, but not on an impeller pump. The impeller pump is designed to push the fuel, so it must be mounted at the tank, below the fuel level.

We have a Carter electric pump on one of our cars that has been humming away for years. It looks as

if it is going to outlast the car, and it requires no attention at all. It is noisy, but any electric pump makes some noise. The Carter electric is available in both regular and high-performance models.

Newest impeller pump on the performance scene is the Holley GPH-110. As the name indicates, it pumps 110 gallons per hour, which is more than any of the pumps described in this chapter. It pumps so much that it must be used with a pressure regulator to keep from overriding the float and turning the engine into a fuel fountain. The GPH-110 will work in any application, but its high cost will probably limit it to the drag strip and race track.

All electric fuel pumps are rated according to pressure and output. The manufacturers know what is needed in most applications, so their recommendations should be followed. Some pumps are made in

different models, for normal or high output installations. About 45 gallons per hour is the capacity usually furnished for most hot rod installations.

With all the pumps available, deciding which one to buy can really be a problem. The first question you should answer is whether you really need a pump that is any better than the stock one. Late-model engines have fuel pumps that put out a lot a fuel. If the pump is in good shape, there probably isn't any reason to change it. However, if you are running multiple carburetion on an early engine, such as a flathead Ford, then the stock pump probably will not do the job.

If you decide to get a special pump, do a little checking on specifications. Some special pumps are designed for dependability. They will last forever, but they don't have the high output required in a multiple carburetor installation. ♛

4

5

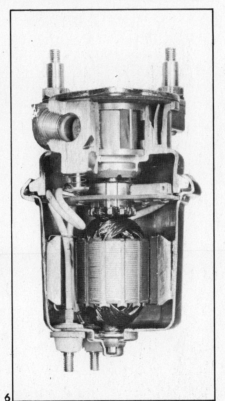

6

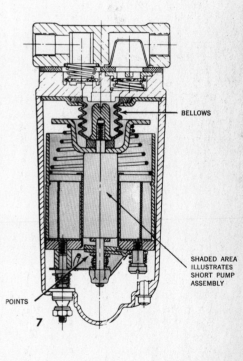

BELLOWS

SHADED AREA ILLUSTRATES SHORT PUMP ASSEMBLY

POINTS

7

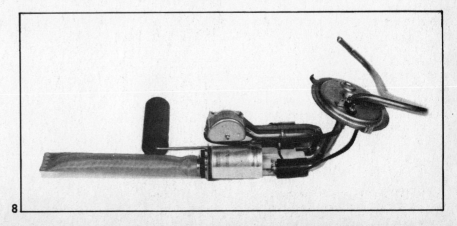

8

EDELBROCK'S ELECTRONIC FUEL INJECTION

BY JIM McFARLAND

As a concept, electronic fuel injection is not altogether new. For that matter, neither is port injection. But what Edelbrock is on the threshold of producing is new, because their electronic fuel injection (EFI) is capable of injector nozzle operation that follows the engine's firing order. And this is a little different.

Essentially, the system concerns itself with gathering information on a variety of operating engine variables. These include intake manifold vacuum, engine rpm, ignition rate of advance and total lead, inlet air and coolant temperatures, environmental pressure (altitude compensation) and related engine data. Each of these factors is continously monitored and the resulting information is fed to the mini-computer.

In the computer these data bits are processed to produce a single electronic pulse that is transmitted to an injector nozzle for actuation. As driving conditions change (road load, acceleration, deceleration, etc.), pulses are conditioned electronically to meet the engine's fuel requirements. Since more fuel is delivered the longer each injector nozzle remains on (open), pulse duration becomes critical to both fuel economy and drivability.

There is another important feature. In carbureted engines for which the intake manifold flows wet (both air and fuel), problems of air/fuel separation (or wet-out) inside the intake manifold and inlet ports are common. This tends to upset the quality of mixed air and fuel in the combustion chamber. In many instances, it increases production of unburned hydrocarbons, since raw fuel is being passed right through the engine.

In Edelbrock's EFI system, injectors are turned on well into the induction cycle, after most of the influence of reversion pressures (backflow) is subdued. This backflow condition, brought about by cylinder pressures that are much higher than those inside the intake manifold (above atmospheric pressure in the cylinder vs. below atmospheric pressure in the intake manifold) at the time the intake valve begins to open, can be quite disruptive to engine efficiency.

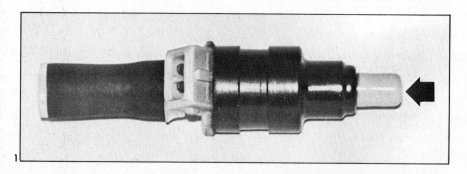

1

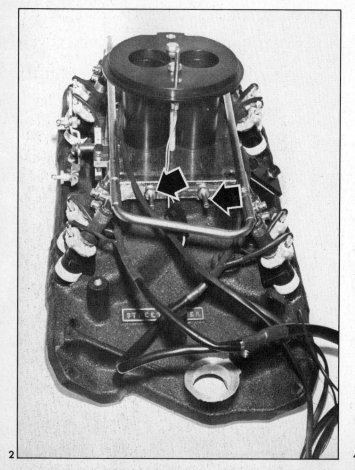

2

3

4

1. Bosch injector nozzles are used on the Edelbrock EFI. Principle of nozzle operation includes solenoid-actuated plunger that is unseated in the nose of the nozzle (as shown), allowing a measured portion of fuel to be admitted to the passing airstream.

2. Of the various parameters sensed by the system, both intake manifold vacuum and distributor advance vacuum are taken from the base of the air valve body. Only manifold vacuum, however, becomes one of the several inputs to the mini-computer. Vacuum advance functions as in a normal Kettering battery ignition.

3. Carburetor (or air valve) inlet air temperature is sensed at the top of the air valve and delivered as electrical input to the mini-computer. This is a typical thermocouple/temperature measuring element.

4. Heat insulators separate the injector nozzles from the intake manifold. They also provide seating surfaces for the screw-type nozzle clamps (as shown). O-rings are used at the interface between the insulators and the nozzles.

5. A dual magnetic-pickup distributor (also an Edelbrock design) is used in the system. A carefully-dimensioned "shutter" triggers pulses for both ignition timing and injector timing.

6. Included in the special distributor is a stock-type centrifugal advance mechanism. A certain amount of "tailoring" was necessary to provide the correct rate of advance for the EFI system, due in part to the very high rate of response that the electrical components provide in fuel delivery control.

5

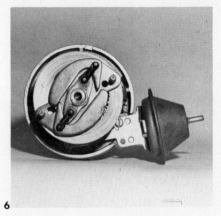

6

On engines that have a carburetor, these backflow pulses or velocity spikes can make the carburetor deliver unwanted fuel. Physically, these pressures are the result of combustion residue finding its way back into the intake manifold, where it can mix with the fresh air/fuel mixture that's being let into another cylinder. The net effect here is that the residue (actually exhaust gas) reduces the amount of heat produced by a given air/fuel mixture . . . and power is lost. This is the intent on vehicles that use exhaust gas recirculation (EGR) to reduce the level of oxides of nitrogen (NOx) produced at the tailpipe.

However, Edelbrock's EFI unit incorporates injector "on" times (periods when the nozzle opens) that begin well after the piston has passed top dead center on the intake stroke, so most of the disruptive pressures and/or dilution are significantly reduced. In addition, the spray or atomization patterns offered by the injector nozzles deliver fuel in particle sizes considerably finer than those found in carbureted engines. There is also more uniformity of particle size. This permits establishing and maintaining much leaner air/fuel ratios over a broader range of engine rpm. To a large extent, this accounts for the fuel economy benefits offered by the EFI system.

On the basis of mathematical calculation and measured levels of carbon monoxide, carbon dioxide and unburned hydrocarbons, air/fuel ratios with the Edelbrock unit have been found to be in the 17.5:1-18.0:1 range during highway cruising conditions. This puts the engine in a lean-burn condition but still allows adequate power for both pulling and safety.

In place of a carburetor as we know it today, Edelbrock's EFI uses an air valve that merely opens and closes like conventional throttle blades. This regulates the amount of air entering the engine. Since airflow is being sensed by other means, the specific amount of fuel needed to maintain a predetermined air/fuel ratio is computed and the injector nozzles are "told" when to turn on and off. Obviously the engine will not be static in terms of rpm or load, so the mini-computer has been designed to recompute injector "on" times very rapidly. That way there is no lag in fuel delivery instruction. In fact, the system updates its "on" times at the rate of one injector pulse every millisecond. This means that the system computes (or updates) its injector nozzle instructions at the rate of 1000 times per second! That's a little faster than most of us are able to move our throttle foot.

Fuel delivery to the nozzles is provided by a Bosch pump operating at a maintained pressure of 35 psi. Regulated at this pressure, the fuel is filtered and passed into a set of fuel rails that tie all of the nozzles together. It then returns to the fuel tank by way of a bypass system. In this fashion, there is a constant pressure head of fuel at each nozzle. The time when the injector is open is so brief that there isn't enough time for line pressure to drop due to flowing pressure changes when fuel leaves each nozzle.

And then there's the system's ability to follow the firing order. By way of comparison, the Bendix system on late Cadillac Seville models is a so-called "batch" system. Only sufficient fuel for four of the eight cylinders is injected at one time. The resulting loose fuel in the system was believed by Edelbrock to contribute to wasted fuel (poor combustion efficiency) and/or air/fuel separation within the inlet paths.

So, for the first time, Edelbrock has developed a system whereby injector nozzles turn on and off in the same sequence as the engine's firing order, changing the intake manifold into a dry-flow manifold (no more mechanical separation of air and fuel in the manifold) in which very high velocities can be generated without fear of centrifuging fuel out of the airstream in corners and bends of the runners. For this reason, special consideration was given to the intake manifold design. The result is a package that is

EDELBROCK

extremely sharp and crisp in throttle response with very good low-rpm torque capability.

The distributor contains some rather interesting features too. It is a dual magnetic pickup unit that can provide data pulses both to the spark plugs, via the ignition system, and to the injectors, via the mini-computer and driver circuits—each independently. That way, injector pulse timing can be separate from that needed to fire the spark plugs. Consequently, the injectors can be operated well ahead of the point of ignition.

A scallop-shaped shutter is mounted just below the distributor rotor (like an inverted bowl) in such a way that it can pass by each of the magnetic pickups while the distributor shaft rotates. As you might expect, the relationship between the shutter's vanes and the magnetic pickups is

critical, but this dimension is fixed in the manufacture of the system and is not adjustable by the consumer.

The remainder of the ignition system is basically a high-energy ignition system (as designed by Edelbrock). It is solid-state and integrated with the magnetic pickup distributor. Since lean-burn conditions are a reality with the complete EFI system, higher-than-stock ignition output was necessary and was therefore included.

From the standpoint of performance (including fuel economy), data are still being gathered and fuel curves fitted to common vehicle uses. Typically, low-rpm torque is greatly increased. This seems to be the result of both much-improved air/fuel handling at engine speeds where conventional carburetion is not capable of providing good atomization of fuel and preventing (or reducing) air/fuel separation. At lower engine speeds, mixture velocity is ordinarily not as high as necessary to help

maintain fuel suspension. It's purely a matter of low kinetic energy in the inlet system. However, the atomization efficiency provided by the injector nozzles is such that rpm do not affect nozzle performance. In fact, the nozzles don't know how fast the engine is going, anyway—all they're told is how long to stay on.

So vehicles equipped with Edelbrock's EFI system feel better in the low and middle rpm ranges. They also drive much smoother. This is a direct consequence of an intake manifold design that provides very good air distribution among the engine's cylinders. Stated another way, the intake manifold does not allow very much port-to-port airflow variation. Each cylinder receives about the same amount of air as the next.

With the control provided by the mini-computer and nozzles, this means the engine can be operated at air/fuel ratios (cylinder-to-cylinder) that are about the same. The amount of power each cylinder produces is therefore comparable to that of any other cylinder . . . and the engine runs smoother. There is also less chance for the roughness that comes from random misfiring, because the tendency to misfire is significantly decreased by the system.

One other aspect of the Edelbrock EFI system is the fact that the fuel curves (or fuel delivery instructions)

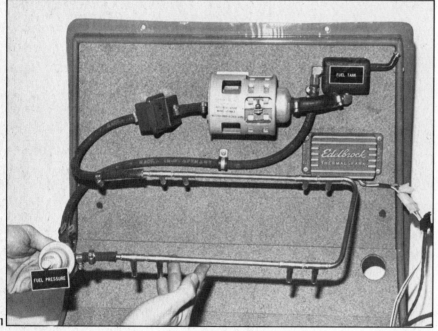

1

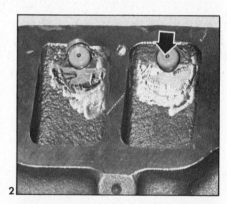

2

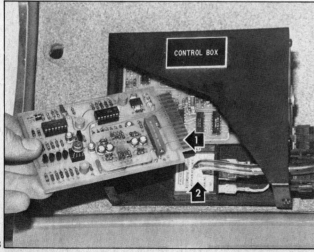

3

4

1. *Other than the scaled-down fuel tank, this is the basic fuel-handling system. A Bosch fuel pump and regulator couple through a filter and hook to a fuel rail that ties all of the injector nozzles together. The operating pressure is 30-35 psi, so understandably this part of the system was designed with considerable care.*

2. *Location of the discharge side of the nozzles is in the roof of the manifold's runner, at the junction of the manifold and cylinder heads. Much experimentation led to selection of the rather critical angular relationship between flow paths and nozzle attitude.*

3. *Plug-in printed circuit (P.C.) boards (1) comprise the mini-computer, which, among other requirements, determines the length of injector "on" time, thereby providing varying amounts of fuel for a variety of driving conditions. A vacuum pressure transducer(2) senses intake manifold depression, which is another of the variables monitored to determine the amount of fuel to be delivered*

4. *Working in conjunction with the mini-computer is the injector nozzle driver box. It actually operates the injectors, though how long they are to be left on is determined by the mini-computer. These signals are electric pulses that vary in duration.*

5. *Schematic of Edelbrock's EFI shows relationship of the system's parts. Price of the setup had not been announced by press time, nor had an estimate of when it would be available off-the-shelf. Contact Edelbrock Equipment Co., 411 Coral Circle, El Segundo, CA 90245 for more complete information.*

come from one little electronic chip that plugs into the mini-computer. Thinking ahead a little, it might be possible to design chips that would produce fuel curves compatible with racing engines, off-road engines or ''fill-in-the-blank'' engines. Certainly there would be other minor alterations to make, but not many.

Right now Edelbrock is concerned with the production of systems that materially improve the drivability and fuel economy potential of passenger cars. Initially they plan to release systems for small-block Chevys. Other systems are being developed for Fords and Chryslers, but right now it's a ''let's walk before we run'' situation, and Edelbrock isn't ready yet to say much.

When asked about what sort of fuel economy improvements and exhaust emissions benefits were being obtained, Edelbrock personnel indicated that the emissions performance of the system was very good and that fuel economy gains were pretty solid. One spokesman said, ''Well, one of the development cars is a '74 Chevy wagon that baselined about 11.4 mpg just before we installed one of the EFI systems on it over a year ago. Right now, correctly trimmed, it gets a little more than 16 mpg. But what you must keep in mind is that fuel economy as such is really a tricky subject. It isn't just how far you've traveled in

making the measurement, but how long the engine has been running. You might travel 15 miles going to and from work every day. One day you might make the trip in 25 minutes, the next day it could take 40, if the traffic is heavy. It doesn't take a raving genius to figure out which trip used the most fuel. So the odometer doesn't tell you everything, and the figures like those we're talking about here are under well-controlled test conditions where the data is both good and repeatable. But we feel that a 15-20% gain is not going to be out of reach if the car is properly driven. The problem is that the system makes the car feel so good that it's hard to keep your foot out of the throttle. And you don't have to jack the throttle around much to kill the economy. In that respect, it's not much different from a carburetor.''

Slated for general production by the end of 1977, several dozen Edelbrock systems will be released by midsummer of the same year as a preproduction wrap-up to the final design. But judging from the way the program has already developed, despite its rather ambitious nature for a company the size of Edelbrock, success is only a matter of time. And when you consider that the system will run upside down as well as right side up, even aircraft are possible users. Off-road, anybody?

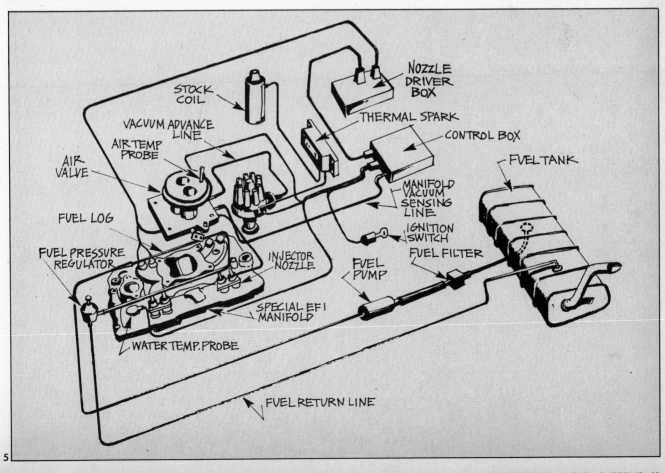

TURBOCHARGING

BY BILL CORYELL

PHOTOS BY THE AUTHOR AND ERIC RICKMAN

Let's face it: The primary objectives of virtually every serious engine builder are increased power combined with good flexibility, a smooth idle and acceptable reliability. However, we often find ourselves so possessed with wringing the last possible drop of power from an engine that we give these other objectives amazingly little consideration. Or sometimes we compromise the total power output just enough to provide levels of flexibility, smoothness and reliability that are barely adequate for the engine in a certain very specific application.

When you really stop to think about it, it would certainly be nice if there were some way to obtain very high power outputs but still retain the tractability, reliability and smoothness of a stock engine. This would be particularly valuable in high-performance street applications, where there are no rules to limit what can be done to an engine and where the need to use the vehicle for day-to-day transportation makes the aforementioned qualities almost mandatory.

Supercharging, or forcing fuel and air into the engine at pressures greater than one atmosphere, has long been accepted as a means of dramatically increasing power throughout the entire rpm range of the engine. However, like many other power-producing techniques, conventional supercharging does have its drawbacks. First, mechanically driven superchargers must be mounted to the engine in a position that allows use of a reasonably straightforward drive system. This may or may not be the best position for placement of other objects under the hood. Even worse, it may necessitate changes in the hood profile. Additionally, no matter what type of mechanical drive system is employed, power losses within the drive system are inevitable. Possibly the largest drawback, though, is that a mechanical drive system drives the supercharger at speeds directly proportional to crankshaft rpm.

The supercharger, then, is being driven at a fairly high rpm under most road conditions, regardless of whether the engine is under a light or a heavy load. The result is that a large amount of energy is wasted in driving the supercharger at high rpm during many road situations where full or nearly full power is not called for. This high-rpm operation consumes extra fuel unnecessarily at light and intermediate throttle settings. A final noteworthy point about mechanically driven superchargers is that the most common varieties, particularly roots types and vane types, add noticeably to the noise level of the engine and have no tendency whatever to reduce exhaust noise.

Certainly, conventional superchargers can be used to advantage in some automotive applications, but there now appears to be an alternate approach. It derives the same power, range and evenness available via supercharging yet with none of the aforementioned disadvantages of the conventional mechanical drive arrangement. This alternate approach to high performance is turbocharging.

Let's look at how it works. The turbine wheel of a turbocharger is driven by the escaping exhaust gas. A

common shaft joins the turbine to the compressor wheel. The turbine/compressor speed is therefore determined by the exhaust flow and temperature. This is important, because the turbocharger output increases or decreases according to the throttle position (or power demand on the engine), not just the engine speed. In

1. Turbocharging may well be the way to go to achieve substantial horsepower and torque outputs from the ever-smaller engines Detroit is forced to give us. Once regarded as the ultimate addition to a big-inch racing V-8, turbos also provide significant performance increases for small street engines.

2. This is the AiResearch 1⅝-in. wastegate. The poppet valve "wastes" excess exhaust to level off boost at a predetermined value. Manifold pressure is plumbed to fitting (1). A "horsepower screw" (2) provides boost level adjustment.

3. The wastegate disassembled. A variety of springs (1) and shims (2) are available to control the range of boost adjustment.

4. AiResearch Model T-04 turbocharger. The dark section is ductile iron turbine housing; the aluminum section is compressor. Rotating assembly is supported by bearings in center.

5. On this reworked Vega cylinder head, note moderate combustion chamber work. Ports have also been matched to the intake manifold.

non-supercharged engines, the exhaust energy is almost completely wasted. This makes the turbocharging system more flexible and also much more efficient, because turbocharging does not utilize engine crankshaft horsepower. Furthermore, since the turbocharger is exhaust-driven and only needs to be plumbed into the engine's intake and exhaust systems, mounting it in a convenient location and maintaining a low hood profile is generally easier than with conventional supercharging.

In addition to harnessing an engine's otherwise wasted exhaust and using it to dramatically increase horsepower, turbocharging offers a number of additional benefits over unblown engines which are not widely known but are extremely important, particularly in high-performance street cars. First of all, turbocharging adds power throughout the entire rpm range of the engine. To gain an equivalent amount of power in a normally aspirated engine, sacrifices must be made in the lower and middle rpm ranges. This is because an engine is essentially an air pump. The more air it can pump, the more power it can produce.

A turbocharged engine, then, is a two-stage air pump, while an unblown engine is only a single-stage pump. To pump an equal amount of air, the single-stage pump must turn more rpm. Also, in order to breathe properly at higher rpm, it must employ an intake system and valve timing which work well at high rpm but are inefficient at lower rpm. The result is a noticeably "peaked" power curve. On the other hand, the turbocharged engine, since it can pump large volumes of air at low rpm as well as high, has a gently rounded power curve, with much greater power in the low- to mid-rpm range.

A broad power curve is not the only advantage of producing peak power at low rpm. An engine's volumetric efficiency (air-pumping ability per revolution) is definitely greater at low rpm, because there is more time per revolution for air movement.

2

4

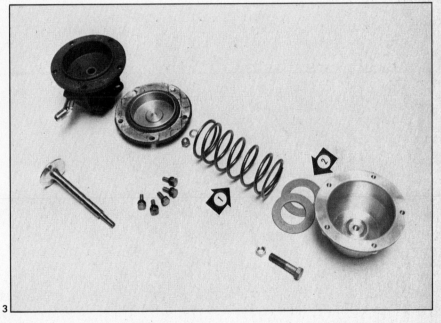

3

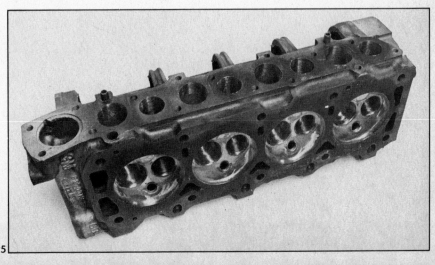

5

TURBOCHARGING

Losses from friction are less at low rpm too, so fuel consumption can be reduced as well as engine wear.

Less friction and greater volumetric efficiency are certainly worthwhile advantages, but possibly the most amazing advantage attributable to decreased rpm is the reduction of stress. For example, a Vega engine with normal hot-rodding modifications—big cam, high compression, high-flow carburetion, porting, etc.—that produces 150 hp at 7000 rpm suffers a stress increase due to its higher rpm and torque of *112%* compared with a turbocharged engine that produces the same power at 5000 rpm. Therefore, the 150-hp turbo engine should last more than twice as long as the unblown one, possibly even three times as long if you consider the reduced friction.

Furthermore, by peaking power at lower rpm, a mild cam can be used, eliminating load-up at idle. It should be noted that 150 hp is by no means the maximum power available via turbocharging. The limiting factor in any maximum-power turbo setup is the basic engine design and the amount of strength that can be built into the engine's cylinder head, valvetrain and bottom-end assembly.

Another secondary benefit not widely known is that even though a turbocharged engine puts out more power and therefore achieves greater BMEP (Brake Mean Effective Pressure, or "average cylinder pressure") than a non-turbocharged engine, the peak cylinder pressures are generally less than those in a normally aspirated engine of the same power. This is the result of the lower static compression combined with a higher-density intake charge which are characteristic of turbocharged engines. Also, less cylinder pressure is "wasted" by the high frictional losses generated at high rpm. These relatively low peak cylinder pressures, in conjunction with lower rpm and resultant lower reciprocating momentum, actually place less load on the bottom ends of turbocharged engines than on unblown engines of the same total power output.

Another important consideration is that turbochargers definitely reduce engine noise. Noise is merely one of the many forms of energy. Installing a turbocharger on the exhaust harnesses much of this energy, converting it to the useful work of pumping a greater amount of air into the cylinders. More air enables the engine to produce more power, and it reduces the amount of noise and heat energy which is normally emitted through the engine's exhaust and thus wasted. In addition to reducing noise by recovering exhaust energy, the additional mass of the turbocharger dampens some of the sharper noises in the exhaust, further reducing the total amount of noise emitted.

Finally, even at light road loads, a turbocharger will freewheel at several thousand rpm. This freewheeling generates considerable turbulence in the intake tract, which atomizes the fuel droplets more finely and more evenly in the air, providing extremely uniform mixture distribution to all four cylinders. Under these conditions, the carburetor may be leaned down with less chance of any single cylinder go-

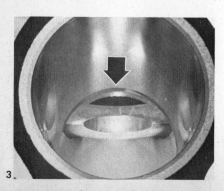

ing too lean. If other engine components such as the camshaft are left the same, fuel consumption with a turbocharger will actually be less at street and highway speeds than it is without one.

A number of turbocharger kits are currently available for the Chevrolet Vega. Among the more noteworthy manufacturers are Accel Performance

1. This is the Arias 6:1 blower piston and its taper-bored wristpin. Cast iron cylinder liners allow use of conventional piston and ring arrangement.

2. Vega aluminum engine block is sleeved with iron cylinder liners. Cylinder barrels protrude .007-in. above the outer part of water jacket to improve head gasket seal.

3. Iron cylinder liners butt against shoulder near lower end of cylinder (arrow) to keep the sleeve from sliding downward and interfering with the crankshaft counterweights.

4. Stock Vega crankshaft was shot-peened, micropolished and balanced, and the oil holes in journals were chamfered. Rods were magnafluxed, and big ends were resized to improve roundness and bearing insert register.

5. Here's the Gale Banks Engineering intercooler. Cooling element is merely a specialized radiator, fabricated from cupro-nickel alloy. This optional part of GBE kit allows higher boost levels at a given compression ratio and with fuel of a given octane.

Systems (a division of the Echlin Corp.) in Branford, Conn.; Crane Cams, Inc. in Hallandale, Fla.; and Turbo Systems, Inc. in Akron, Ohio.

Another turbo kit manufacturer that is currently prototyping a kit for the Vega is Gale Banks Engineering in San Gabriel, Calif. Gale is already well known in the field of high-performance boat turbocharging. The firm produces a line of kits, plus an impressive array of marine turbo engines ranging up to 2200 hp. Over the years Gale has also turbocharged a number of race cars and street machines, including the Vega.

Banks' prototype Vega system is novel in that he uses a wastegate, which provides simple adjustment of the boost level over a fairly broad range of manifold pressures. It's also unusual because he uses an optional intercooler for improved efficiency via intake charge cooling. We were fortunate enough to be allowed to observe the modification of the core engine used with his prototype kit.

Because Gale's system allows adjustment of boost to fairly high levels, a number of internal modifications were performed to enable the engine to undergo prolonged dyno testing at high boost levels without danger of failure. Gale points out though, that these engine modifications are only necessary for Vega owners who plan on running their systems at or near

full available boost. He has found that with the advantages his optional intercooler offers, the system can be set for as much as 8 psi manifold pressure on a stock engine without drastically overtaxing the engine's bottom end or cylinder-head sealing capabilities. He also feels that with the intercooler, 8 psi boost will still be below the detonation threshold, using the stock compression ratio and 95-octane pump gasoline.

Before we look into the details of Gale Banks Engineering's Vega turbo kit, let's follow the engine assembly through Banks' machine shop. A brief review of the modifications done to the core engine reveals some interesting practices that should help any high-boost turbocharged Vega survive under sustained high loads.

Starting with the bottom-end assembly, the crankshaft was magnaflux-inspected, then shot-peened for fatigue resistance. Next, the journals were reground to provide a .0020-in. rod and main bearing clearance. The oil holes were then chamfered and the journals micropolished. A number of stock Vega connecting rods were magnafluxed, and non-perfect units were rejected until four flawless rods were at hand. These were also shot-peened, and the big ends were resized to improve the stock roundness and bearing insert register. Since this engine was

5

TURBOCHARGING

not to be used for racing, where frequent disassembly would be required, the stock pressed-in-rod wristpin arrangement was retained.

The cylinder block area definitely departs from standard hot-rodding techniques. After align-honing the main bearing webs, the cylinders were bored and dry-sleeved with cast iron liners. This was done for two purposes. First, the iron liners allow the use of heavy-duty, forged aluminum Arias 6:1 blower pistons without having to worry about piston skirt and ring compatability with the stock aluminum cylinder walls. Second, after the liners were pressed into the cylinders and milled flush with the top of the block, the entire top of the block, except for the sleeved cylinder walls, was again milled . . . this time .007-in. lower than the tops of the cylinder walls. "In this manner," states Banks, "the tops of the cylinders serve the same function as O-rings. Increasing the pressure between the head and the block peripherally around the cyl-

inders creates a more effective head gasket seal."

Additionally, when the block was bored to receive the sleeves, a short step was left at the bottom of each cylinder. After installation, the sleeves butt against this step, which eliminates any possibility of the sleeves sliding downward and interfering with the crankshaft counterweights. The finished cylinders were power-honed to provide .0072- to .0075-in. skirt clearance.

Other noteworthy points about the bottom end are the retention of the stock lubrication system (except for a slightly enlarged oil pan) and the use of standard-width Speed Pro chrome rings with an end gap of .018- to .020-in.

The cylinder head received much less romancing than did the bottom-end assembly. The combustion chambers were ground out around the valves to minimize shrouding, and the floors of the chambers were ground upward slightly to improve mixture flow at near-zero valve lifts. The valve seats were given a three-angle seat job with .060-in. intake and .080-in.

exhaust seat widths The chambers were polished to reduce heat loss into the cooling system and to keep carbon deposits and hot spots to a minimum. Also, the intake ports were matched to the intake manifold.

Finally, upon reassembly of the head (using the stock valves), a Crower VX-16 cam and kit were installed. This particular camshaft provides .470-in. lift, with 292° intake and exhaust duration on 110° lobe centers. Banks feels that although the Vega GT cam provides good performance in turbocharged applications, the Crower VX-16 offers a little more mid-range and top-end power with virtually no noticeable sacrifices in idle quality and low-speed tractability.

The primary ingredients in Gale Banks Engineering's turbo conversion kit are: an AiResearch Model T-04 turbocharger with an AiResearch 1⅝-in. wastegate to control manifold pressure; a 46mm Hitachi carburetor; and an intercooler, exhaust system and turbocharger mount that Banks designed himself.

The most important consideration when choosing a turbocharger for a

1

2

3

1. Radiator, used under hood adjacent to right fenderwell, maintains 70° F above ambient temperature for intercooler system.

2. Electric fan forces air through radiator in intercooler system. Fan and water/glycol recirculation pump are switched on by Hobbs-type switch on intake manifold whenever the boost reaches 1-2 psi.

3. The 46mm Hitachi carburetor bolts to the manifold, and V-band coupling attaches manifold to the turbocharger's compressor inlet. Carburetor throat, intake manifold and compressor inlet all have nearly identical inside diameters.

4. Exhaust header is of mild steel. Bellows unit allows the turbo to be mounted directly to intake manifold and also accommodates thermal expansion.

5. Optional intercooler is mounted on top of the intake manifold.

6. Cast aluminum intake manifold employs large, 3-bolt lug outside intercooler flange for mounting the turbocharger bracket.

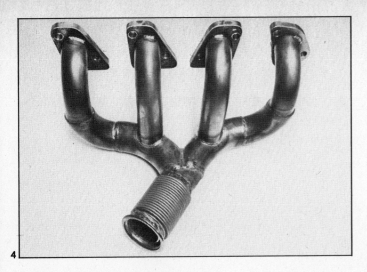

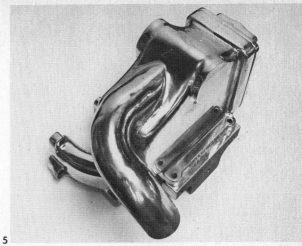

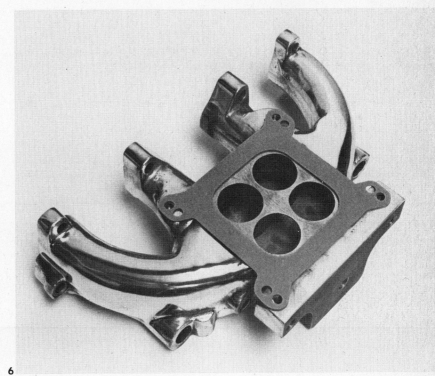

specific application is turbocharger sizing. Gale cautions, "Many 'home brew' turbocharger installations have proved less satisfactory than expected because the wrong size turbo was chosen. If the turbo selected is too small, turbine/compressor overspeeding and inefficiency will result. This can seriously damage the engine and the turbocharger. Conversely, if the turbo is too large, insufficient rpm, inefficiency, poor throttle response and possible surging are likely."

Proper sizing is accomplished by calculating the airflow of the engine (based on displacement and volumetric efficiency, or "breathing ability") at the rpm at which it is planned to achieve peak power. This airflow is then plotted against the intended boost pressure on "compressor maps" of the various models of turbochargers. These maps are available through the turbo manufacturers. The selected turbocharger must operate at high efficiency, yet not be near its surge threshold at the calculated airflow and intended boost pressure.

The AiResearch Model T-04 unit satisfies these requirements for the Vega engine. For general-interest information, its turbine and compressor have approximately 2¾-in. diameters and turn at speeds of up to 120,000 rpm. Additionally, its turbine housing is cast of ductile iron to contain it in the unlikely eventuality of turbine failure at high rpm.

The AiResearch wastegate is merely a poppet-type blowoff valve that is modulated by manifold pressure. In this instance, a 1⅝-in. poppet valve opens and closes to "waste" excess exhaust pressure and thus maintain boost at a predetermined level. The actual boost level at which the poppet leaves its seat is a function of the setting of a spring-loaded diaphragm. This diaphragm serves as the poppet valve actuator. The diaphragm section of the wastegate is plumbed to the intake manifold in such a way that manifold pressure acts against

one side of the diaphragm while a coil spring acts against the opposite side. When the manifold pressure gets high enough to displace the diaphragm against the spring, the diaphragm raises the poppet off its seat to "waste" excess exhaust gases. This in turn levels off the turbocharger speed and limits the boost level.

A "horsepower screw" is built into the regulator housing to allow adjustment of the spring pressure on the diaphragm. Indirectly, this screw allows adjustment of the maximum boost level of the system over a broad range of manifold pressures.

The Hitachi carburetor is a Japanese version of the venerable SU carburetor, used on many English sports cars for years. It is particularly well suited to street car turbocharging for several basic reasons. First, its 46mm throttle bore diameter is almost the same diameter as the turbocharger's

compressor inlet annulus. This provides excellent breathing without any changes in airflow velocity between the carburetor and the turbocharger. Second, the Hitachi is a constant-velocity type of carburetor with a piston dampener to provide temporary tip-in enrichment. With this arrangement, you can change mixture strength by changing a single needle in the carburetor. Also, a relatively constant velocity is maintained across the main fuel discharge orifice. This promotes accurate fuel metering at all off-idle throttle settings. Finally, the piston damper eliminates the need for an accelerator pump, which adds to the already excellent fuel economy that a turbocharger gives.

The final major component of the Banks turbo kit is the optional intercooler, which is Gale's own design. An intercooler is no more than a specialized radiator that cools the intake

TURBOCHARGING

charge and therefore increases its density. The octane requirement for a given engine output can be reduced significantly by intercooling, because the detonation limits of gasoline engines are quite sensitive to intake charge temperature. This is extremely important in a street application, where the engine must run on ordinary 95-octane gasoline. What's more, the tendency for a combustion chamber to develop a hot spot and ignite the intake charge before the plug fires is reduced by intercooling. Lower engine operating temperature is a further benefit.

In the case of this Vega, the cooling element is located in a housing which bolts to the intake manifold. Fuel and air are forced through this specialized radiator element and cooled before entering the intake ports. A water/glycol mixture is pumped through the intercooler by a small, 12-volt electric water pump. The pump operates on current from the car's battery. The current that powers the pump is switched on and off by a Hobbs-type switch on the intake manifold that closes whenever the manifold pressure exceeds 1 or 2 psi. A second small radiator is mounted adjacent to the fenderwell, under the hood. Air is forced through this radiator and out the fenderwell by an electric fan, also powered via the intake manifold pressure switch.

Water heated by the hot intake charge passing through the intercooler is cooled by air flowing through this second radiator, and the cooled water is then recirculated back through the intercooler. This system maintains a temperature of approximately 70° F above ambient, and it

definitely raises the maximum boost pressure that can be run without detonation on a given octane fuel.

When they're all bolted together, the turbocharged engine and intercooling systems fill the engine compartment, but they do fit comfortably beneath the stock Vega hood. The turbine inlet of the turbocharger bolts neatly to a welded, mild steel exhaust header. The system taps lubricating oil for the turbo from the engine's oil pressure gauge boss, runs it through a full-flow filter, through the turbo and then returns it via a flexible hose to the engine's oil pan. Mixture from the compressor is fed through a 2-in. aluminum intake pipe to the intercooler, which is bolted atop the modified aluminum intake manifold. The Hitachi carburetor is mounted directly to the compressor inlet with a Banks-fabricated adapter and a V-band coupling. The exhaust pipe fastens to the turbine exducer with another V-band coupling.

Because the prototype vehicle was going to be tested at high boost levels and high power outputs, the entire exhaust system was fitted with 2½-in. O.D. pipe and a Corvair 2½-in. turbo muffler. The stock Vega clutch and flywheel were replaced with a re-

cently developed Weber clutch system. The Weber clutch features a forged aluminum flywheel, a larger 10½-in. driven plate and a 2200-lb. diaphragm-type pressure plate.

What type of power levels are attainable with a turbocharger system such as this one? After initial sorting out, dyno tests performed on the en-

1. The Crower cam and kit provide better mid-range and high-rpm power than the Vega GT cam with virtually no sacrifices in bottom-end power and idle quality.

2. Weber clutch and flywheel features a larger-than-stock disc, 2000-lb. pressure plate. The flywheel is made from forged aluminum.

3. Simplified schematic shows basics of how a turbo works, utilizing exhaust gases to force air into cylinders.

4. With the turbo and its components in place on the reworked Vega engine, the resulting powerplant takes on an impressive appearance. And it should; it produces a maximum of 309 hp!

5. Plumbing for the turbo is evident here. As significant as the maximum 309-hp figure is the 226-hp reading on the non-intercooled dyno test, because that's what can be expected from a virtually bolt-on turbo kit without serious block or lower-end work.

1

2

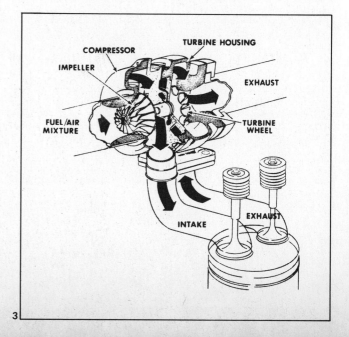

3

gine yielded some very significant results. The tests were run at three different levels, two with the intercooler system and one without. The test without the intercooler is closer to a street-use application, because it allows the turbo to simply be bolted on an otherwise almost stock engine. The non-intercooler test was run with 10 psi of boost, and it yielded 226 hp at 5800 rpm. With the intercooler and a boost pressure of 15 psi, 260 hp at 5800 rpm was achieved. After turning the "horsepower screw" on the wastegate to 20 psi of boost, the engine reached 309 hp at 6000 rpm.

Significant as these power gains were, they are all on the conservative side. More horsepower would certainly be realized after initial break-in of the newly built engine.

Though the maximum power output of 309 hp at 6000 rpm with 20 psi of boost pressure reached during the tests is impressive, the lower numbers noted are also highly significant. At 10 psi of boost without the intercooler, the reading of 226 hp at 5800 rpm is what the street-driven Vega can be expected to produce merely by bolting on the turbo kit. It's a notable improvement over the stock en-

gine, yet no major internal engine reworking is needed. Furthermore, this boost level doesn't require O-ringing the cylinder head to maintain an adequate head gasket seal. What this boils down to is that 226 honest crankshaft horsepower is attainable by merely changing cams, doing some very minor head work and bolting one of these kits, less intercooler, onto a stock bottom end. Banks also points out that at 8 psi of boost, if you use the optional intercooler, the stock 8:1 pistons won't cause detonation and will give slightly more power at low rpm than the 6:1 pistons will.

There's a second significant factor. Regardless of boost pressure, very high power levels were achieved at low and intermediate rpm. Also, it wasn't necessary to resort to extremely high rpm in order to develop peak power outputs.

Additional noteworthy results came out of this dyno testing session. The engine's idle was steady, with only a mild lope at 700 rpm. This very slight idle roughness was not enough to hinder drivability, even with an an automatic transmission. Finally, throttle response was quite crisp, even slightly quicker than stock. Banks contends that this is due primarily to the wastegate, which allows use of a turbo that builds boost quickly yet prevents the system from overboosting at full throttle and high rpm.

All in all, turbocharging is an extremely appealing approach to high performance. The overall size of the system is relatively small, and every bit as much power is available from turbocharging as from conventional supercharging; in fact, even more. Instead of adding power and at the same time making the car noisier, turbocharging adds power and makes the car *quieter*. A quiet car draws less attention—which allows more extensive use of the power available. Turbocharging also provides exceptional low- and mid-range power compared to unblown engines of similar outputs. Turbocharging produces this power at relatively low peak cylinder pressures, too, easing the burden on the engine's bottom end. On top of all this, the fact that a turbocharger merely freewheels at light road loads can actually result in better road-load mileage. That's quite impressive when you consider how much power turbocharging gives at wide-open throttle.

It certainly *would* be nice if there were a way to obtain a very high power output, combined with the flexibility, smoothness and reliability that every serious engine builder would like to achieve. Let's face it: Turbocharging may well be the answer. ⚙

MOTORCRAFT-FORD

In the early '60's, what is now called the Motorcraft Parts Division (formerly Autolite-Ford) of FoMoCo started making its own carburetors. Their 1-, 2-, and 4-bbl. designs were called the 1100, 2100 and 4100, respectively. All were similar and easily recognizable because of the funny looking accelerator pump mounted on the end of the bowl.

The 1100, and a slightly different model—the 1101—were kicked out the door in favor of single-barrel carburetors supplied by Carter. This wasn't the first time Ford had used Carter carbs and it probably won't be the last. Ford also used a Rochester 4MV Quadrajet in 1970 and a Carter Thermo-Quad TQ in 1974—so you can't say that they don't give other carburetors a chance.

Some years back, the 4100 was displaced by the 4300, a completely new design. The 4300's main claim to fame was that it frightened mechanics for a long time because of the numerous parts it contains and the unfamiliarity of its design. For the 1975 model year, both the 2100 and 4300 have been revamped, appearing now as the 2150 and 4350. The facts of life—as well as emissions control requirements—finally caught up to the Motorcraft 2- and 4-bbl. carbs; but that leaky power valve—characteristic of the 2100 and 4300 for so long—still leaks just as much in the 2150 and 4350.

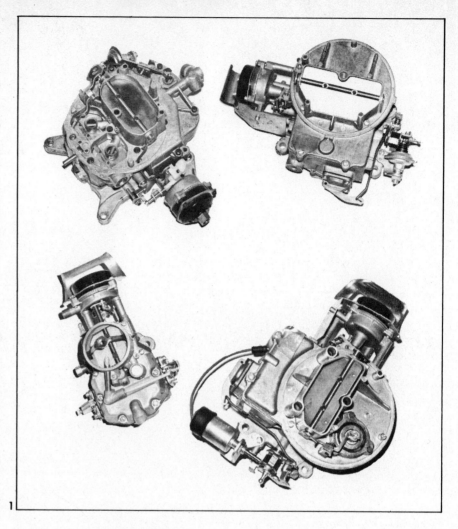

1

1. Clockwise from lower left we have the 1100, the 4300, an early 2100, and a late 2100 equipped with solenoid throttle positioner and a vacuum break unit that is built into the top of the carburetor.

2. Motorcraft's 4300 has had several variations in its design, but the basic shape has not been changed.

3. Motorcraft 4300 4-barrel is a fairly recent design. The secondaries are mechanical, with an air valve.

2

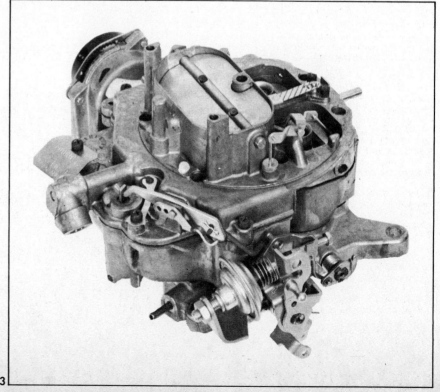

3

MOTORCRAFT-FORD/1100,1101

4

5

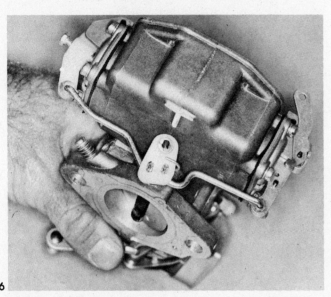

6

7

4. *Motorcraft's 1100 has its choke attached to the side of the main body. The 1101 is much the same carburetor, except that the choke is attached to the air horn. The gadget at the side of the bowl with the funny linkage is the accelerating pump.*

5. *The other side of the 1100 looks as though it has another accelerating pump. In reality, that second diaphragm is the dashpot for the slow closing throttle. Most dashpots operate on air, but this one uses fuel out of the bowl. The hole indicated by the arrow was formerly used to mount the spark valve, in the days when Ford's distributor advance was controlled by venturi vacuum.*

6. *Underneath the 1100 bowl, we can see how the accelerating pump on the right and the dashpot linkage hook up to the throttle shaft. The idle-mixture screw is at the left on the mounting flange.*

7. *With bowl cover off the 1100, we see the plastic venturi staked into the main body. Clip next to the choke cover holds the heater hose. The idea is to have the hot water heat up the choke coil for quicker choke opening.*

8. *Arrow indicates the main jet on the 1100 which is removable. Next to it is the power assembly, which is not removable. Actually, you can remove the power valve, but you will quite probably ruin it when you do.*

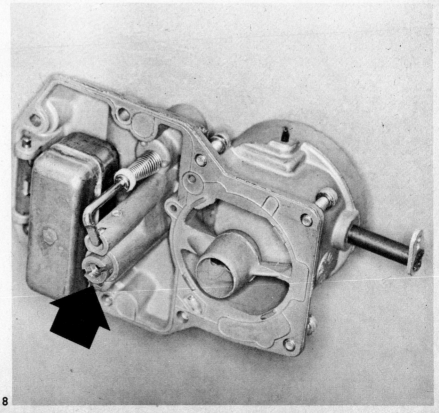

8

MOTORCRAFT-FORD/2100, 4100

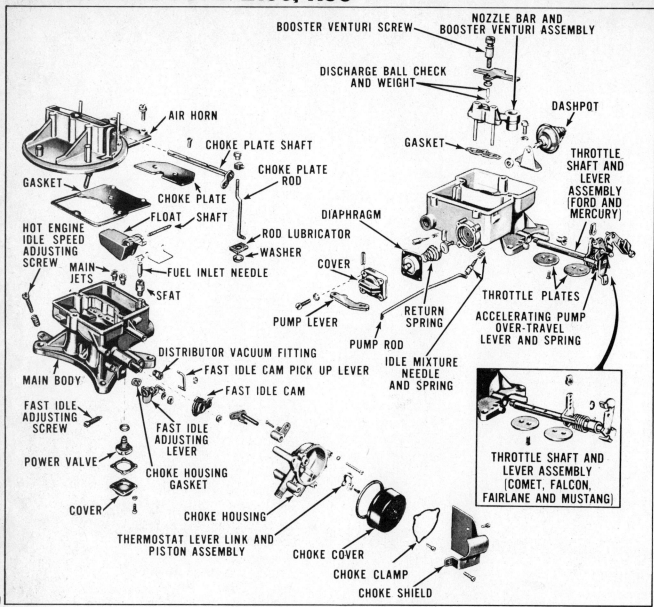

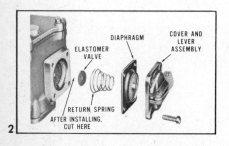

1. This is a 2100 2-barrel, but a 4100 4-barrel uses many of the same parts and has similar construction.

2. Late model carbs with side-mounted pumps use the elastomer valve, which works a lot better than the older steel check ball. The long stem of the valve is for installation so you can pull it through the hole with a pair of pliers. It should be cut off after installation or it might interfere with the float.

3. The 2100 main jets are in the bottom of the bowl; right next to them you can see the top of the power valve.

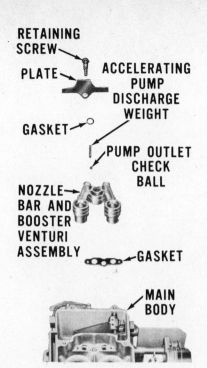

RETAINING SCREW

PLATE — ACCELERATING PUMP DISCHARGE WEIGHT

GASKET

PUMP OUTLET CHECK BALL

NOZZLE BAR AND BOOSTER VENTURI ASSEMBLY — GASKET

MAIN BODY

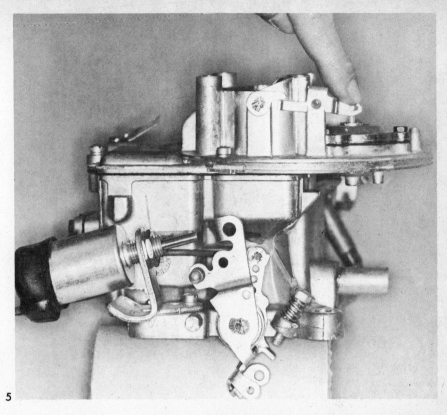

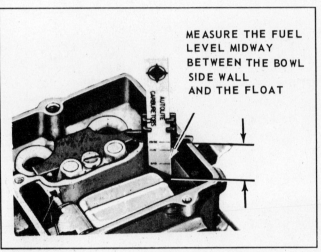

MEASURE THE FUEL LEVEL MIDWAY BETWEEN THE BOWL SIDE WALL AND THE FLOAT

JET WRENCH

MAIN METERING JET

4. Discharge weights are necessary in some cases to keep the check ball seated, as seen on this 2100.

5. One of the latest changes in the 2100 is the vacuum break mounted on the cover. It connects through an internal passage to manifold vacuum and pushes the choke open—as shown—when the engine starts.

6. When overhauling a 2100 or 4100 carb, it's a good idea to leave the cover off and check the actual wet fuel level, after you get the carburetor mounted on the engine.

7. A "jet wrench" is not necessary if you are careful to get a screwdriver that fits the slot in the jet.

8. Here's the way the solenoid throttle positioner works. When the solenoid is energized, the throttle is lifted off the normal idle-speed screw, as shown by the gap (arrow).

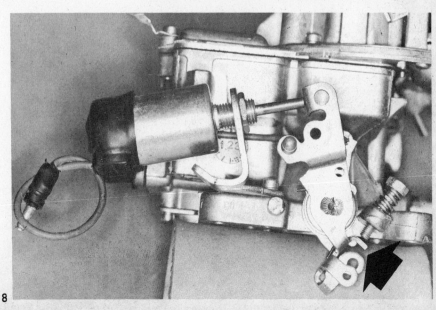

MOTORCRAFT-FORD/2150

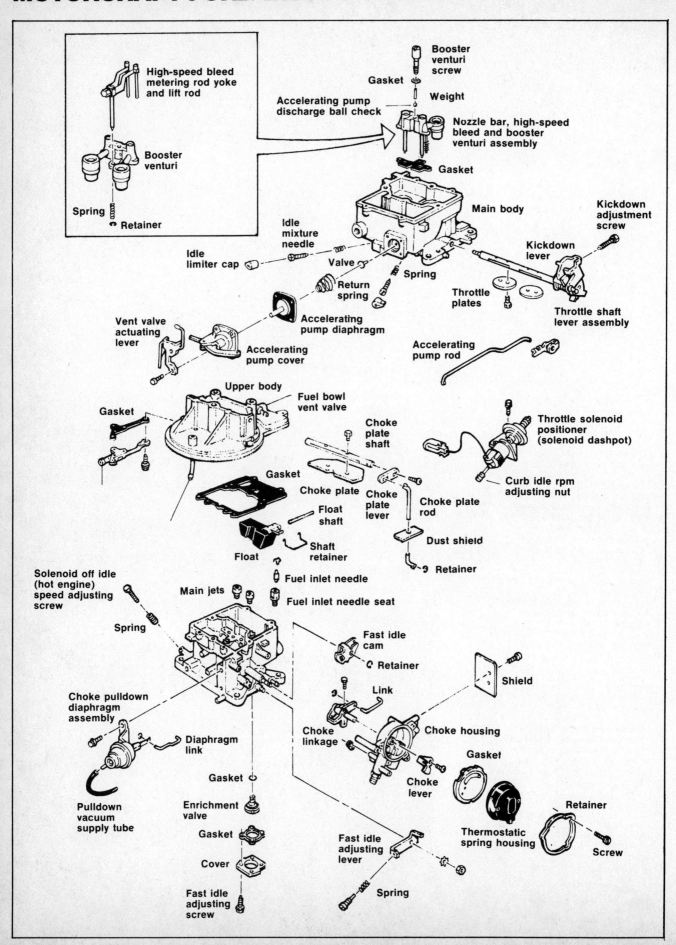

High-speed bleed metering rod yoke and lift rod

Booster venturi

Spring

Retainer

Booster venturi screw

Gasket

Weight

Accelerating pump discharge ball check

Nozzle bar, high-speed bleed and booster venturi assembly

Gasket

Main body

Kickdown adjustment screw

Idle mixture needle

Kickdown lever

Idle limiter cap

Valve

Spring

Return spring

Accelerating pump diaphragm

Throttle plates

Throttle shaft lever assembly

Vent valve actuating lever

Accelerating pump cover

Accelerating pump rod

Upper body

Gasket

Fuel bowl vent valve

Choke plate shaft

Throttle solenoid positioner (solenoid dashpot)

Gasket

Choke plate

Choke plate lever

Choke plate rod

Curb idle rpm adjusting nut

Float shaft

Shaft retainer

Dust shield

Retainer

Float

Solenoid off idle (hot engine) speed adjusting screw

Fuel inlet needle

Main jets

Fuel inlet needle seat

Spring

Fast idle cam

Retainer

Shield

Link

Choke pulldown diaphragm assembly

Choke linkage

Choke housing

Diaphragm link

Gasket

Choke lever

Pulldown vacuum supply tube

Enrichment valve

Gasket

Thermostatic spring housing

Retainer

Screw

Cover

Fast idle adjusting lever

Fast idle adjusting screw

Spring

2

3

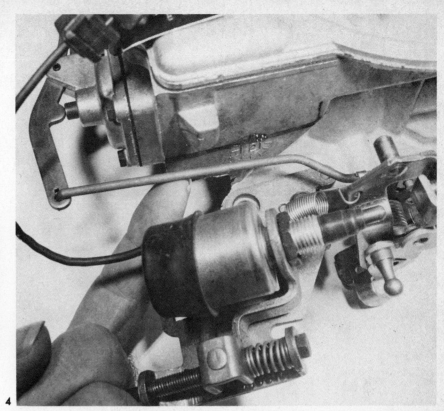

4

1. Major internal design changes are detailed in this exploded drawing of 2150—note mechanical metering rod system.

2. Externally, new Motorcraft 2150 bears a marked resemblance to 2100.

3. One of first differences you'll note is the mechanical vent valve and its actuating lever, which operates off the accelerator pump arm. Vent valve should be open to the vapor canister whenever the engine is off, and closed when it's running.

4. Accelerator pump arm adjustment is made by bending this linkage up or down, as in the past, but any adjustment here may affect operation of the vent valve, which must then be adjusted.

5. Here we can see the velocity fuel feed, or pullover enrichment system— two tiny nozzles in air horn that are connected to a small tube which dips into the fuel bowl to pick up fuel at high rpm, richening the mixture at open throttle.

6. Throttle shaft cam operates the mechanical high-speed bleed control. As throttle plates open, cam pushes up a lift rod connected to the metering rods, reducing the air flow and richening the mixture. Note that the leaky power valve is still used.

7. As in former versions, air horn gasket must fit over an alignment pin at each end. The 2150 will surprise no one who's worked on the 2100.

8. A throttle solenoid positioner is used on some; others also have a dashpot. TSP adjustment remains as in past at A. Off-idle adjustment (A) is factory set and should not be disturbed. Don't confuse it with the kickdown adjusting screw above it.

5

6

7

8

MOTORCRAFT-FORD/4300

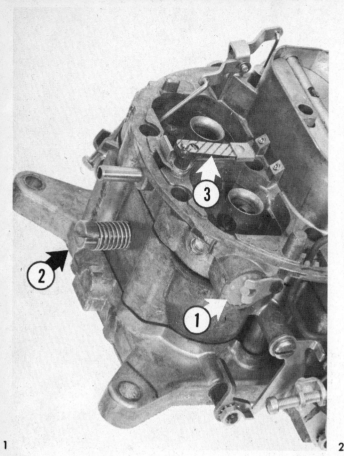

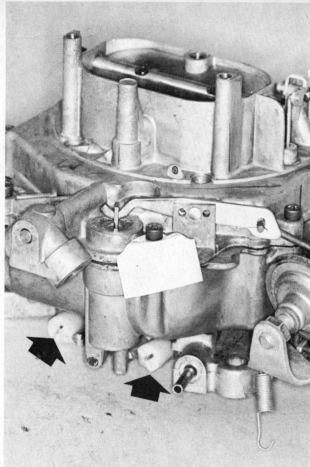

1. Here's the 4300 that uses the air valve spring (1), has an idle air screw (2) instead of a throttle cracking screw, and also has the hot idle compensator (3).

2. The idle-mixture screw limiter caps are plain to see on this late model 4300. Note the three hole positions for the fulcrum pin in the acceleration pump arm. The different positions give a longer or a shorter stroke.

3. Shown here is an early model 4300 without the limiter caps on the idle-mixture screws.

4. When you see this large screw in the end of the carburetor, it means that the throttles close almost completely at curb idle. This screw is the air bypass that regulates the idle speed of the engine.

5. *The power valve is easily removable if you have a socket that is deep enough to clear the stem.*

6. *Located in the bottom of the bowl are the two main jets with the power valve positioned between them.*

7. *Screw at arrow on the 4300 is for fast idle adjustment only.*

8. *Float level on the 4300 is set with the bowl cover inverted, and the float resting on the closed needle. Measure distance from the bowl cover surface to the top of the float.*

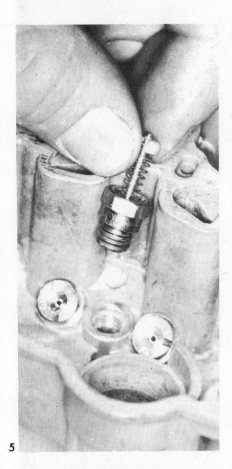

5

6

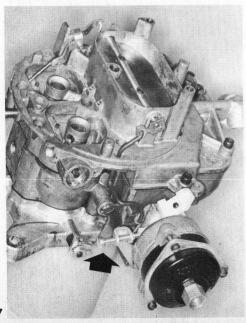

7

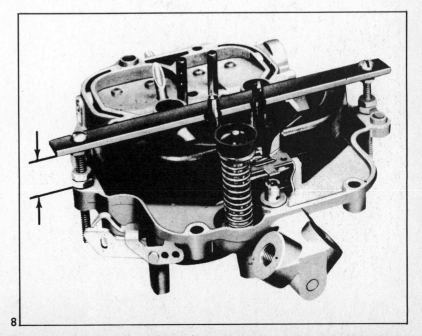

8

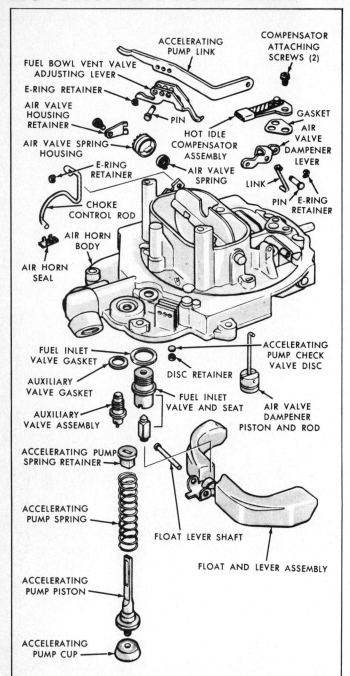

Fuel Bowl Vent Valve Adjusting Lever
E-Ring Retainer
Air Valve Housing Retainer
Air Valve Spring Housing
E-Ring Retainer
Choke Control Rod
Air Horn Body
Air Horn Seal
Accelerating Pump Link
Pin
Hot Idle Compensator Assembly
Air Valve Spring
Compensator Attaching Screws (2)
Gasket
Air Valve Dampener Lever
Link
Pin
E-Ring Retainer

Fuel Inlet Valve Gasket
Auxiliary Valve Gasket
Auxiliary Valve Assembly
Disc Retainer
Fuel Inlet Valve and Seat
Accelerating Pump Check Valve Disc
Air Valve Dampener Piston and Rod

Accelerating Pump Spring Retainer
Accelerating Pump Spring
Accelerating Pump Piston
Accelerating Pump Cup
Float Lever Shaft
Float and Lever Assembly

1

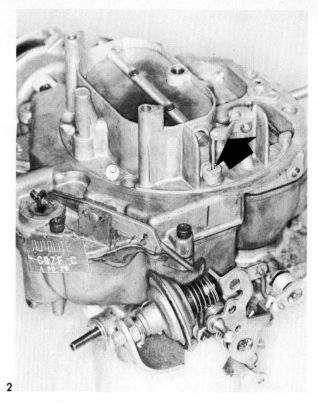

2

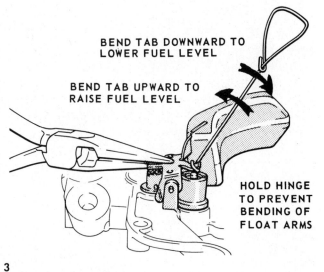

BEND TAB DOWNWARD TO LOWER FUEL LEVEL

BEND TAB UPWARD TO RAISE FUEL LEVEL

HOLD HINGE TO PREVENT BENDING OF FLOAT ARMS

3

1. The air horn of the 4300 is quite a bit more than just a simple bowl cover. This is an early model which used the external air valve spring.

2. This little link on the 4300 connects to a piston in a well of fuel. Secondary air valve works against the piston, opens slowly to eliminate bog.

3. Changing the float level on a 4300 is pretty tricky. It will be a lot easier to do if you first make this little bending tool from a piece of stiff wire.

4. Most carbs only have a single-needle valve, but the 4300 has two. It requires an additional adjustment for the second valve. With the float gauge in place holding up the floats, the second valve should clear by a certain amount according to your carb's specifications.

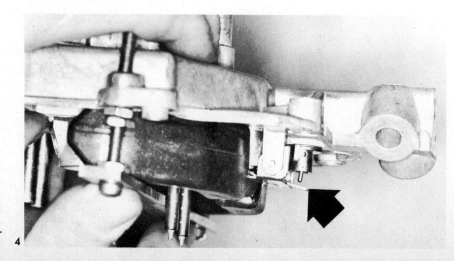

4

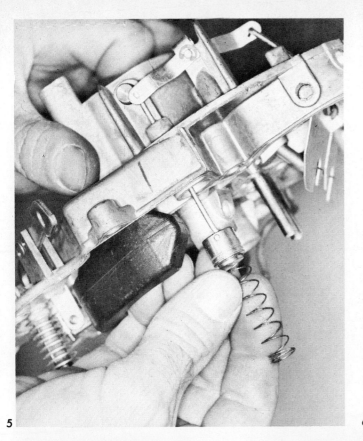

5

6

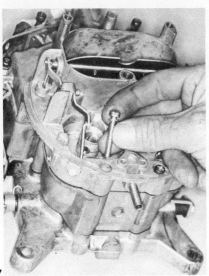

7

8

5. *Early model carburetors used a spring on the other side of the carburetor to close the air valve. Late models have done away with that external spring and instead use a spring underneath the piston. If your 4300 does not have the external spring, it must have this one under the piston, or the valve will stay open all the time.*

6. *On the underside of this bowl cover we see the stem of the vacuum piston which operates the power valve.*

7. *All of the bowl cover screws in the 4300 are the same, except this one — and it must go in this location.*

8. *Here's how they can use the same model carburetor on two different engines. The venturis are a different size, as pointed out by the arrows.*

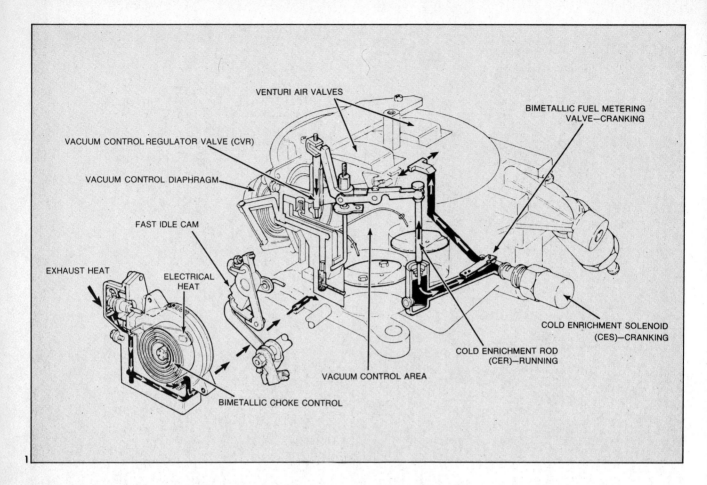

VENTURI AIR VALVES

BIMETALLIC FUEL METERING VALVE—CRANKING

VACUUM CONTROL REGULATOR VALVE (CVR)

VACUUM CONTROL DIAPHRAGM

FAST IDLE CAM

EXHAUST HEAT

ELECTRICAL HEAT

COLD ENRICHMENT SOLENOID (CES)—CRANKING

COLD ENRICHMENT ROD (CER)—RUNNING

VACUUM CONTROL AREA

BIMETALLIC CHOKE CONTROL

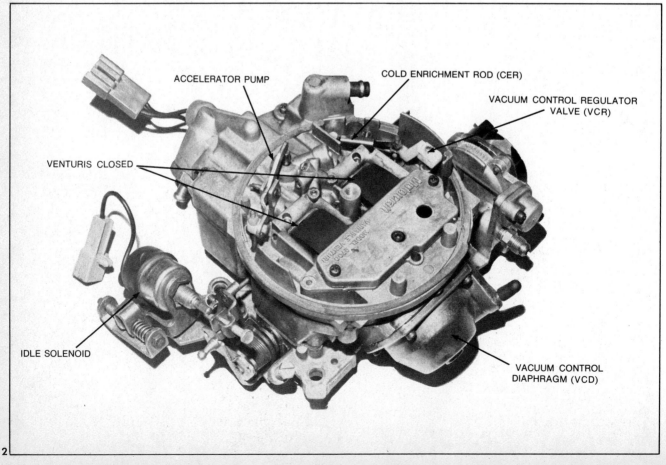

ACCELERATOR PUMP

COLD ENRICHMENT ROD (CER)

VACUUM CONTROL REGULATOR VALVE (VCR)

VENTURIS CLOSED

IDLE SOLENOID

VACUUM CONTROL DIAPHRAGM (VCD)

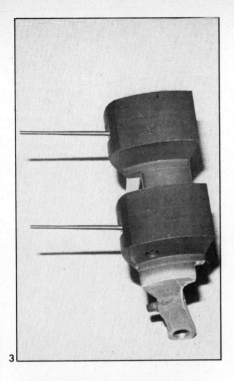

3

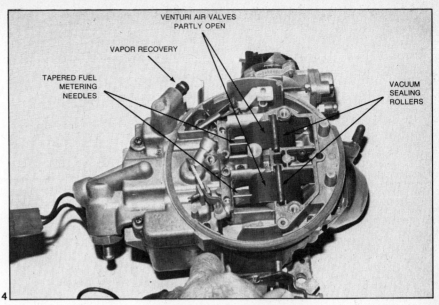

VENTURI AIR VALVES PARTLY OPEN

VAPOR RECOVERY

TAPERED FUEL METERING NEEDLES

VACUUM SEALING ROLLERS

4

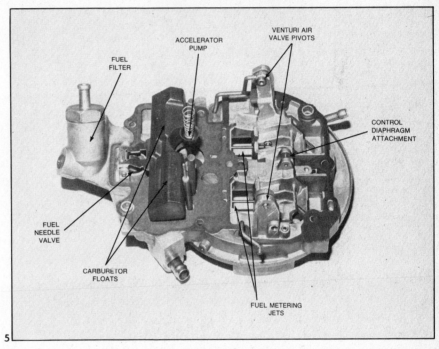

ACCELERATOR PUMP

VENTURI AIR VALVE PIVOTS

FUEL FILTER

CONTROL DIAPHRAGM ATTACHMENT

FUEL NEEDLE VALVE

CARBURETOR FLOATS

FUEL METERING JETS

5

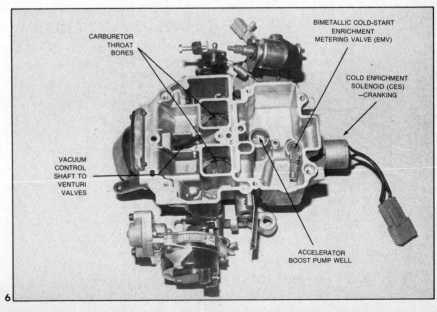

CARBURETOR THROAT BORES

BIMETALLIC COLD-START ENRICHMENT METERING VALVE (EMV)

COLD ENRICHMENT SOLENOID (CES) —CRANKING

VACUUM CONTROL SHAFT TO VENTURI VALVES

ACCELERATOR BOOST PUMP WELL

6

1. On cold start, bimetallic choke coil lifts CER, metering more fuel to the enrichment system. The CES opens when key is in crank mode, as bimetallic valve adds more fuel while cranking. The CER holds the venturi slightly open to stop flooding and gives a slighty rich mixture for cold drive-away.

2. You can't tinker with this carb. The CER and VCR controls must be set to within .005-in. with a dial indicator. The VCD senses the amount of vacuum between the venturi air valves and throttle butterflies and controls the venturi air valves. The idle solenoid closes the throttle butterflies completely when ignition is off.

3. This is the secret. Venturi air valves have curved leading edges on left. The air is squeezed between carburetor throat wall and edge of venturi valve. Free-floating tapered needles meter exact air/fuel ratio for any air valve position. The needles pass through calibrated jets in carb body.

4. Venturi air valves withdraw the tapered fuel-metering needles from calibrated jets on left side of venturi. Controlling the size of the venturi opening maintains high air velocity at all throttle settings. Rollers seal cover.

5. Underside of carb cover reveals floats and venturi air valve pivots. Air valves must move freely. As air valve moves, changing the size of the venturi opening, incoming air is accelerated as it squeezes past the restriction. Fuel from the jets is mixed with high-velocity air. The air/fuel ratio is controlled by the position of the tapered needles in the calibrated jets.

6. Cover off carb bowl reveals the square carb throats. The control vacuum is drawn from between throttle butterflies (bottom of throats) and the venturi air valves in carb cover. CES opens as engine is cranked, while EMV opening is controlled by fuel temperature. The colder the start, the greater the amount of fuel admitted to the starting enrichment system.

CARTER

Despite the fact that most Carter 4-bbl. carbs look alike, there are so many variations of them that we couldn't possibly show them all in the space available. The AFB-based line of performance and emissions carburetors offers one of the widest selections on the market. Most O.E.M. use of Carters is on Chrysler Corp. cars, although some of the 1-bbl. and 2-bbl. models are used on Ford and GM cars as well. The aftermarket carburetors Carter sells are calibrated for many engines.

The latest configurations in the AFB series are the 9400, 9500 and 9625 carburetors. These are easy to understand, since the last three digits refer to the cfm airflow. Thus the 9400 is a 400-cfm carburetor, suitable for small V-8's or performance use on 6-cylinder engines. The three carburetors mentioned are federally certified for use on 1972 350-cu.-in. Chevrolet engines. By adding one to the last digit of the model number, you get the part number for a Chrysler V-8-certified carb. A 9501 is therefore a 500-cfm 4-bbl. for Chrysler engines. This trio will soon be available for Ford small V-8's; on them you add two to the last digit. For example, the 625-cfm model for Ford engines will then be called the 9627.

From our photos it may appear that the venturis are interchangeable between the basic carb bodies. Although they can physically interchange, Carter warns that all of the systems in each carb are calibrated for a specific use. Just changing to a larger (or smaller) venturi won't automatically give you proper carburetion with a change only in cfm rating.

Carter's 800-cfm Thermo-Quad carburetor remains one of their most popular 4-bbls. for performance use, with a spread-bore (small primary, large secondary) design for good around-town economy. We've selected a few of the most popular Carters here for detailed views to show you how they work.

1. *Simplest of the Carters is the 1-bbl. YF model, which is used mostly on 6-cylinder Ford engines.*

2. *Another 6-cylinder, 1-bbl. design is the BBS model shown here.*

3. *The new series of AFB-based 4-bbls. shares same body, but the guts differ. Note differences in venturi sizes of the three cfm ratings (shown by last three digits of model number).*

4. *The BBD 2-bbl. carburetor is used in a number of O.E.M. applications. There are two sizes; this one is the 1¼-in. throttle plate size. The 1½-in. BBD is quite different from other BB's.*

5. *Although "performance" became a dirty word after this carburetor was introduced, Thermo-Quad is still one of the best for mileage via the primaries and performance on the secondaries.*

1

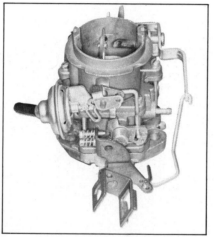

2

3

9625   9500   9400

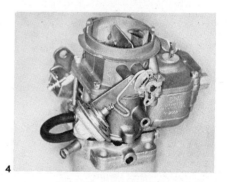

4

5

CARTER/YF

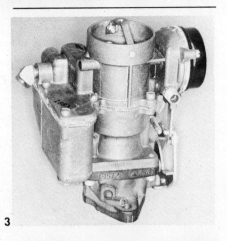

3

4

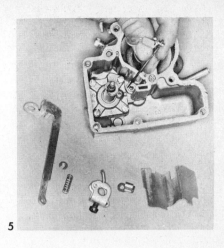

5

6

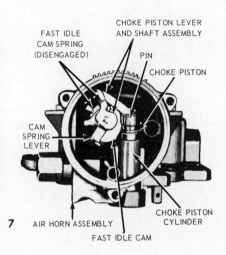

7

FAST IDLE
CAM SPRING
(DISENGAGED)

CHOKE PISTON LEVER
AND SHAFT ASSEMBLY

PIN

CHOKE PISTON

CAM
SPRING
LEVER

AIR HORN ASSEMBLY

CHOKE PISTON
CYLINDER

FAST IDLE CAM

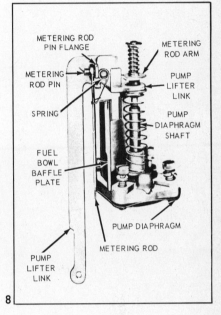

8

METERING ROD
PIN FLANGE

METERING
ROD ARM

METERING
ROD PIN

PUMP
LIFTER
LINK

SPRING

PUMP
DIAPHRAGM
SHAFT

FUEL
BOWL
BAFFLE
PLATE

PUMP DIAPHRAGM

METERING ROD

PUMP
LIFTER
LINK

3. *One nice thing about working on 6-cylinder automobiles is the simplicity of their single-barrel carburetors.*

4. *Carter's YF carburetor is used on Ford's 6-cylinder engines, except the 250. The tag on the carburetor says Autolite, but that's because Autolite sells it through Ford dealers, and independent outlets.*

5. *Here's where the YF gets a little bit tricky. The metering rod is both mechanically and vacuum controlled, which makes the linkage hookup somewhat difficult.*

6. *If you remove the choke housing, look carefully at the parts before you take any of them out. There are several pivots and links that can easily be put in the wrong place.*

7. *With the choke trip lever and the fast idle link removed, the choke linkage is exposed. To remove the piston, you must remove the choke plate. Later model YF's have a much simpler linkage arrangement.*

8. *Accelerating pump and lifter link is quite an accumulation of parts. Note position of fuel baffle plate.*

9. *Various designs have been used to operate the metering rod. There is even one model with an adjustable screw to change metering rod height.*

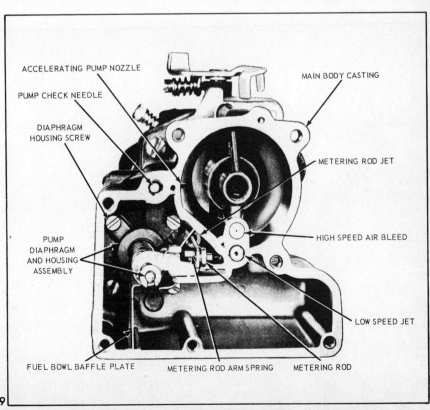

9

ACCELERATING PUMP NOZZLE

MAIN BODY CASTING

PUMP CHECK NEEDLE

DIAPHRAGM
HOUSING SCREW

METERING ROD JET

PUMP
DIAPHRAGM
AND HOUSING
ASSEMBLY

HIGH SPEED AIR BLEED

LOW SPEED JET

FUEL BOWL BAFFLE PLATE

METERING ROD ARM SPRING

METERING ROD

CARTER/BBS

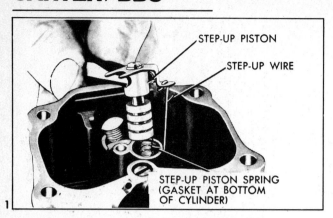

STEP-UP PISTON

STEP-UP WIRE

STEP-UP PISTON SPRING
(GASKET AT BOTTOM
OF CYLINDER)

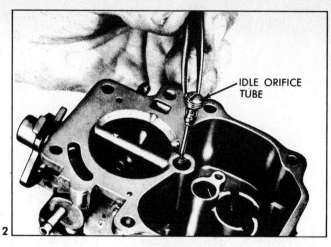

IDLE ORIFICE
TUBE

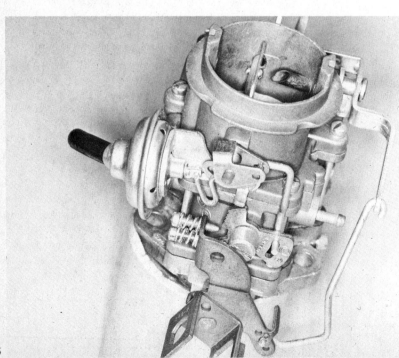

1. The BBS step-up piston and wire works like a power valve. At high vacuum it may leak if you don't have a little gasket underneath the piston.

2. A lot of carburetors have an idle jet similar to this BBS idle orifice tube. The calibrated idle jet is the hole which is located in the bottom end of the tube.

3. The Carter BBS has been around on 6-cylinder applications for quite a few years. Note how the screws for the bowl cover go clear through the bowl flange and then thread directly into the throttle body.

4. Fast idle cam mounts on main body with special large-head screw. Idle speed screw bears against head of screw.

5. The Carter BB carbs can be exasperating, because the fast idle and curb idle screws are right next to each other. It's easy to get on the wrong one.

6. The BBS accelerating pump is spring controlled. The arm does not really push the plunger down. Instead, it merely allows the spring to do that particular job.

7. Position the fast idle cam with the screw on the slowest step. Then set fast idle rpm according to specifications.

8. The spring around the pump plunger is the one that pushes it down when the linkage allows it to on the BBS.

9. The gauge is handy but not really necessary when checking float level on a BBS. You can use a scale if you are careful. You may have to put your thumb on the retainer to keep everything from falling out.

10. Note the two ports above the throttle valve on this BBS throttle body. An old carburetor often doesn't run well because the throttle shaft wears and allows the plate to get out of line with the idle and spark ports.

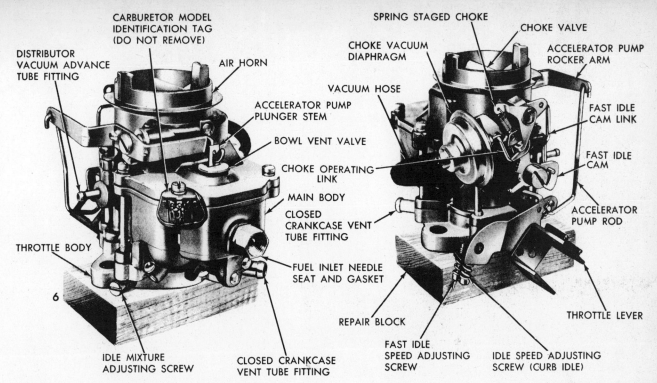

DISTRIBUTOR VACUUM ADVANCE TUBE FITTING

CARBURETOR MODEL IDENTIFICATION TAG (DO NOT REMOVE)

AIR HORN

ACCELERATOR PUMP PLUNGER STEM

BOWL VENT VALVE

CHOKE OPERATING LINK

MAIN BODY

CLOSED CRANKCASE VENT TUBE FITTING

THROTTLE BODY

FUEL INLET NEEDLE SEAT AND GASKET

6

IDLE MIXTURE ADJUSTING SCREW

CLOSED CRANKCASE VENT TUBE FITTING

SPRING STAGED CHOKE

CHOKE VALVE

CHOKE VACUUM DIAPHRAGM

ACCELERATOR PUMP ROCKER ARM

VACUUM HOSE

FAST IDLE CAM LINK

FAST IDLE CAM

ACCELERATOR PUMP ROD

REPAIR BLOCK

FAST IDLE SPEED ADJUSTING SCREW

IDLE SPEED ADJUSTING SCREW (CURB IDLE)

THROTTLE LEVER

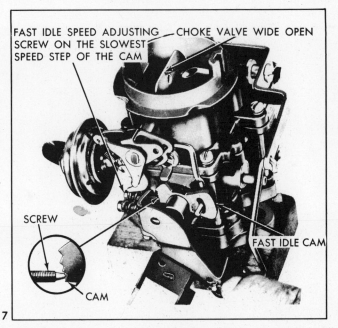

FAST IDLE SPEED ADJUSTING SCREW ON THE SLOWEST SPEED STEP OF THE CAM

CHOKE VALVE WIDE OPEN

SCREW

CAM

FAST IDLE CAM

7

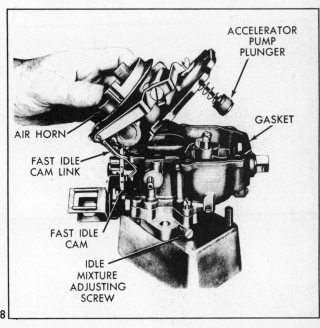

ACCELERATOR PUMP PLUNGER

GASKET

AIR HORN

FAST IDLE CAM LINK

FAST IDLE CAM

IDLE MIXTURE ADJUSTING SCREW

8

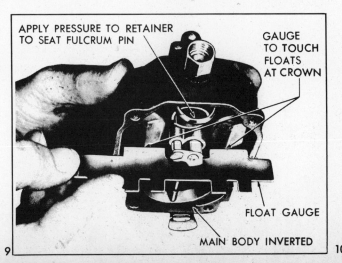

APPLY PRESSURE TO RETAINER TO SEAT FULCRUM PIN

GAUGE TO TOUCH FLOATS AT CROWN

FLOAT GAUGE

MAIN BODY INVERTED

9

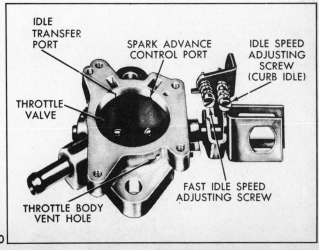

IDLE TRANSFER PORT

SPARK ADVANCE CONTROL PORT

IDLE SPEED ADJUSTING SCREW (CURB IDLE)

THROTTLE VALVE

FAST IDLE SPEED ADJUSTING SCREW

THROTTLE BODY VENT HOLE

10

CARTER/BBD 1¼"

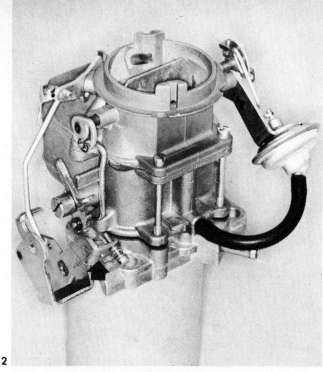

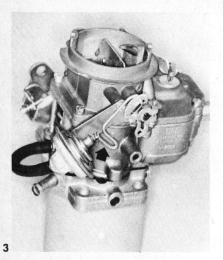

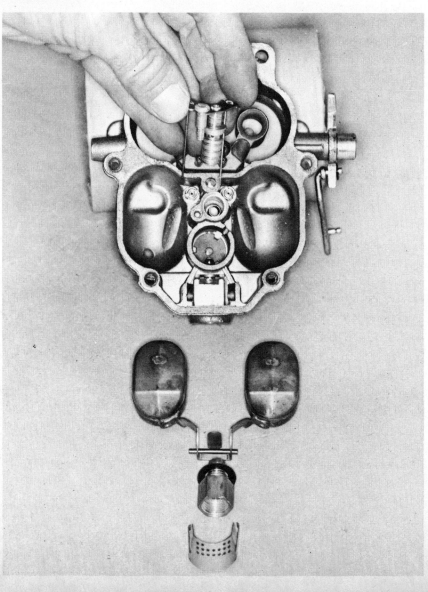

1. The BBD 1¼" is very similar to the BBS. Notice the well-type choke that was a mark of Chrysler products for many years, is now used on other makes too.

2. The large screw on the BBD that holds the fast idle cam on the side of the bowl is necessary to provide a resting place for the idle speed screw. The idle speed screw is missing on this carburetor; it gave the owner fits because the engine would start and run well while on choke, but the minute the choke went off it would die.

3. When you see a vacuum break with a funny bend in the middle of it, it was put there for adjustment purposes. Changing the shape of the bend lengthens or shortens the rod to control the vacuum break opening on the choke.

4. The similarity between the BBD and the BBS is obvious. The main jets are in the middle of the bowl on each side of the vacuum piston well. The accelerating pump check ball rests loose on the bottom of the pump well.

CARTER/BBD 1½"

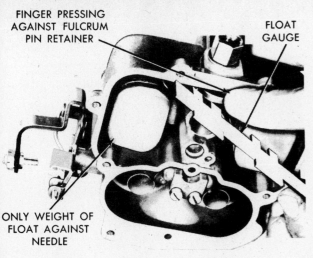

FINGER PRESSING AGAINST FULCRUM PIN RETAINER

FLOAT GAUGE

ONLY WEIGHT OF FLOAT AGAINST NEEDLE

5

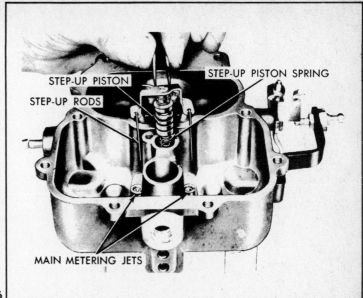

STEP-UP PISTON

STEP-UP PISTON SPRING

STEP-UP RODS

MAIN METERING JETS

6

5. To check float level, invert the bowl but keep your thumb on the retainer so that the float doesn't fall out.

6. The 1½-inch BBD has the same general appearance inside, although the shape of the bowl is different.

7. Some step-up rods used in BB carburetors are straight, but these are like a metering rod with steps that meter fuel according to how much the rod is in or out of the jet.

8. There is little outward similarity between the BBD 1½-inch and the other BB's. It's only when you get inside that you see the familiar BBD design.

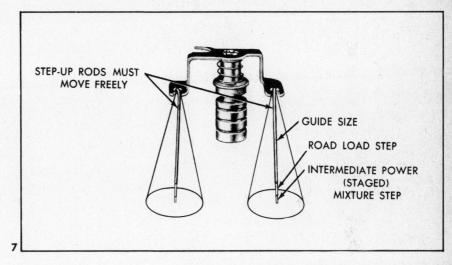

STEP-UP RODS MUST MOVE FREELY

GUIDE SIZE

ROAD LOAD STEP

INTERMEDIATE POWER (STAGED) MIXTURE STEP

7

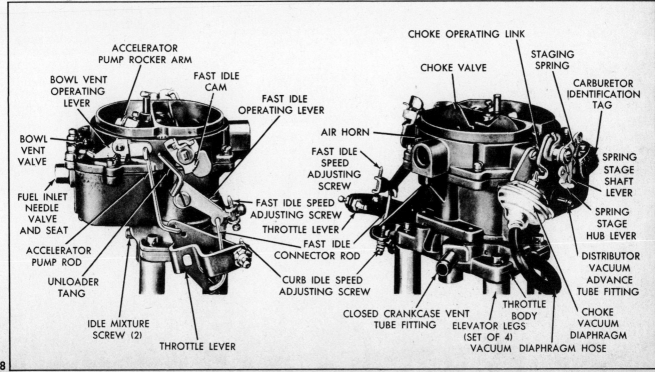

ACCELERATOR PUMP ROCKER ARM

FAST IDLE CAM

CHOKE OPERATING LINK

CHOKE VALVE

STAGING SPRING

BOWL VENT OPERATING LEVER

FAST IDLE OPERATING LEVER

CARBURETOR IDENTIFICATION TAG

BOWL VENT VALVE

AIR HORN

FAST IDLE SPEED ADJUSTING SCREW

SPRING STAGE SHAFT LEVER

FUEL INLET NEEDLE VALVE AND SEAT

FAST IDLE SPEED ADJUSTING SCREW

THROTTLE LEVER

SPRING STAGE HUB LEVER

ACCELERATOR PUMP ROD

FAST IDLE CONNECTOR ROD

DISTRIBUTOR VACUUM ADVANCE TUBE FITTING

UNLOADER TANG

CURB IDLE SPEED ADJUSTING SCREW

IDLE MIXTURE SCREW (2)

THROTTLE LEVER

CLOSED CRANKCASE VENT TUBE FITTING

THROTTLE BODY ELEVATOR LEGS (SET OF 4)

VACUUM DIAPHRAGM HOSE

CHOKE VACUUM DIAPHRAGM

8

CARTER/AFB

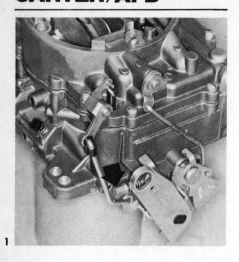

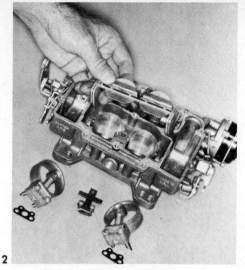

1. Still thriving, the AFB is one of the best carbs Carter ever made. Arrow points to the idle speed screw.

2. Remove the secondary clusters on an AFB and then the secondary air valve will come out.

3. Idle-mixture screws on an AFB are usually found in this position. The small hole next to the screws (arrow) is a pin that keeps you from removing them; it is a smog control item to prevent richening the mixture.

4. It's an AFB all right, but it has a different arrangement using a second shaft to manipulate the choke valve. This model was also used on Chevys.

5. Late model Chrysler AFB has divorced choke and vacuum diaphragm mounted on the side of the carburetor.

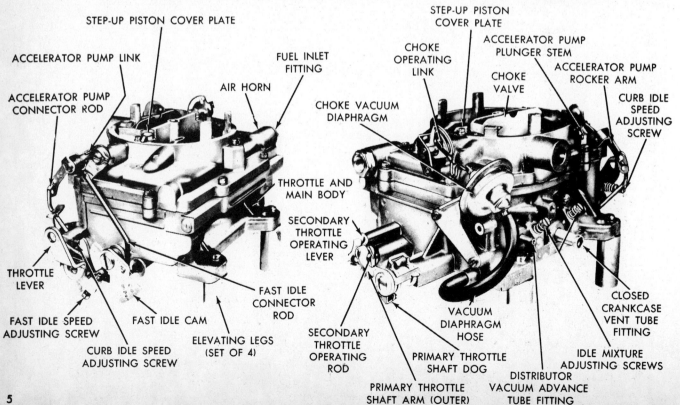

STEP-UP PISTON COVER PLATE

ACCELERATOR PUMP LINK

ACCELERATOR PUMP CONNECTOR ROD

AIR HORN

FUEL INLET FITTING

THROTTLE LEVER

FAST IDLE SPEED ADJUSTING SCREW

CURB IDLE SPEED ADJUSTING SCREW

FAST IDLE CAM

ELEVATING LEGS (SET OF 4)

FAST IDLE CONNECTOR ROD

THROTTLE AND MAIN BODY

SECONDARY THROTTLE OPERATING LEVER

SECONDARY THROTTLE OPERATING ROD

PRIMARY THROTTLE SHAFT ARM (OUTER)

STEP-UP PISTON COVER PLATE

CHOKE OPERATING LINK

ACCELERATOR PUMP PLUNGER STEM

CHOKE VALVE

ACCELERATOR PUMP ROCKER ARM

CURB IDLE SPEED ADJUSTING SCREW

CHOKE VACUUM DIAPHRAGM

VACUUM DIAPHRAGM HOSE

PRIMARY THROTTLE SHAFT DOG

DISTRIBUTOR VACUUM ADVANCE TUBE FITTING

CLOSED CRANKCASE VENT TUBE FITTING

IDLE MIXTURE ADJUSTING SCREWS

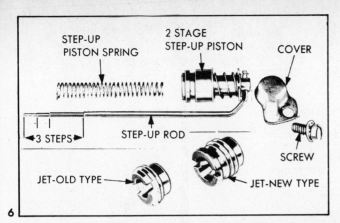

STEP-UP PISTON SPRING

2 STAGE STEP-UP PISTON

COVER

STEP-UP ROD

3 STEPS

SCREW

JET-OLD TYPE

JET-NEW TYPE

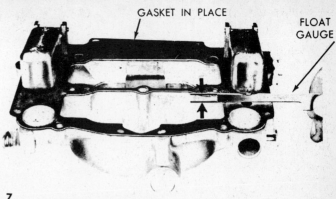

GASKET IN PLACE

FLOAT GAUGE

6

7

8

9

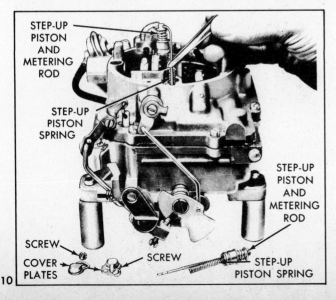

STEP-UP PISTON AND METERING ROD

STEP-UP PISTON SPRING

STEP-UP PISTON AND METERING ROD

SCREW

COVER PLATES

SCREW

STEP-UP PISTON SPRING

10

6. Some AFB models on Chrysler products used a 2-stage step-up piston. Step-up rod is called a metering rod.

7. Checking float level on an AFB. You don't have to use a float gauge; if you are careful a scale will do as well.

8. Looking into the AFB bowl, we see the two primary jets in the cutouts and the secondary jets on the floor of the bowl. This AFB is the larger type with the velocity valve. Some models do not have this valve.

9. This particular model AFB was used on Chevrolets. To lengthen or shorten the accelerating pump stroke, you bend the rod indicated, as there is no choice of holes.

10 Metering rods and pistons on an AFB are always put into the carb after the bowl cover has been installed. Wiggle them slightly as you push down and they will go in easily.

CARTER/AVS

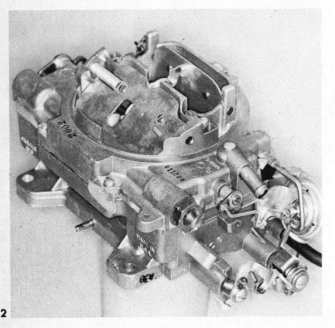

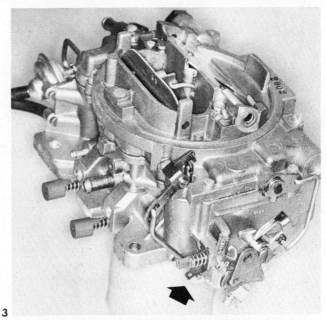

1. Inside the AVS there isn't much difference from an AFB. Note that there are no secondary clusters in the AVS.

2. The bowl vent tube identifies this as the vapor control AVS carburetor. Smog control demands that gasoline fumes are not allowed to evaporate into the air anymore.

3. Electrical connection on this AVS is for the solenoid retard on the distributor. It retards the spark at closed throttle.

4. Carter AVS vacuum break unit is connected by a rubber hose to the base of the carburetor. The vacuum break unit pulls the choke open as soon as the engine starts.

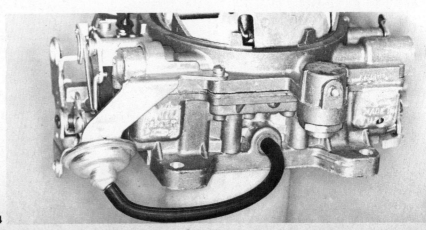

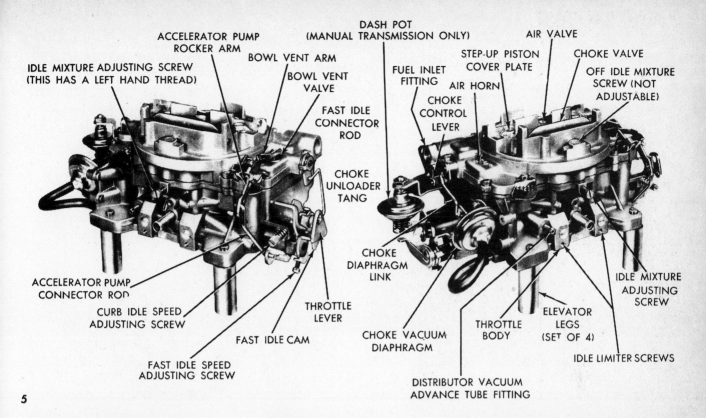

ACCELERATOR PUMP
ROCKER ARM

IDLE MIXTURE ADJUSTING SCREW
(THIS HAS A LEFT HAND THREAD)

BOWL VENT ARM

BOWL VENT
VALVE

FAST IDLE
CONNECTOR
ROD

CHOKE
UNLOADER
TANG

CHOKE
DIAPHRAGM
LINK

ACCELERATOR PUMP
CONNECTOR ROD

CURB IDLE SPEED
ADJUSTING SCREW

FAST IDLE CAM

THROTTLE
LEVER

FAST IDLE SPEED
ADJUSTING SCREW

DASH POT
(MANUAL TRANSMISSION ONLY)

FUEL INLET
FITTING

AIR HORN

CHOKE
CONTROL
LEVER

STEP-UP PISTON
COVER PLATE

AIR VALVE

CHOKE VALVE

OFF IDLE MIXTURE
SCREW (NOT
ADJUSTABLE)

IDLE MIXTURE
ADJUSTING
SCREW

CHOKE VACUUM
DIAPHRAGM

THROTTLE
BODY

ELEVATOR
LEGS
(SET OF 4)

IDLE LIMITER SCREWS

DISTRIBUTOR VACUUM
ADVANCE TUBE FITTING

5

5. *The AVS looks like an AFB at first glance, but it's different enough to merit the new name.*

6. *Here's how the vapor control bowl vent works on the AVS. At throttle, the idle linkage opens the vent and fuel vapors are allowed to go out the tube to the crankcase.*

7. *On the AVS, like the AFB, the metering rods and pistons are inserted after the bowl cover is on the carb.*

8. *When the throttle comes back to closed position on this AVS, it touches the idle adjustment screw, which is the grounding contact for the idle retard solenoid.*

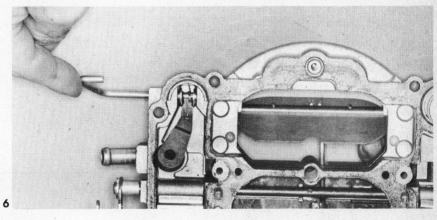

6

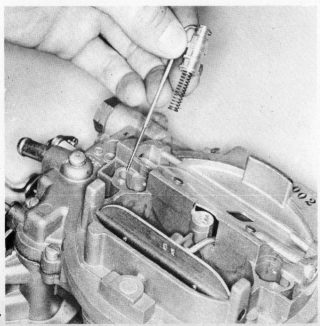

7

8

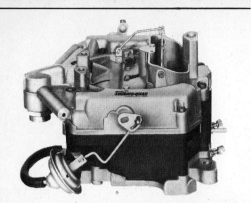

1

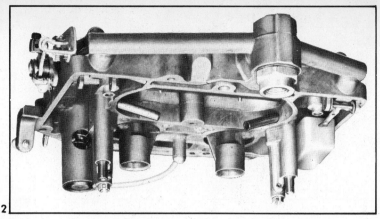

2

3

4

5

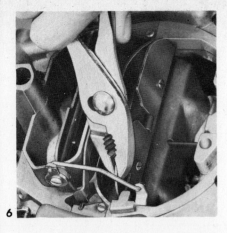

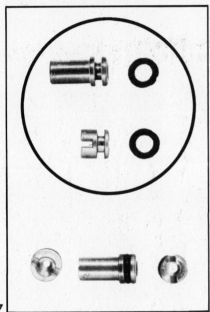

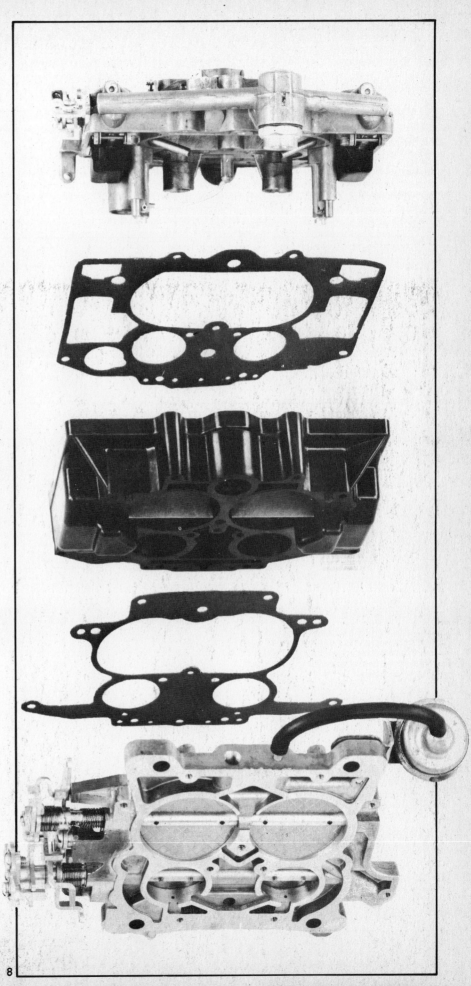

1. On the Thermo-Quad 4-barrel the damper diaphragm acts as a slow opener for the air valve. It's a must if you're considering street applications.

2. Thermo-Quad is radical design. Suspended accelerating pump has low, center fuel intake. Large holes in the cylinder below the fuel level increase pump efficiency.

3. Air horn assembly is heart of T.Q. Neat package makes modifications quick and easy. Jets slip in with O-rings.

4. "Free breathing" manual choke puts carburetor at "fast idle" and controls clever secondary latching mechanism. Air valve spring adjustment can be seen next to choke levers on air horn.

5. Top removed from 850 CFM Thermo-Quad shows air valve torsion spring which enables the fuel to feed from large secondary nozzles.

6. Corner of air valve is notched for adjustment of wide-open position.

7. Closeup of the jets shows how the O-rings fit. Jets should be worked out with fingers, if possible. Pliers can crush them.

8. Exploded view shows unique fuel bowl and "suspended" metering system which keeps Thermo-Quad cool.

HOLLEY

From a manufacturer of small carburetors of the O.E.M. (Original Equipment Manufacturer) type for several decades, Holley emerged in the 1960's as *the* name in 4-bbl., high-performance carburetion. Holleys were used on virtually all of the "hot" production muscle cars. The '70's have seen many changes in the automobile industry, but Holley has maintained its firm position in aftermarket sales with its line of emissions-calibrated 2- and 4-bbls. You can pick up a Holley catalog and choose a suitable carburetor for virtually any engine or purpose. There are still the performance models for which the company is famous—the center-squirters, the dual-feeds, the mechanical-secondary models, huge-cfm 2-bbls. and even the big, racing-only 4500's. In addition, Holley offers a complete line of 4-bbls. that replace O.E.M. spread-bore (small primary, large secondary) designs, in cfm's ranging from the new 450 to the 650 and 800.

Of course, Holley also manufactures the rest of the components that make up a fuel system. Their high-performance fuel pumps and fuel pressure regulators have been around for several years now, but they are also making spark plugs, and in 1976 the company introduced a complete line of aluminum intake manifolds of their own design. All Holley parts are grouped under their integrated heading of "The System," with equipment available for performance/competition uses as well as for street/emissions purposes. ♟

1

2

3

4

1. Newest in the Holley line is the model 4360 shown here. This 450-cfm 4-bbl. is designed for today's engines, providing emissions/economy benefits along with good performance.

2. The 4360's spread-bore design uses mechanical secondaries for crisp response. The three-piece carburetor body is unlike any other Holley, because the float bowls are integral and jets are not in a separate metering block.

3. The 6619 remains one of the most popular 600-cfm 4-bbls. for street use with emissions calibration. The secondaries are vacuum-operated on this single-feed model 4160.

4. Holley offers two spread-bores that directly replace Quadrajets. The 4175 shown here features 650-cfm flow and vacuum secondaries, while the 4165 is a double-pumper with mechanical secondaries and 650 or 800 cfm.

5. The 4175 spread-bore uses standard metering block and replaceable jets on the primary side, with a drilled metering plate for the secondaries. The performance 4165 features jets and metering blocks at each end.

5

HOLLEY/1920

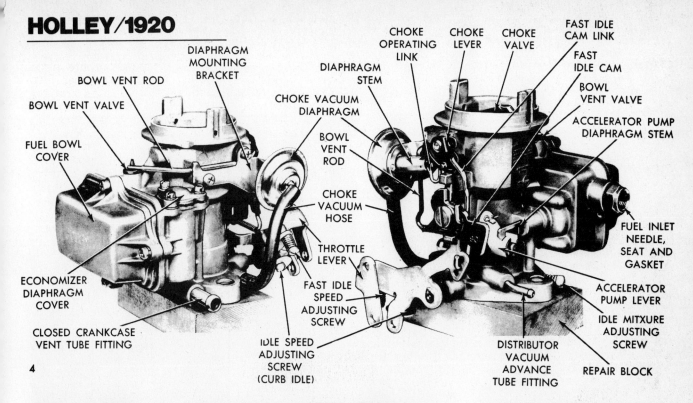

DIAPHRAGM MOUNTING BRACKET
BOWL VENT ROD
BOWL VENT VALVE
FUEL BOWL COVER
ECONOMIZER DIAPHRAGM COVER
CLOSED CRANKCASE VENT TUBE FITTING

CHOKE OPERATING LINK
CHOKE LEVER
CHOKE VALVE
DIAPHRAGM STEM
CHOKE VACUUM DIAPHRAGM
BOWL VENT ROD
CHOKE VACUUM HOSE
THROTTLE LEVER
FAST IDLE SPEED ADJUSTING SCREW
IDLE SPEED ADJUSTING SCREW (CURB IDLE)

FAST IDLE CAM LINK
FAST IDLE CAM
BOWL VENT VALVE
ACCELERATOR PUMP DIAPHRAGM STEM
FUEL INLET NEEDLE, SEAT AND GASKET
ACCELERATOR PUMP LEVER
IDLE MITXURE ADJUSTING SCREW
DISTRIBUTOR VACUUM ADVANCE TUBE FITTING
REPAIR BLOCK

4

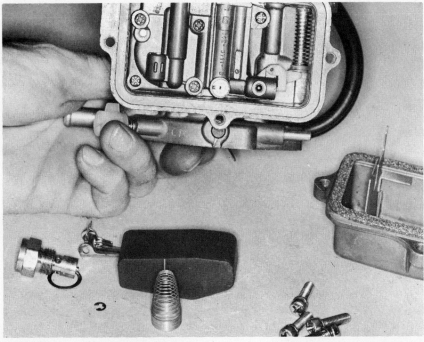

5

4. The model 1920 shown here has an exposed idle-mixture adjusting screw. The later models use the limiter caps that will prevent you from unscrewing the needle past a certain point.

5. With the bowl off the 1920, the float and needle seat will come out easily. You must remove the needle seat before attempting to remove the float. Note the spring that holds up the float to keep it from bouncing.

6. The screw indicated is for adjusting the bowl vent, but is open only at idle position. Above idle the external vent should close so that the internal vent in the air horn can balance the pressure in the bowl.

7. If you want to measure the actual wet fuel level while the carburetor is on the car, you can manage to do it down through the economizer hole.

8. Needle and seat on the 1920 cannot be inspected for wear, so it's a good idea to replace it whenever the carburetor is torn down for cleaning or overhaul.

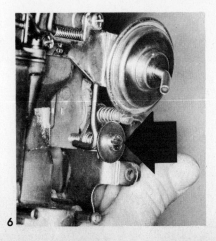

6

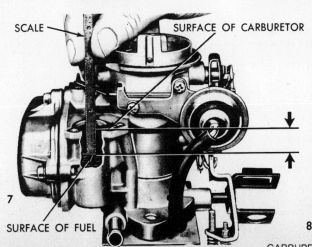

SCALE
SURFACE OF CARBURETOR
SURFACE OF FUEL

7

8

HOLLY/1945

1. A single bore, concentric downdraft design, Holley Model 1945 carburetor was introduced in '74. This '75 version has a remote automatic choke system and fits standard trans Chrysler Corp. cars as factory equipment.

2. A vacuum-operated choke actuator and throttle positioner solenoid are part of the new emissions controls. The vacuum diaphragm pulls the choke open when the engine is started; the throttle positioner solenoid protects the catalytic converter from overheating during deceleration from high rpm by holding the throttle open slightly and allowing airflow to dilute the otherwise rich mixture.

3. This vacuum tap at the throat of the carburetor venturi provides a control signal for the EGR amplifier.

4. Automatic transmission models of 1945 will have an idle enrichment valve located here, with an idle enrichment passage system in bowl cover.

1

2

3

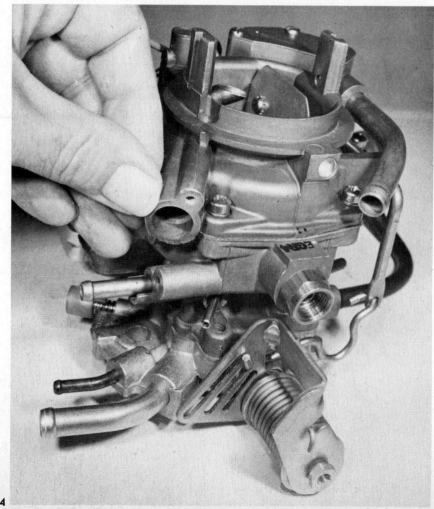

4

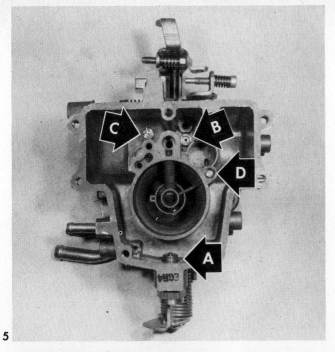

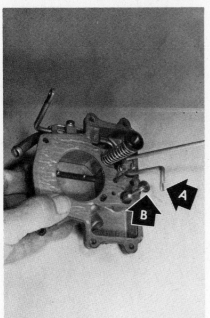

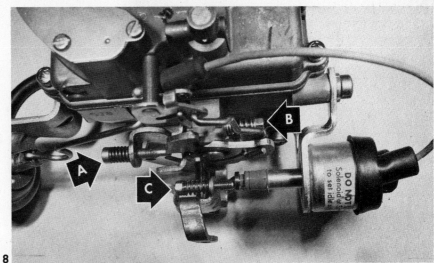

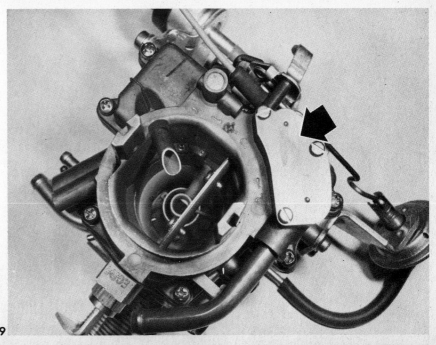

5. With carburetor bowl off, you can see the fuel inlet needle (A), main jet (B), power valve (C) and pump discharge weight (and ball) (D).

6. The power valve is a 3-piece unit consisting of the valve, a removable valve stem and a spring.

7. The main difference between the 1945 and its predecessor, the 1940, is a gradient fuel enrichment system. As the throttle approaches wide open, spring-loaded rod (A) contacts vacuum piston stem (B), fully opening the valve. This is a mechanical action unrelated to engine vacuum.

8. Fast idle (A), curb idle (B) and throttle position solenoid stop (C) are all set on one side of carb.

9. A mechanical fuel vent is located under this cover (arrow) and vents directly to the vent tube.

HOLLEY/2200

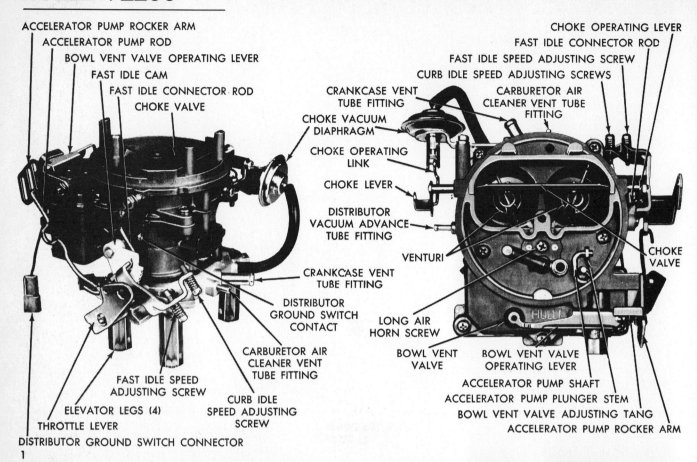

ACCELERATOR PUMP ROCKER ARM
ACCELERATOR PUMP ROD
BOWL VENT VALVE OPERATING LEVER
FAST IDLE CAM
FAST IDLE CONNECTOR ROD
CHOKE VALVE

CHOKE OPERATING LEVER
FAST IDLE CONNECTOR ROD
FAST IDLE SPEED ADJUSTING SCREW
CURB IDLE SPEED ADJUSTING SCREWS

CRANKCASE VENT TUBE FITTING
CHOKE VACUUM DIAPHRAGM
CHOKE OPERATING LINK
CHOKE LEVER
DISTRIBUTOR VACUUM ADVANCE TUBE FITTING

CARBURETOR AIR CLEANER VENT TUBE FITTING

VENTURI

LONG AIR HORN SCREW

CRANKCASE VENT TUBE FITTING

DISTRIBUTOR GROUND SWITCH CONTACT

CARBURETOR AIR CLEANER VENT TUBE FITTING

CHOKE VALVE

BOWL VENT VALVE

BOWL VENT VALVE OPERATING LEVER

FAST IDLE SPEED ADJUSTING SCREW

CURB IDLE SPEED ADJUSTING SCREW

ELEVATOR LEGS (4)
THROTTLE LEVER
DISTRIBUTOR GROUND SWITCH CONNECTOR

ACCELERATOR PUMP SHAFT
ACCELERATOR PUMP PLUNGER STEM
BOWL VENT VALVE ADJUSTING TANG
ACCELERATOR PUMP ROCKER ARM

1

2

3

4

5

6

1. Holley's 2210 doesn't look like we might expect a Holley to look. It is used on Chrysler products.

2. The 2210 is a conventional carburetor. Note how close together the fast idle and curb idle speed screws are.

3. The idle retard solenoid is controlled by the electrical contact that is under the idle speed screw.

4. Vacuum break diaphragm is connected to vacuum source by a hose. It's a handy place to check engine vacuum.

5. Cleaner float bowls are hard to find. The power valve is at the bottom of the bowl between the two main jets.

6. Inverting the bowl reveals the two idle jets sticking up with the power piston and the spring between them. The spring on the accelerating pump assists the linkage when it operates the pump.

7. Limiter caps on the idle-mixture screws are universal nowadays. The Holley caps do allow some adjustment.

7

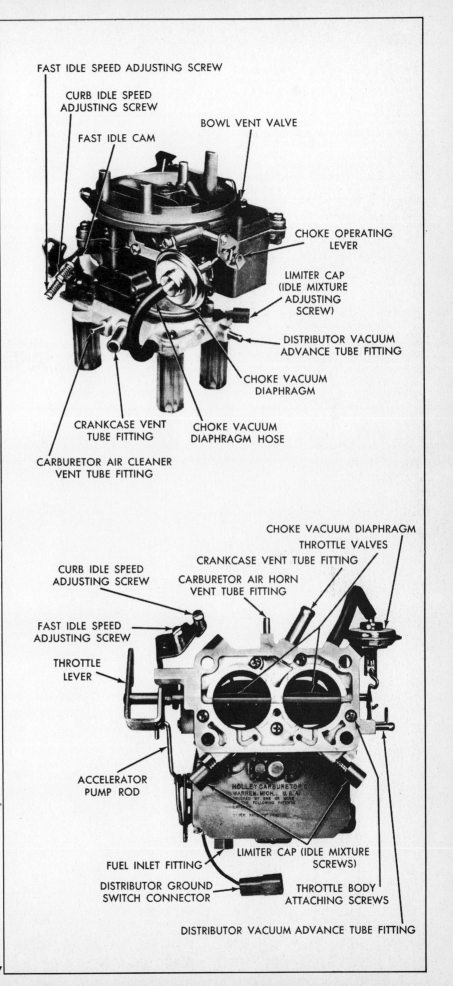

FAST IDLE SPEED ADJUSTING SCREW

CURB IDLE SPEED ADJUSTING SCREW

FAST IDLE CAM

BOWL VENT VALVE

CHOKE OPERATING LEVER

LIMITER CAP (IDLE MIXTURE ADJUSTING SCREW)

DISTRIBUTOR VACUUM ADVANCE TUBE FITTING

CHOKE VACUUM DIAPHRAGM

CRANKCASE VENT TUBE FITTING

CHOKE VACUUM DIAPHRAGM HOSE

CARBURETOR AIR CLEANER VENT TUBE FITTING

CHOKE VACUUM DIAPHRAGM
THROTTLE VALVES

CRANKCASE VENT TUBE FITTING

CARBURETOR AIR HORN VENT TUBE FITTING

CURB IDLE SPEED ADJUSTING SCREW

FAST IDLE SPEED ADJUSTING SCREW

THROTTLE LEVER

ACCELERATOR PUMP ROD

FUEL INLET FITTING

DISTRIBUTOR GROUND SWITCH CONNECTOR

LIMITER CAP (IDLE MIXTURE SCREWS)

THROTTLE BODY ATTACHING SCREWS

DISTRIBUTOR VACUUM ADVANCE TUBE FITTING

HOLLEY/2245

1. Holley 2245 2-bbl. carburetor uses gradient power enrichment system instead of single or 2-stage power valve of the previous 2210 model. It's a dependable carburetor, and very easy to work on.

2. Principal feature of the '75 model is this idle enrichment valve found on carburetors used with automatic transmission-equipped cars. Valve gets a vacuum signal from coolant thermal switch, provides around 35 secs. of enrichment for cold starts.

3. Gradient power enrichment of 2245 uses a one-piece staked vacuum piston instead of the two-piece power valve piston/spring assembly of previous 2200 models. This is not adjustable and is usually not removed during rebuild unless piston malfunctions.

4. Twin idle enrichment ports are in the air horn near enrichment valve. System is designed to reduce cold stalling by using a metering system instead of the choke.

1

2

3

4

5. Vacuum tap at throat of carburetor venturi (A) gives a control signal to EGR vacuum amplifier. Vacuum fittings below it connect to air cleaner heated inlet air system (B), PCV valve (C).

6. Throttle positioner solenoid is used on '75 carbs fitted to catalytic converter-equipped cars. It's part of converter protection system and works to hold throttle plates open slightly during deceleration to increase air-flow, reduce otherwise too rich mixture.

7. With the air horn off, we can see power valve seat and needle (A), two main jets (B), pump discharge needle (C) location. Main jets may differ in size, depending upon application of the carburetor.

8. Orifice spark advance control (OSAC) valve to distributor (A) and charcoal canister purge port (B) can be seen easily by turning carburetor over.

HOLLEY/2300

1

1. The 2300 is really half of a 4150 or 4160. In the Chrysler Six-Pack setup, the center carb has the thick metering block, and the end carbs have the thin.

2. End carbs have a sealed idle system. The adjusting screws are under these lead plugs. From the factory the carbs are set to idle lean for emission control. The plugs can be removed and the idle richened if you are going to use the car on the drag strip.

3. Comparison of a Holley 2300 2-barrel on the left with the double pumper 4-barrel on the right. Similarity of the two designs is quite obvious. The 2-barrel has a slightly different bowl vent baffle, whereas the double pumper has the white whistle.

2

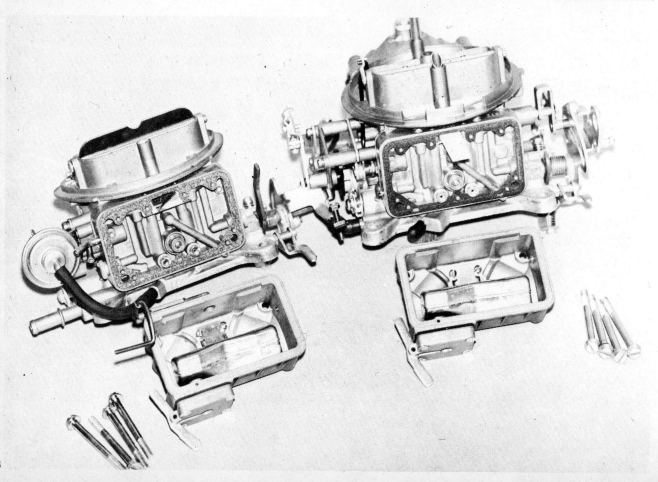

3

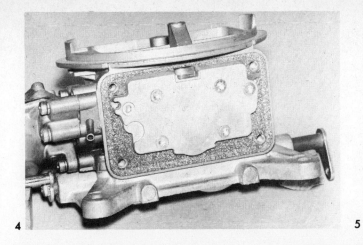

4

5

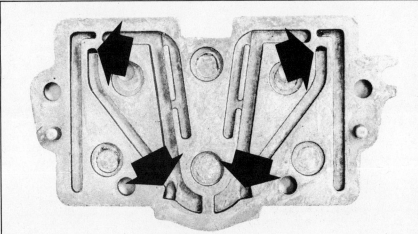

6

4. Here's what we mean by the thin metering block on the outboard 2300 carburetors. The 4160 4-barrel uses a similar metering block on the secondary side.

5. Spread bore pattern of base is obvious in this bottom shot.

6. Thin metering block on end carbs has fixed main jets (lower arrows). Upper passageway shows path of fuel after it has gone through the main jets.

7. Stock Chrysler setup was on an Edelbrock manifold. The Six-Pack came on both 440 and 340 Chrysler engines.

7

HOLLEY/4150, 4160

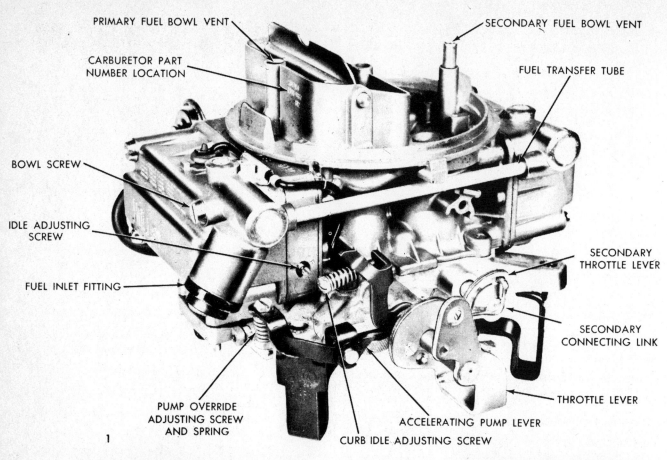

PRIMARY FUEL BOWL VENT

CARBURETOR PART NUMBER LOCATION

BOWL SCREW

IDLE ADJUSTING SCREW

FUEL INLET FITTING

PUMP OVERRIDE ADJUSTING SCREW AND SPRING

CURB IDLE ADJUSTING SCREW

ACCELERATING PUMP LEVER

SECONDARY FUEL BOWL VENT

FUEL TRANSFER TUBE

SECONDARY THROTTLE LEVER

SECONDARY CONNECTING LINK

THROTTLE LEVER

1

2

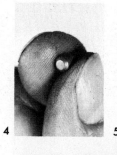

3

4

5

6

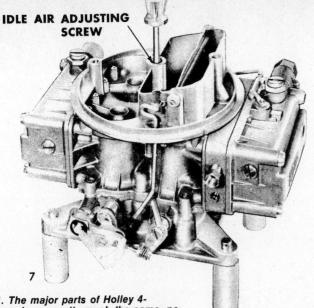

IDLE AIR ADJUSTING SCREW

7

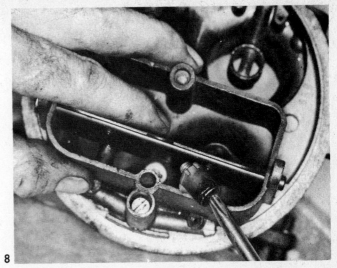

8

9

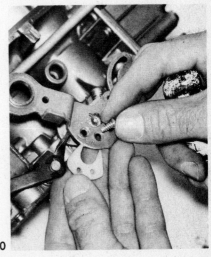

10

1. *The major parts of Holley 4-barrels are pretty much the same, no matter whose engine the carburetor is designed to fit. This is a 4160 with the thick metering block on the primary side only.*

2. *Holley 4-barrels come in many different shapes and sizes. This — for Chrysler — has a balance tube running between the two bowls behind the fuel transfer tube.*

3. *Screw in accelerating pump is adjustable. It should be screwed out just enough to take up all play. If it's either too tight or too loose, you will lose part of the pump stroke.*

4. *Underneath this pump nozzle is this outlet check. This one is a short plunger. It could also be a ball and weight, or a needle.*

5. *Older Holley 4-barrels used Phillips-head screws to hold the accelerating pump on the bottom of the bowl. Later ones used clutch-type screws for added clearance between the pump and the manifold.*

6. *Accelerating pump housing comes off the bottom of the bowl, reveals the diaphragm and spring. Ball check is held in position, not removable.*

7. *The idle air screw is a means of supplying air to run the engine when the design of the carb allows the throttle plates to close completely at idle. You'll never find this one if you don't know it's there, because the air cleaner stud screws in on top of it. A disadvantage is that idle adjustments must be made with air cleaner off.*

8. *Accelerating pump nozzle is down below the choke valve.*

9. *Early model carbs had the pump cam encircling the throttle shaft. It could still be adjusted, but not removed, unless you removed the shaft.*

10. *Pump cam can be put in two different positions, for short or long stroke. Cam is plastic, so don't tighten the screw too much, or it may strip out.*

11. *Adjusting the fast idle speed on late-model Holley 4-barrels is done by twisting this little link that is hidden in behind everything else. It can be twisted with a screwdriver in the slot.*

11

HOLLEY/4150, 4160

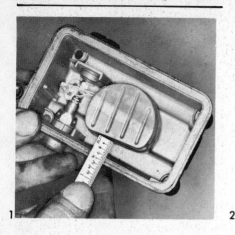

1

2

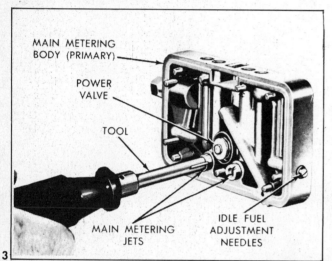

MAIN METERING
BODY (PRIMARY)

POWER
VALVE

TOOL

MAIN METERING
JETS

IDLE FUEL
ADJUSTMENT
NEEDLES

3

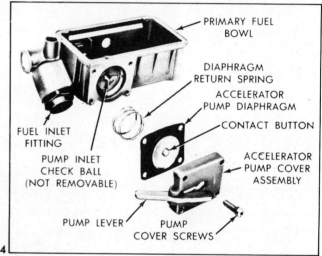

PRIMARY FUEL
BOWL

DIAPHRAGM
RETURN SPRING

ACCELERATOR
PUMP DIAPHRAGM

CONTACT BUTTON

ACCELERATOR
PUMP COVER
ASSEMBLY

FUEL INLET
FITTING

PUMP INLET
CHECK BALL
(NOT REMOVABLE)

PUMP LEVER

PUMP
COVER SCREWS

4

5

6

7

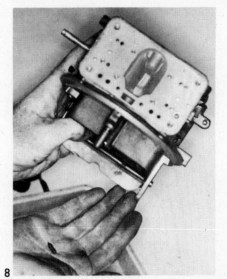

8

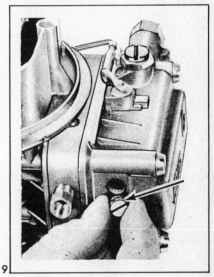

9

1. Float level is the only internal adjustment on a Holley. The measurement is made at the location shown, but it differs with other models of carburetors, so you should check your shop manual for correct specifications.

2. To remove Holley throttle body, take out the Phillips-head screws from the bottom.

3. Note that they are using a special tool to remove the Holley main jets rather than a screwdriver. Sometimes a screwdriver doesn't fit right and will damage the jets.

4. Holley pumps are not difficult to disassemble, but make sure you get the spring on correct side of diaphragm.

5. A Holley 4-barrel for use on a Chevy. There is no balance tube running between the bowls, behind the fuel tube.

6. Be sure you have a full gasket set available when you take the carb apart. The old gaskets will probably fall apart in your hands, as here.

7. Choke side of Holley made for Chevys. Note how the diaphragm rod pulls on the lever to open the secondary throttles.

8. Part most easily lost is the pump outlet check. After removing the pump nozzle, it will fall out easily.

9. Here, when the float is adjusted correctly, gasoline should just wet the bottom of the threads in the sight plug hole. Note the float-adjusting nut and lockscrew atop the bowl of this 4-barrel Holley. If you have already set the float with a gauge and the fuel level doesn't reach the bottom of the sight plug hole, you should reset the float with the lockscrew and nut until the wet fuel level is correct. Best results are achieved with the adjustment being made while the engine is running at a normal idling speed on level ground.

10. Four long screws hold the Holley 4-barrel bowl in place. This is center-pivot float bowl, for racing.

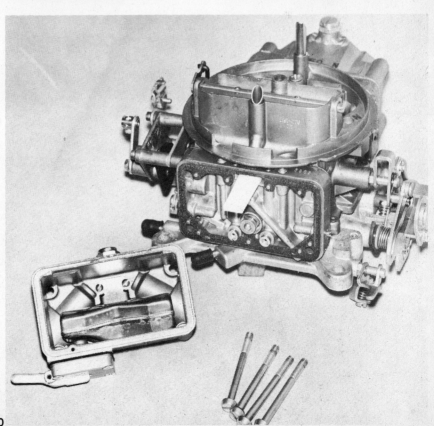

10

HOLLEY/5200

1. Manufactured under license to Weber, Holley 5200 series is used on Pinto 2000cc and Vega L-4 engine options. This is Pinto version, which differs somewhat from the more sophisticated Vega 5210-C.

2. The Holley 2-bbl. 5200 has a number of unusual features not common to American-designed 2-bbl. carbs—a primary/secondary system and a water-heated bimetal thermostatic choke housing are two.

3. Vega L-4 option is equipped with 5210-C and has idle stop solenoid with curb idle adjustment at stem, making throttle linkage somewhat more complex. Carb for standard transmission car is slightly different than this one used with automatic.

4. To make curb idle—low idle adjustment on Vega carb, disconnect idle stop solenoid and adjust low idle screw (1) to specs. Set dwell and timing, recheck speed and reconnect solenoid. Then adjust curb idle screw (2) to specs. Final speed setting should be made with a tach.

1

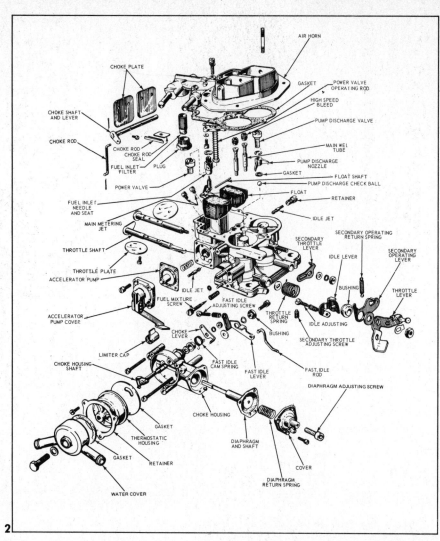

2

3

4

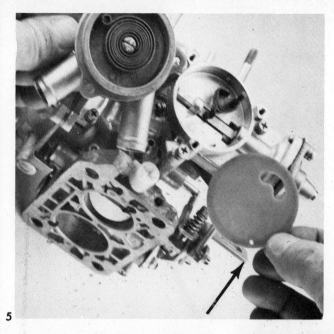

5

6

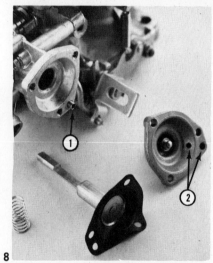

7

8

9

5. Removal of three hex head screws provides access to the choke plate for adjustment. When replacing the cover, make certain that the housing pin engages the tiny hole at 5:00 position on gasket.

6. Choke plate pulldown can be measured with screwdriver behind vacuum diaphragm stem as shown. You'll need to insert a gage rod or drill between lower edge of choke plate and air horn wall for correct measurement.

7. Adjustment of choke plate-to-air horn clearance is made as shown. Remove the outside screw and you'll find a vacuum diaphragm adjusting screw inside the housing. On some Pinto models as well as the Vega carbs, a hex head screw is used that operates directly on the diaphragm instead of the external/internal screw arrangement.

8. Three screws hold the vacuum diaphragm housing and spring in place against the diaphragm stem. Vacuum is applied via inlet (1) and passes through chamber (2) in housing cover to exert suction on diaphragm to operate choke pulldown.

9. Float shaft is a press fit that's a bit too tight to remove by hand but loosens nicely with a gentle tap on punch. Nitrophyl float has a tendency to absorb fuel and can give problems.

10. Power valve operating rod is equipped with a rather fragile diaphragm that likes to wrinkle and curl when pressure is removed.

10

HOLLEY/5200

1. When replacing the operating rod, you'll find it necessary to exert sufficient force to flatten the diaphragm before tightening screws or diaphragm will get crimped and leak.

2. Vega 5210-C uses bowl vent (1) system to reduce percolation. Internal venting to air cleaner is provided by dual vents (2) cast into air horn.

3. Vega carb uses an adequate-sized fuel inlet filter of standard pleated paper design (left) while Pinto version has an undersized plastic container with a wire mesh screen located on underside of air horn fuel inlet (right). It bears frequent checking.

4. Accelerator pump diaphragm and return spring are identical on both Pinto and Vega carbs and are held in place by cover assembly and four screws.

5. Accelerator pump arm adjustment can be made by removing pin and relocating the arm-to-pump cover position.

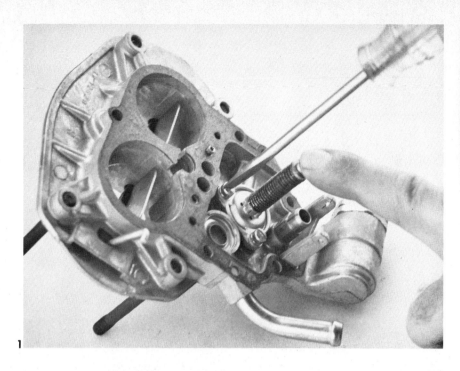

1

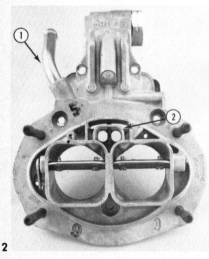

2

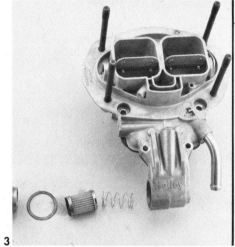

3

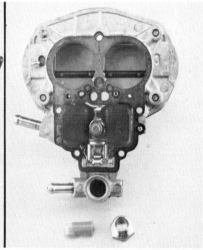

4

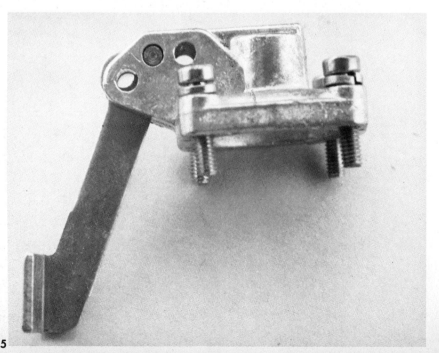

5

6. *Twin main metering jets (1) are positioned inside of float bowl at base of main well tubes. Idle jets (2) are positioned at each end of throttle body under retainer plugs.*

7. *Three types of pump discharge valve assemblies have been used: cage, single ball and double ball. Use of second ball is unusual; it functions only as a weight.*

8. *Vega carb uses timed vacuum ports on EGR control; Pinto has none. Main port (1) is located just above the throttle plate; other port cannot be seen here but is positioned near the lower idle air bleed.*

9. *Side-by-side comparison of Pinto 5200, Vega 5210 (right) versions of Holley-Weber design reveals major differences—except for EGR porting setup.*

ROCHESTER

If you have a General Motors car, the chances are excellent that a Rochester carburetor is doing the mixing for you.

Rochester started out with the model B single-barrel; the model M is a later 1-bbl. The Rochester 2G 2-bbl. has been joined by a new 2MC 2-bbl. for 1975, created from a Quadrajet casting. The 4-bbl. Quadrajet model is called the 4M and has been joined for 1975 by a variation called the Mod-Quad, or Modified Quadrajet. If a Rochester carburetor has a manual choke, it uses the basic designation only, such as B or 2G. If a choke coil is added to the carburetor itself, the letter C becomes part of the model code, as in BC or 2GC. Later-model carbs had the choke on the intake or exhaust manifold and the carburetor's code included a "V" added to the basic lettering, such as BV, 2GV or 4MV; for '75, they're back on the carburetor—the remote choke is gone, at least temporarily. ♕

1

2

3

4

1. The two lower carburetors are model MV's, also called the Monojet. At left we have a BC and above it a 2GV. At upper right are two big quadrajets; in the middle is the peculiar Buick 2GV with the double vacuum break unit.

2. Most Rochester carbs have a paper or bronze filter behind the fuel line fitting. The filter should be changed every time the carburetor is overhauled.

3. Rochester 4-barrel has 2¼-inch secondary holes, which should make any V-8 come alive. But it's not considered a performance carb.

4. Rochester 4-barrel with anti-dieseling solenoid. Curb idle is set with the solenoid adjustment.

ROCHESTER/MV

5. The Monojet is the latest Rochester design. However, most of its features are conventional. Note the idle-mixture screw located at base of carburetor.

6. With the bowl cover off and the float removed, we can see the main jet in the bottom of the bowl on the left with the metering rod inserted in it.

7. The rod for the accelerating pump goes through the bottom of the bowl on the Monojet model.

8. On the side of the carburetor is a little cover with two screws; underneath it is the hot idle compensator.

9. You can push the little spring down on the metering rod and it will pop right off the arm.

10. External bowl vents are now out, so the MV model bowl vent has been changed to a pressure relief valve that vents only when the pressure in the bowl is high.

11. The vacuum break unit is built into the side of the carburetor, underneath this cover. It's a rubber diaphragm, so don't dunk it in the cleaning fluid.

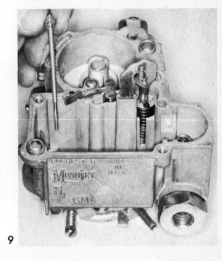

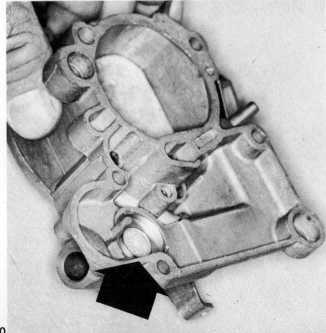

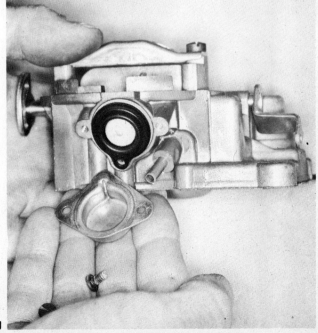

ROCHESTER/MV

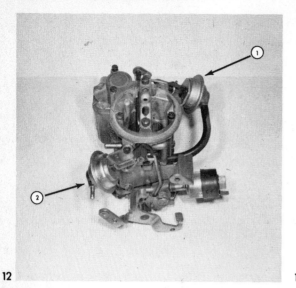

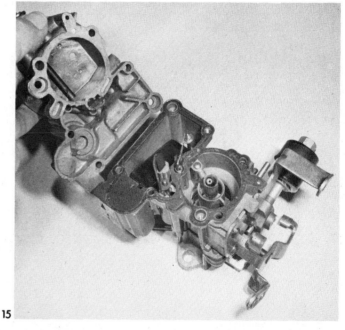

12. Recent MV models use an external dual vacuum break system (1 & 2) for improved choke control. The auxiliary diaphragm unit (2) is controlled by a coolant operated vacuum switch.

13. Curb idle is set by a threaded plunger in the end of anti-dieseling solenoid.

14. Alphabetical code letters on MV are now used to identify vacuum and clean air tubes for correct hose connections; of course, if you don't know what code letters stand for, they're not much help.

15. Internally, the MV hasn't changed very much over the years, but some 6-cylinder models use two timed EGR ports—one in the base of throttle body and one in the lower venturi area in the bowl—to provide a vacuum signal to the EGR valve.

16. Removing and replacing the float can be a bit tricky, as fuel inlet needle must be fitted into inlet valve at same time float is installed.

ROCHESTER /BC, BV

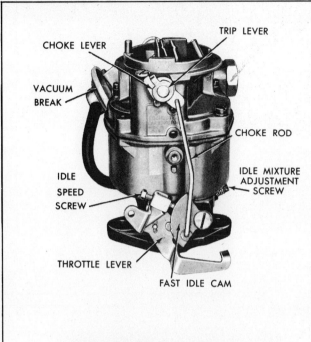

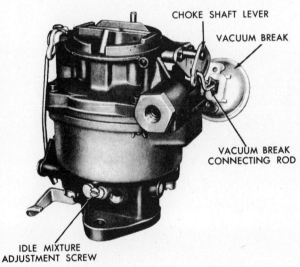

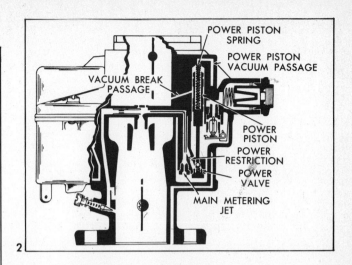

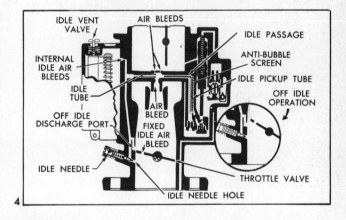

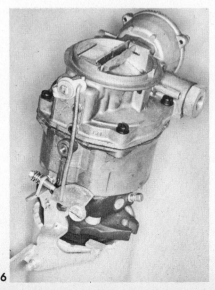

1. BV with choke coil mounted down on the exhaust manifold.

2. Note location of the power restriction or power jet on the model B. It is not in the power valve itself.

3. Next to the model B main jet is a hex cap covering the power valve. Underneath that is the stem of the vacuum piston that opens the valve.

4. Main nozzle on the model B is a peculiar shape, but it does the job well. Note that the idle mixture crosses over to the opposite side of the carburetor on its way to the idle port.

5. Main metering parts on the model B, as illustrated in this photo, are contained in the bowl cover itself.

6. The BC ran on the old 6-cylinder Chevys for years. It is one of the few carburetors that uses one screw for both its fast idle and its slow idle.

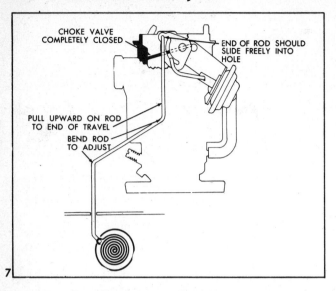

CHOKE VALVE COMPLETELY CLOSED

END OF ROD SHOULD SLIDE FREELY INTO HOLE

PULL UPWARD ON ROD TO END OF TRAVEL

BEND ROD TO ADJUST

7

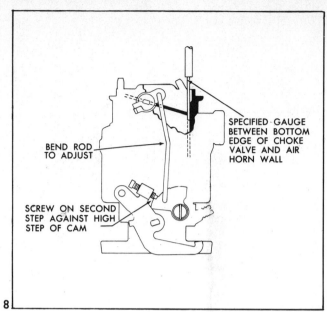

BEND ROD TO ADJUST

SPECIFIED GAUGE BETWEEN BOTTOM EDGE OF CHOKE VALVE AND AIR HORN WALL

SCREW ON SECOND STEP AGAINST HIGH STEP OF CAM

8

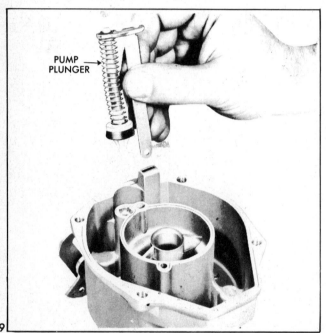

PUMP PLUNGER

9

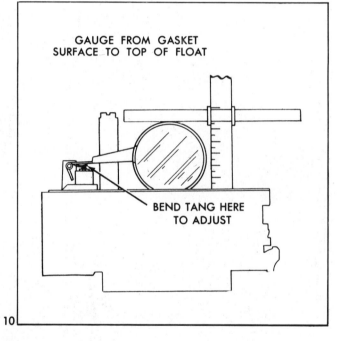

GAUGE FROM GASKET SURFACE TO TOP OF FLOAT

BEND TANG HERE TO ADJUST

10

11

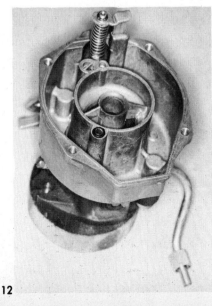

12

7. Here's the way the choke hooks up to a BV. This setup is common on all General Motors 6-cylinder engines.

8. Note the choke rod adjustment on a BV. This adjustment for the length of the rod insures that the fast-idle cam will end up in the right position for proper operation.

9. Remove the link underneath the bowl and then the complete accelerating pump plunger assembly will come out.

10. Float level on the BC and BV is set with the bowl cover inverted.

11. Instead of being built into the carburetor casting, the BC uses an external line that comes up from the throttle body to supply the choke piston with the vacuum it needs.

12. As can be seen here, the float bowl completely surrounds the venturi on the model B Rochester.

ROCHESTER /2GC, 2GV

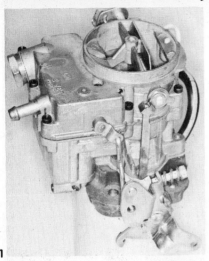

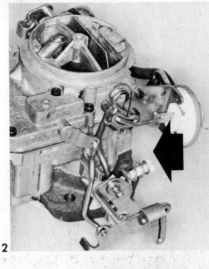

1. The tube sticking out of the bowl cover on this Pontiac 2GV is not a fuel connection; it merely allows vapors to go to a carbon canister for storage.

2. Arrow indicates idle-speed screw on this Buick 2GV. Notice internal bowl vent tube sticking into the air horn.

3. Here's a 2GC with the choke coil mounted on the throttle body. It was used on some Pontiacs.

4. 2GV's used on '71 Oldsmobile have an auxiliary fuel feed that allows additional fuel to flow into the throat when the engine is at high rpm. It works about the same way a power valve does.

5. Inside the bowl, most 2G models are alike. The two main jets are nestled close together with power valve in front.

6. Three screws hold the cluster in position. Accelerating pump, idle, and main jet fuel pass through the cluster.

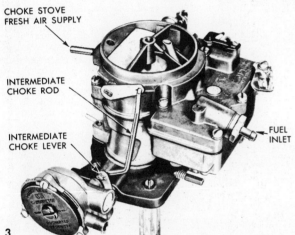

CHOKE STOVE
FRESH AIR SUPPLY

INTERMEDIATE
CHOKE ROD

INTERMEDIATE
CHOKE LEVER

FUEL
INLET

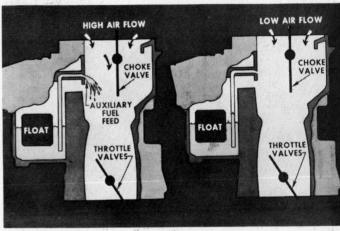

HIGH AIR FLOW

LOW AIR FLOW

CHOKE VALVE

AUXILIARY FUEL FEED

FLOAT

THROTTLE VALVES

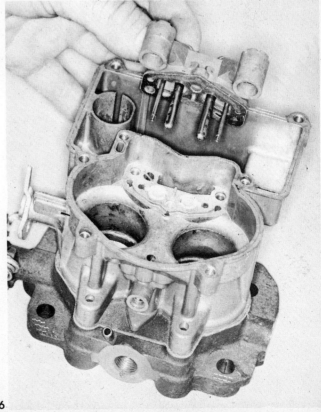

ROCHESTER/2GC, 2GV

7. Business end of a Rochester metering cluster. Pen points to the end of the idle tube. This is actually the idle jet for one barrel.

8. Buick's 2GV for 1970 with double vacuum break units. One of the units comes into action a little later than the other in order to give a progressive choke opening.

9. Pontiac uses this more conventional 2GV on its 1970 models. It only has one vacuum break unit.

10. Here's the underside of the bowl cover on the Buick model with the double vacuum break setup.

11. Float level on the 2G carbs is set with the bowl cover inverted. Measure to the sharp edge of the seam on the float. Later floats are plastic, but they still have a seam.

12. With the bowl cover off a Pontiac 2GV and the float removed, we can see all the mechanism that operates the bowl vents. The right-hand arrow indicates the internal vent which goes into the air horn. At the left is the external vent. In between the two of them is a vacuum diaphragm that closes the external vent and opens the internal. When the engine is shut off there is no vacuum, so a spring on the other side of the diaphragm closes the internal vent and opens the external. At wide-open throttle there would be no vacuum, allowing the internal vent to close and the external to open. But we can't have this, so a little tang on the accelerating pump arm keeps the internal vent open and the external vent closed whenever the carburetor is at wide-open throttle.

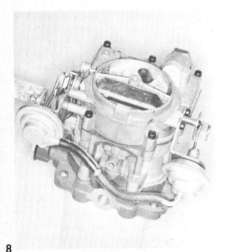

8

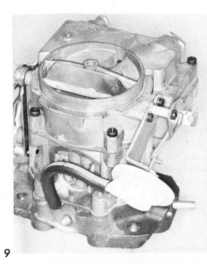

9

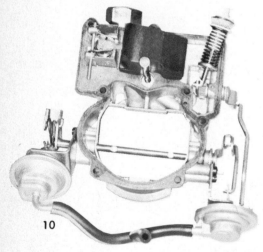

10

11

12

13

14

15

16

13. The 2GC for '75 is fitted with an integral choke and dual vacuum break diaphragms for better control of carburetor mixtures during engine warmup.

14. 2GC models used on '75 350-cu.-in. engines have a bowl vent valve adjustment located under this cover. With the idle-speed screw on the second step of fast idle cam, valve should just be closed. When idle-speed screw moves to next lower step, valve should just begin to open.

15. Like all recent Rochester carbs, the newer 2GC models use an expander spring under the pump plunger cup for better pump fuel delivery. You can't see it, but it's there.

16. The retaining clip on accelerator pump plunger stem has been eliminated in favor of "clipless" retaining setup. Plunger is removed by twisting with pliers until upset end breaks; replacement assemblies have a grooved end along with a retaining clip.

17. An auxiliary fuel feed tube operates in conjunction with a combination vacuum/mechanical power system. When manifold vacuum drops to the power cut-in level, the power piston (arrow) moves downward to force the power valve plunger off its seat, giving enough fuel for light power requirements. A second power valve, located at pump well base, is mechanically actuated by accelerator pump plunger.

17

ROCHESTER/2MC

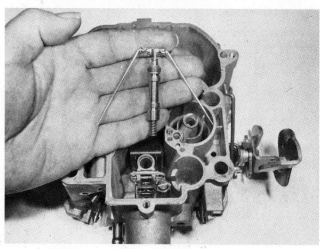

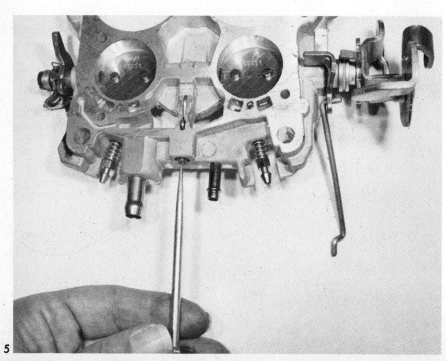

1. New for 1975, Rochester 2MC is a 2-bbl. carburetor made from a Quadrajet casting, with secondary throttle bores and metering equipment left out. GM uses it only on new 260 V-8.

2. With all secondary equipment gone, it seems that there's a lot of wasted area, but tooling up for a brand-new carb these days is costly; however, using a triple venturi similar to that of the Quad's primary side—but with 1 ⅜-in. bores—makes the 2MC better adaptable to smaller engines.

3. An adjustable part throttle (APT) feature is used to keep a very close control on fuel mixtures during part throttle operation.

4. The APT uses a special power piston and primary metering rods; you can interchange it with any other.

5. With fuel bowl removed, you can see the pin on which the power piston rests. As the adjustment screw is screwed in, the pin expands, raising the piston and lowering the metering rods. Rod taper can be set precisely in the metering jet for the required air/fuel ratio.

6. The Pull-Over Enrichment system makes use of twin supplemental fuel feeds connected to a calibrated hole in each bore to provide fuel required at high rpm for good performance.

7. With the pin and adjusting screw removed, you can get a better idea of its operation. As screw enters the open end of the pin, it expands. APT is factory-set, with a capped adjustment screw that should not be readjusted.

8. Like its 4-bbl. brother, the 2MC's accelerator pump piston utilizes an expander (garter) spring under the pump cup for proper wall-to-wall contact during operation.

9. The 2MC uses a single vacuum break with spring-loaded plunger, or bucking spring; this offsets the tension of the choke coil to balance greater opening of choke valve with tension of the thermostatic coil.

10. Overhauling and adjusting 2MC is similar to, but far simpler than, same procedure with Quadrajet.

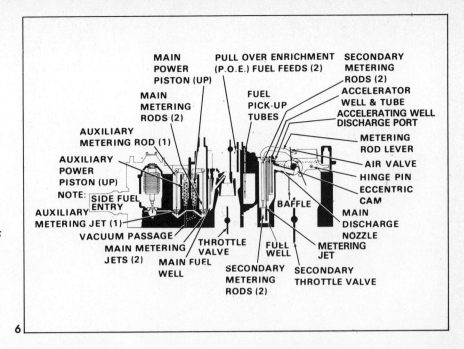

6

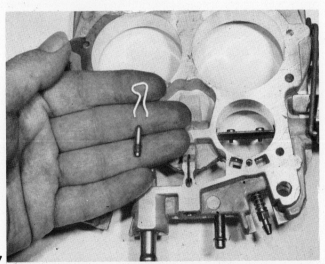

7

8

9

10

ROCHESTER /4MV

1

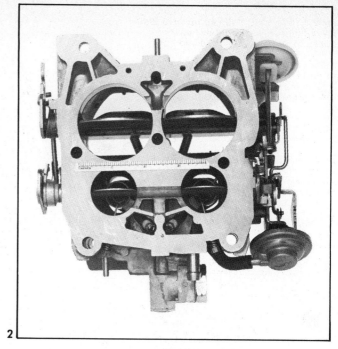

2

3

4

5

1. Secondary metering rods on 4MV's can be removed without removing the bowl cover. Just take out little screw in middle of arm between two air valves.

2. Maybe this is one reason why the Rochester is not considered a performance carburetor. There is just too much garbage in the bores for it to do any serious breathing.

3. The secondary metering rods on this 4MV are operated by the air valve itself. Here the valves are open and the arm connected to the metering rod is up in the air, thereby lifting the rods out of the jets.

4. This 4MV has two vacuum diaphragms. The one on the right is for choke vacuum break and also to control the secondary air valves. The left one is an air-conditioning idle-speed-up device. This carb came off a Cadillac.

5. You won't see many of these around. It's one of the first models of the quadrajet design. Note the secondary throttle lock-out on the throttle body.

6. The arrow indicates the idle-speed screw on this 4MV. You can observe that this one has an external bowl vent hooked to the accelerating pump arm.

7. The idle-mixture screws on the 4MV are down on the front of the carburetor close to the manifold. This is an early model without the limiter caps.

8. Secondary linkage on Rochester 4-barrel is a rod, adjusted by bending. Screw (arrow) is for curb idle adjustment.

9. The little link that sticks out over the air valve is the choke lock-out, which prevents the valves from operating when the choke is on.

10. Like all late-model quadrajets, the one shown here uses the choke vacuum break unit to help control the air valves in the secondary bores.

6

7

8

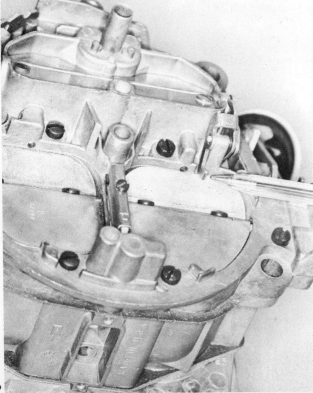

9

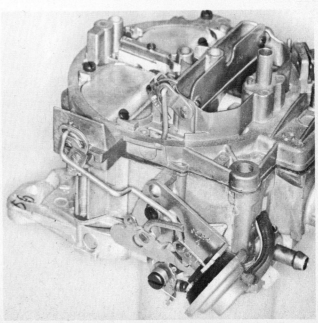

10

ROCHESTER /4MV

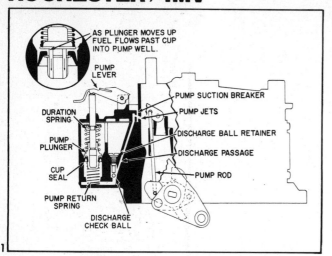

AS PLUNGER MOVES UP FUEL FLOWS PAST CUP INTO PUMP WELL.

PUMP LEVER

PUMP SUCTION BREAKER

PUMP JETS

DURATION SPRING

DISCHARGE BALL RETAINER

PUMP PLUNGER

DISCHARGE PASSAGE

CUP SEAL

PUMP ROD

PUMP RETURN SPRING

DISCHARGE CHECK BALL

1

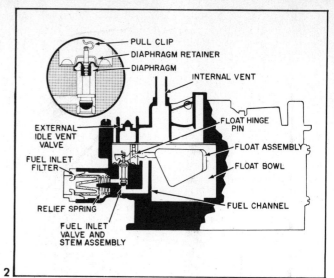

PULL CLIP

DIAPHRAGM RETAINER

DIAPHRAGM

INTERNAL VENT

EXTERNAL IDLE VENT VALVE

FLOAT HINGE PIN

FUEL INLET FILTER

FLOAT ASSEMBLY

FLOAT BOWL

RELIEF SPRING

FUEL CHANNEL

FUEL INLET VALVE AND STEM ASSEMBLY

2

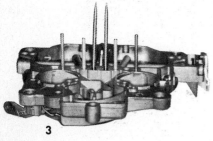

3

1. *Accelerating pump system on the 4MV. In this lower model, fuel flows past the accelerating pump cup as it moves up in the well. There is no inlet ball check.*

2. *Some 4MV's used a diaphragm needle valve. Replacing it is tricky. Luckily, the later models use a conventional needle and seat assembly.*

3. *Here we have removed the bowl cover from the 4MV without taking the trouble of removing the rods first.*

4. *The gasket covers up everything on the 4MV, and a cutout in it fits in between the two primary metering rods.*

5. *Lift the gasket off and then remove the fuel baffle that fits around the needle and the seat.*

6. *The float and pin easily lift right out, and then you can just pull the needle out of the seat.*

7. *With the float bowl clear, we can see the primary metering rods in the jets. Note how full the venturis are with the added second and third venturis.*

8. *To remove the primary metering rods and pistons, just let the piston snap up against the spring a couple of times, and it will pop the plastic retainer out.*

9. *Rochester primary metering rods all have the same diameter on the power or wide-open throttle portion. The part-throttle portion, or the "A" diameter varies with the rod. The clue here is that if you change the main jet, you are changing the mixture throughout the entire range. However, if you change the rod only, then you are only affecting the part-throttle mixture. Power can sometimes be gained by using a richer rod for a little bit more gasoline at part-throttle setting.*

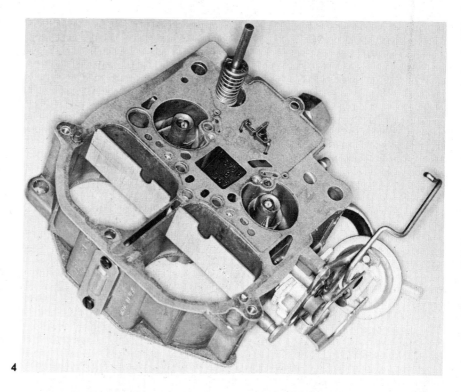

4

5

6

7

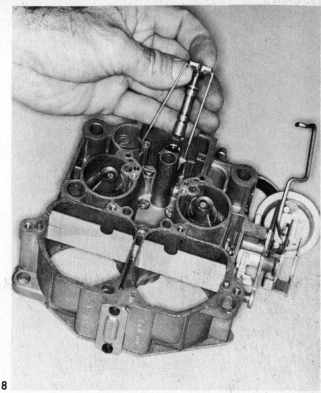

8

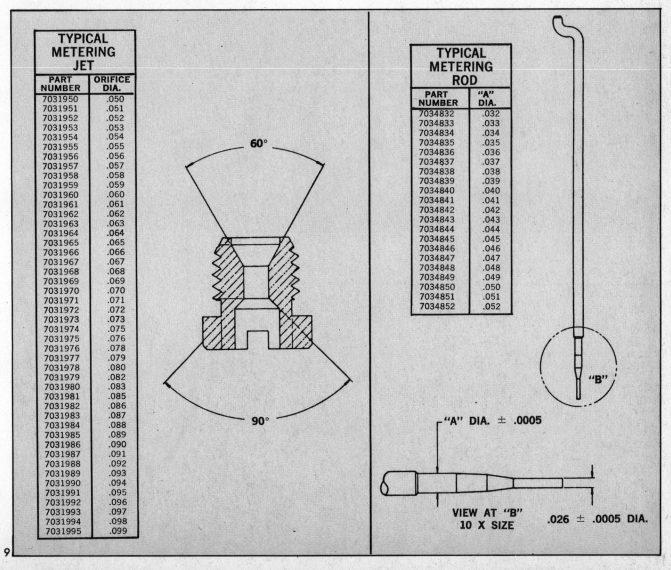

TYPICAL METERING JET	
PART NUMBER	ORIFICE DIA.
7031950	.050
7031951	.051
7031952	.052
7031953	.053
7031954	.054
7031955	.055
7031956	.056
7031957	.057
7031958	.058
7031959	.059
7031960	.060
7031961	.061
7031962	.062
7031963	.063
7031964	.064
7031965	.065
7031966	.066
7031967	.067
7031968	.068
7031969	.069
7031970	.070
7031971	.071
7031972	.072
7031973	.073
7031974	.075
7031975	.076
7031976	.078
7031977	.079
7031978	.080
7031979	.082
7031980	.083
7031981	.085
7031982	.086
7031983	.087
7031984	.088
7031985	.089
7031986	.090
7031987	.091
7031988	.092
7031989	.093
7031990	.094
7031991	.095
7031992	.096
7031993	.097
7031994	.098
7031995	.099

60°

90°

TYPICAL METERING ROD	
PART NUMBER	"A" DIA.
7034832	.032
7034833	.033
7034834	.034
7034835	.035
7034836	.036
7034837	.037
7034838	.038
7034839	.039
7034840	.040
7034841	.041
7034842	.042
7034843	.043
7034844	.044
7034845	.045
7034846	.046
7034847	.047
7034848	.048
7034849	.049
7034850	.050
7034851	.051
7034852	.052

"B"

"A" DIA. ± .0005

VIEW AT "B"
10 X SIZE

.026 ± .0005 DIA.

9

ROCHESTER M4MC, M4MCA, M4MEA

1. Though basically same as previous Quadrajet models, three new versions for 1975 are now called Mod-Quads, or Modified Quadrajets. This denotes special feature changes added to the standard Quad. All models use the bowl-mounted electric choke housing with thermostatic coil.

2. The deflector plate directs air into the secondary air valves, where an integral baffle has been added to improve mixture distribution from the secondary side at higher airflow.

3. Some models, such as this used on the Chevrolet 455, have a deflector plate mounted to the air horn attachment screws just in front of the secondary plates.

4. Alphabetical code letters are now stamped at external tube locations to help identify air, vacuum and fuel hose routing under the hood. Of course, if you don't know the code, this feature is of little use.

5. Bowl vent valve (A) has been added to the air horn to vent fuel vapors from the carburetor to the collection canister, and requires an adjustment routine. Also used on some Mod-Quads, the altitude compensator device is part of the adjustable part throttle feature (B).

6. Carburetors used on California cars omit the auxiliary power piston with its single metering rod, which operates in a fixed jet.

7. The primary power piston is conventional, using two metering rods which operate in replaceable main metering jets. Where both pistons are used, don't mix up springs, as they're of different lengths/tensions.

8. Two power pistons form multiple stage power enrichment on non-Calif. cars for better air/fuel control during light power demands, while giving a richer mixture when the engine load is moderate to heavy.

9. Those who are at all familiar with the integral type choke will feel right at home with the '75 models. GM abandoned remote choke, feeling float bowl choke to be more precise. A dual vacuum break system is also used to improve choke operation during warm-up.

10. To improve fuel delivery, expander, or garter spring, has been added under accelerator pump plunger cap (A); the spacer (B) is also used with some applications.

6

7

8

9

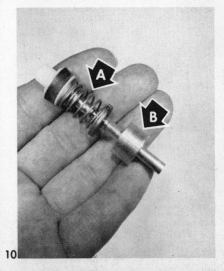

10

EFI, AMERICAN STYLE

When Cadillac introduced their extremely successful Seville for 1976, they also premiered a new electronic fuel-injection system that has now found applications on the larger Cadillacs and which may find still wider use in the future. Driving a car equipped with this system is a dream, especially when compared to the lack of drivability in the rest of Detroit's current line-up.

As emissions regulations and fuel economy quotas get tighter and tighter, the good old carburetor has an uphill fight to accomplish everything asked of it. Electronic fuel injection (EFI), however, appears able to handle the challenges and then some. By metering a precise amount of fuel directly to each cylinder at the precise moment it is required, not only does EFI improve engine operating efficiency, it eliminates difficulties due to altitude changes. Also, such common carburetion faults as stumbling, loading up at idle and vapor lock are no longer a problem.

Most fuel-injection systems employ a constant flow of fuel to the injector nozzles. There are various methods of timing the opening and closing of these nozzles to allow fuel to enter the ports and to route the excess fuel back to the tank. The systems seen on drag racing vehicles are of a continuous-flow type, in that the nozzles are always open to the ports. Only the throttle-blade opening and the fuel flow *rate* are variable. That's fine for all-out racing at high rpm, but emissions and drivability at partial throttle aren't ever considered in such an application.

For passenger car use, the release of fuel must be timed to the firing of each cylinder, which can be done in several ways. The Cadillac system times the injectors in two groups, one for each bank of cylinders. Each of the injectors is connected by steel tubing (called the fuel rail) with cylinders Nos. 1, 2, 7 and 8 in one group and Nos. 3, 4, 5 and 6 in the second group. All of the injectors in the two banks are opened once during every two complete revolutions of the crankshaft, in accordance with the engine's firing order. All of the injectors in a group open at once. A throttle body that looks like a stripped-down 2-bbl. carburetor meters air into the intake manifold, and also contains a thermostatic fast idle valve to aid engine warm-up in cold weather.

The elements of the Cadillac system can be divided into four groups: the fuel delivery system, the air induction system, the sensors and the electronic control unit, which is the real heart of EFI. In addition to those parts of the fuel delivery system already mentioned, there are two electric fuel pumps, a fuel filter and a pressure regulator. One electric pump is located within the gas tank, at the pickup end of the fuel line. It pumps fuel to the larger electric pump mounted on the chassis, which then sends the fuel through the large fuel filter and on to the engine. As fuel under high pressure reaches the engine, the pressure regulator mounted at the beginning of the fuel rail limits this pressure to a constant 39 psi and delivers the excess fuel through another line back to the fuel tank.

The air induction system includes the throttle body, intake manifold and fast idle valve. All of the normal connections for manifold vacuum are lo-

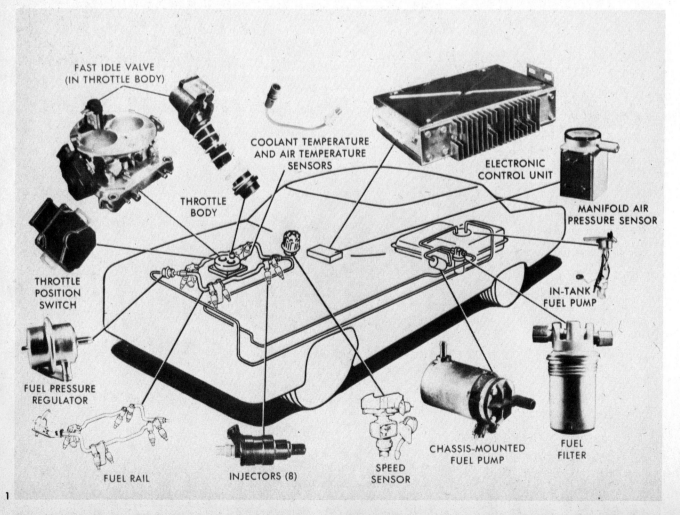

FAST IDLE VALVE (IN THROTTLE BODY)

COOLANT TEMPERATURE AND AIR TEMPERATURE SENSORS

ELECTRONIC CONTROL UNIT

MANIFOLD AIR PRESSURE SENSOR

THROTTLE BODY

THROTTLE POSITION SWITCH

IN-TANK FUEL PUMP

FUEL PRESSURE REGULATOR

FUEL RAIL

INJECTORS (8)

SPEED SENSOR

CHASSIS-MOUNTED FUEL PUMP

FUEL FILTER

cated on the manifold or the throttle body. The manifold itself is much like a standard one, except that it only delivers air and has no exhaust-heat crossover underneath it. The exhaust passage from the right cylinder head *is* connected to the manifold, but only for operation of the EGR (Exhaust Gas Recirculation) valve.

An idle air passage in the throttle body is adjusted by a setscrew to control the warm-engine idle speed. The fast idle valve consists of a plastic housing incorporating a spring and plunger, an electric heater and a thermal-sensitive element. When the engine is started cold, the valve is open and allows enough extra air-flow for a faster idle speed. As the engine warms up, the electric heating element heats the temperature-sensitive device, which expands and

pushes down the plunger (against the pressure of the spring). This closes off the air bleed and slows the idle down to normal. The valve closes completely at 140° F. Depending on the ambient air temperature, the valve may only be open for a minute or so, up to a maximum of full five minutes in -20° F weather.

ELECTRONIC BRAIN

The device which times the delivery of the fuel to the two sets of injectors and judges the length of injection for various engine conditions is the heart of the EFI system, the electronic control module or "brain." A steel box crammed full of special circuits and which amounts to a preprogrammed analog computer makes up this control unit. It's mounted below the radio under the dash. This onboard computer receives information from five sensors on the engine and adjusts

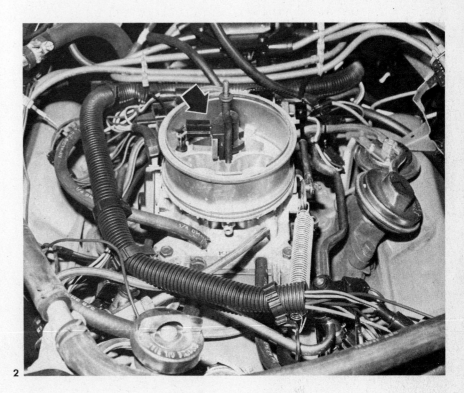

1. Cadillac's system marks first American use of electronic fuel injection. These are the basic components of the system, which improves drivability and economy while corraling emissions.

2. Looking under the hood of a 1977 Seville, things seem normal with the air cleaner in place. Even without the air cleaner, as here, the new throttle body looks like a standard carburetor. Arrow indicates the fast idle valve in the throttle body.

3. Fuel delivery system has a pump within the fuel tank, a second one mounted on the chassis, a fuel filter, two fuel rails and eight valves, a pressure regulator and lastly, a return-to-the-tank line for excess fuel.

2

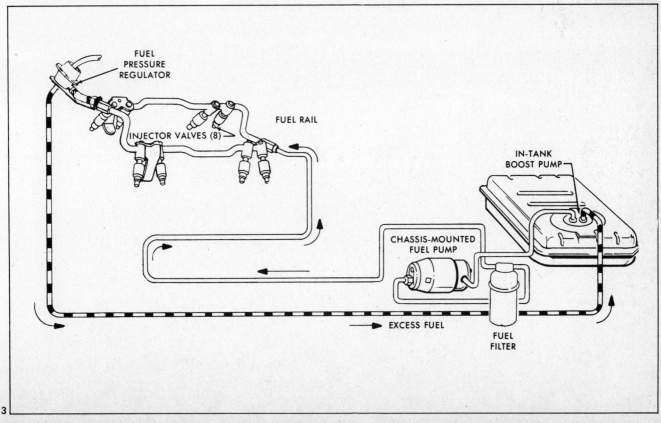

3

AMERICAN EFI

the fuel injection accordingly.

The five sensors detect: intake manifold pressure, throttle position, engine coolant temperature, intake manifold air temperature, and engine speed and firing position. The latter information comes from the speed sensor, located within the HEI (High-Energy Ignition) distributor. This sensor consists of a rotor with two magnets which spins past two reed switches. The throttle position switch is attached to the linkage on the throttle body and tells the control unit when the engine is at idle, partial throttle or full throttle.

The sensor for intake pressure is mounted within the control box. Through a vacuum line connected to the throttle body, it senses minute changes resulting from variations in engine load, speed or barometric pressure, which means the engine is not affected by changes in altitude as an ordinary carbureted engine is. The

sensor converts these pressure changes into electrical impulses, which it feeds to the control unit. The control then calls for more or less fuel according to engine demands.

Information from these sensors plus the engine coolant sensor and intake manifold air temperature sensor is analyzed by the computer, which plans the opening of the injectors according to this information. The Cadillac engineers have programmed the electronic control unit for the most efficient air/fuel ratio under various driving conditions. The result is a car with exceptional drivability and smoothness. To meet emissions standards, there are two differently calibrated control units, one for California cars with their stiffer requirements and another for the rest of the country.

REPAIRS

Like the electronic ignition systems now supplied on all new U.S. cars, it's not recommended that you work on the EFI in your backyard. The sen-

sitive equipment is too delicate for amateur probings, particularly without a factory shop manual to go by. As an example of why you shouldn't fool with the EFI unless you know what you're doing, just loosening one of the injectors (or any connection to the fuel rail) can cause a fire or eye injury. The rail is always full of fuel under pressure, and there is a specific factory procedure to follow to relieve this pressure before working on the system components.

The way technology is moving today, in the future we may not see any more mechanics as we know them. When we have car trouble, we'll call an electronics shop or TV repairman! Actually, an EFI system is long overdue on a production American car. While waiting for all the diesels, gas turbines, electric cars or steam cars that the future probably holds, electronic fuel injection is a dandy interim improvement for the venerable internal combustion engine. Let's hope some of the other manufacturers follow Cadillac's lead.

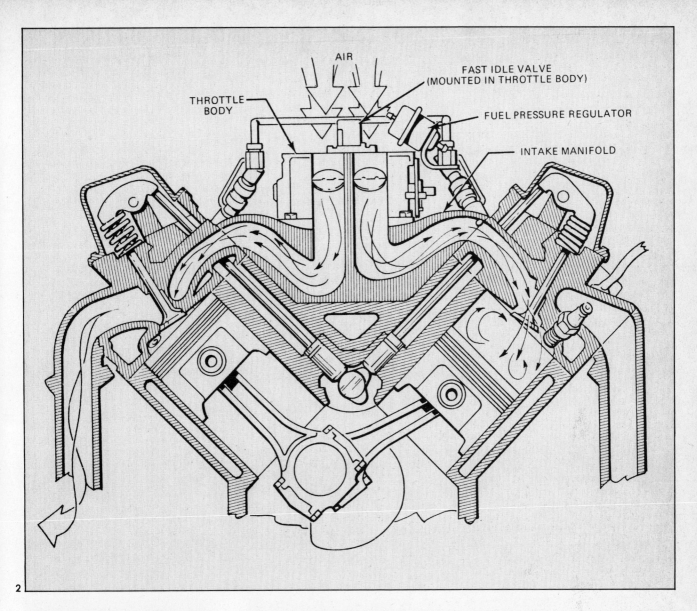

THROTTLE BODY

AIR

FAST IDLE VALVE (MOUNTED IN THROTTLE BODY)

FUEL PRESSURE REGULATOR

INTAKE MANIFOLD

2

1. Fuel in the fuel rail is always under 39 psi pressure, and electronic brain tells these injectors (arrows) when to open and feed each cylinder.

2. This airflow diagram shows how the throttle body takes the place of a carburetor, but flows only air. Fuel is never lost from suspension in the manifold, so car runs smoother and emissions are reduced. Fuel is aimed directly at intake ports.

3. As can be seen in this diagram, the Cadillac EFI electronic control unit receives five function "messages" and in turn sends the appropriate data to five interrelated components. This happens, of course, in milliseconds.

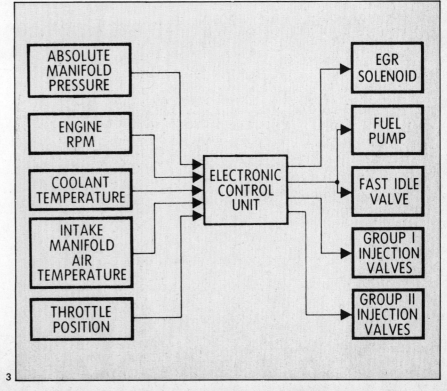

ABSOLUTE MANIFOLD PRESSURE

ENGINE RPM

COOLANT TEMPERATURE

INTAKE MANIFOLD AIR TEMPERATURE

THROTTLE POSITION

ELECTRONIC CONTROL UNIT

EGR SOLENOID

FUEL PUMP

FAST IDLE VALVE

GROUP I INJECTION VALVES

GROUP II INJECTION VALVES

3

SMOG CONTROL SYSTEMS

Smog first started causing trouble in Los Angeles, but now there is eye irritation to some degree in every large city in the United States. Smog affects our breathing, and can even cause death. Scientists tell us that the country is losing millions of dollars every year from damage to plants and farm animals caused by smog. They also tell us that this smog is produced by a photochemical reaction in sunlight between hydrocarbons and oxides of nitrogen that come out of our automobile crankcase and exhaust pipe.

Whether you agree with this or not is unimportant. Arguments about the origin of smog have been going on for years, with everybody pointing the finger at everybody else, and these arguments will probably continue until long after there isn't any more smog, if the world ever reaches that point.

The important thing is that laws have been passed to control hydrocarbon and carbon monoxide emissions from cars. The ordinary car owner will not be too concerned about it, because he leaves mechanical matters up to his mechanic. But the hot rodder must study the law and understand it. The days when engine modifications could be made freely are over. Nowadays, the hot rodder must know the federal and state laws that apply where he lives, and he must comply with them. If he makes an engine modification that is illegal, he might be fined, or he might be unable to get license plates or tabs for his car.

All this smog business started in California, so let's examine the situation in that state. If you live outside of California, don't make the mistake of thinking that the same thing can't happen in your state. It can, and it probably will, even if you have never shed a smog-caused tear or even seen any blue haze of the kind that settles into the Los Angeles Basin.

The hydrocarbons that cause smog are basically unburned gasoline. This unburned gasoline comes out of the crankcase breather and from the tailpipe of an automobile. Most people think the only thing that blows out of the crankcase breather is oil smoke, but they are mistaken. Let's take a look at crankcase devices first, and then we will get into exhaust controls.

There has never been a piston ring yet that was a positive seal between the piston and the cylinder wall. They all leak, even when brand new. You can easily test this by screwing an ordinary pressure gauge, without valve, into the spark plug hole. Crank the engine over until the piston is on top dead center at the end of the compression stroke, then stop. The pressure will rise as the piston goes up, then the pressure will reach a maximum at the top of the stroke.

Watch the pressure gauge after the piston stops, and you will see that it only takes a few seconds for the pressure to leak away.

This leakage occurs between the cylinder wall and rings. While the engine is running it happens fast enough to build up pressure in the crankcase. This "blowby" past the rings is mostly unburned gasoline, with little exhaust or burned fuel.

This happens because the combustion in the chamber does not burn all the fuel. Most of the time it only burns the fuel that is atomized. The remainder clings to the combustion chamber sides and cylinder walls and doesn't burn. In particular, this fuel gets into the little space between the piston top and the cylinder wall.

When combustion happens, the force of the burning gases pushes the piston down and makes everything operate, but the same force also pushes that unburned fuel down past the rings into the crankcase. Scientists with accurate techniques have analyzed the blowby gases and found that they are mostly unburned gasoline.

It's easy to see what would happen if this unburned gasoline were allowed to build up in the oil pan. Pretty soon the oil would be so full of gasoline that it wouldn't be any good as a lubricant. The blowby gases also cause varnish, sludge and acid that

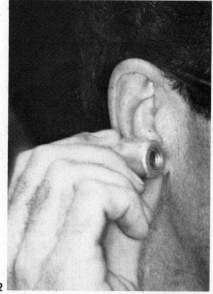

1. Hose connecting the air cleaner to the rocker cover identifies this as a closed crankcase ventilation system.

2. It's not an infallible test, but if the jiggle pin inside the smog valve can be heard rattling around, you at least know it's not gummed up.

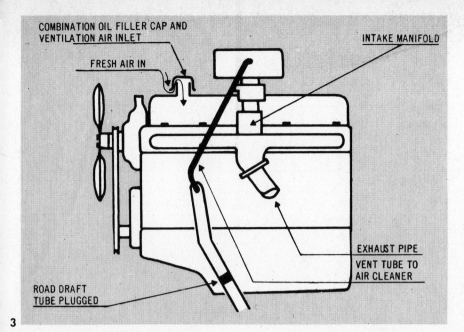

COMBINATION OIL FILLER CAP AND VENTILATION AIR INLET

FRESH AIR IN

INTAKE MANIFOLD

EXHAUST PIPE VENT TUBE TO AIR CLEANER

ROAD DRAFT TUBE PLUGGED

3

3. California PCV systems are classified according to four different types. This setup could be a Type 1 or 2 depending upon the construction of the valve and the size of the hole in the filler cap.

4. For several years Pontiac used this system of double vacuum connections to the smog valve. Double connections give an even pull, so that the engine will idle smoothly.

5. In the good old days, before we worried about poisoning the world from emissions, this is the way crankcases used to breathe. This system depends on the air movement of the car, which creates airflow past the end of the road draft tube and draws the fumes out of the crankcase. On a stationary engine this system would not work unless the road draft tube were positioned in the fan blast.

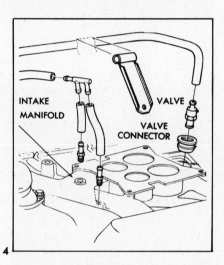

INTAKE MANIFOLD

VALVE

VALVE CONNECTOR

4

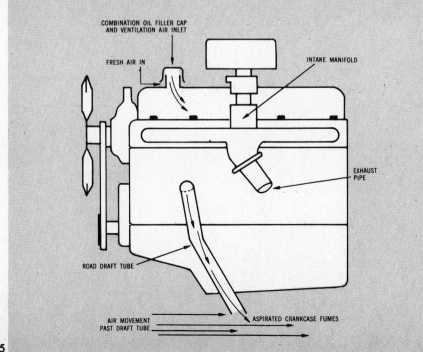

COMBINATION OIL FILLER CAP AND VENTILATION AIR INLET

FRESH AIR IN

INTAKE MANIFOLD

EXHAUST PIPE

ROAD DRAFT TUBE

AIR MOVEMENT PAST DRAFT TUBE

ASPIRATED CRANKCASE FUMES

5

starts eating at the bearing metal.

This problem was recognized at the beginning of the automobile industry, way before anybody ever heard of smog. All kinds of systems were tried to get the vapors out of the crankcase. Finally, almost all manufacturers settled on the road draft system: A tube was connected to the crankcase so that the draft of air flowing under the car would create a slight suction at the end of the tube, thus drawing the vapors out of the crankcase. They called it the "road draft tube." Of course, there had to be a hole somewhere else on the engine for fresh air to enter. This was usually in the oil filler cap, and there was some kind of an oil-wetted mesh inside the cap in order to keep dust out of the engine.

The system worked pretty well, as long as the car was going fast enough to make a draft on the tube. This was usually about 25 mph. Below that, the system didn't work at all, except to let the crankcase vent itself just from the pressure of the gases. Milk trucks really had a problem, because they would go for days without ever getting over 25 mph. Boats had a little trouble, too. It's kind of hard to create a road draft when you don't have a road. So we can see that the problem is not new. Positive crankcase ventilators of various types have been used for many years on those vehicles with a special operating condition.

CRANKCASE DEVICES

Today there are four types of crankcase devices, usually called PCV (Positive Crankcase Ventilation). In all PCV systems, the road draft tube is either plugged or nonexistent. Type 1 has a hose running from the crankcase through a valve to the intake manifold. Manifold vacuum sucks the vapors out of the crankcase, while fresh air enters through the oil filler cap. The vacuum connection to the crankcase does not necessarily have to be directly on the crankcase. It may be on the valve cover, rocker cover, valley cover, intake manifold back of the block or even the oil pan, depending on how the system was designed. No matter where the connection is, the purpose is to suck the vapors out of the crankcase and into the intake manifold, where they are carried into the combustion chamber and burned.

The PCV valve may have a fixed orifice or a spring-loaded plunger in a Type 1 system. Six-cylinder engines usually have the fixed orifice, and V-8's the variable, with the plunger. When the engine is off, the spring closes the valve. If the engine has an intake manifold explosion or "back-

SMOG CONTROL

fire,'' the spring plus the force of the backfire will close the valve to prevent flame from getting into the crankcase and causing an explosion. When the engine is under high vacuum, such as idle or deceleration, the plunger moves against spring pressure to a minimum flow position.

When the engine is under low vacuum, or partial load, the spring moves the plunger to a central position for maximum flow.

During wide open throttle with zero vacuum, the spring closes the valve. But the blowby gases are still going past the rings into the crankcase. The only place they can go under this condition is out through the oil filler cap. The same thing happens on the fixed orifice system, because there is no vacuum to draw the gases into the intake manifold. You can see that the Type 1 system is not perfect, because at zero vacuum it allows the crankcase gases to escape into the atmosphere.

The Type 2 system is basically the same as Type 1, except that a special PCV valve and oil filler cap are used. The valve is a diaphragm type that regulates the amount of flow according to how much vacuum is in the crankcase. If the crankcase is under pressure most of the time, as it would be on a worn engine, the valve opens up to take care of the blowby.

The Type 2 oil filler cap has a small, calibrated hole, big enough to let the fresh air in, but small enough to keep the crankcase under vacuum. Type 2 systems can only be installed on an engine with a ''tight'' crankcase. Any air leaks in the oil pan gasket, rocker cover gasket or anyplace that air can enter the crankcase will allow the valve to open wide, which may lean the fuel mixture to a dangerous level.

Type 3 is the kind of breather that backyard mechanics have used for years to cure an engine of excessive crankcase smoking. It is simply a tube from the crankcase to the air cleaner. Fresh air enters the engine through the oil filler cap and is drawn through the tube into the air cleaner and down through the carburetor into the engine. Because blowby gases are mostly unburned gasoline, this system tends to richen the mixture. This must be taken into account when designing the carburetor.

The suction of the Type 3 system depends on the airflow through the carburetor. At idle it doesn't work very well, but as engine speed picks up, and airflow increases through the air cleaner, the suction on the crankcase increases. Some foreign cars use a Type 3 system with the oil filler cap sealed. This means that there is no actual ventilation of the crankcase, but the gases are allowed to flow into the air cleaner under crankcase pressure and as a result of air cleaner suction.

Type 4, sometimes called CCV (Closed Crankcase Ventilation), is a combination of Type 1 and Type 3. You remember we said that under zero vacuum Type 1 would allow gases to escape. With Type 4 this is not possible, because the filler cap is sealed. A tube from the air cleaner goes to the rocker cover. Fresh air enters the air cleaner, goes through the tube, into the rocker cover and down into the crankcase. From there, just like a Type 1, blowby gases go through the hose, into the PCV valve and into the manifold.

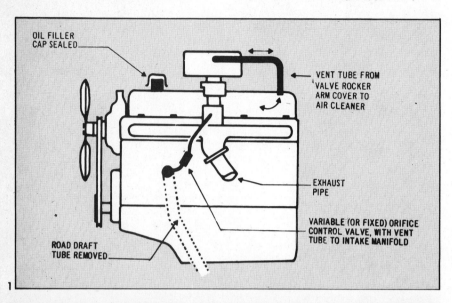

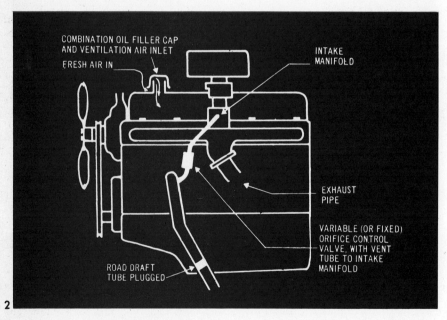

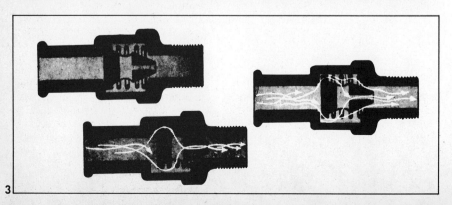

1. *The Type 3 system does not use a valve. It relies on a small amount of suction in the air cleaner to draw fumes out of the crankcase. The Type 3 system, like Types 1 and 2, is open to the atmosphere through the oil filler cap.*

2. *The Type 4 system is also known as the closed system, because the filler cap is not open to the atmosphere. This diagram shows the valve connection where the road draft tube used to be. On late model cars, the valve connection can be on the rocker cover or anywhere that is convenient to pick up the crankcase gases.*

3. *Here's the way the spring-loaded type of PCV valve works. At the top is the closed position, which occurs whenever the engine is off or during zero vacuum, such as at wide-open throttle, or whenever the engine backfires. At the bottom is the flow during high vacuum, as at idle, and at the right we have the flow during medium vacuum. The strength of the spring, balanced against engine vacuum, determines the flow. Because some engines pull more vacuum than others, the spring is tailored to fit a particular engine. This means you must have the correct smog valve if you want your engine to idle right.*

4. *The shape of a smog valve can vary with the manufacturer, but the result is the same. This valve, with the little hood attached by a nut, is used on Chrysler products.*

5. *GM and many other carmakers use this valve that connects by slipping hoses over both ends.*

6. *Flame arrestors prevent a backfire from causing a crankcase explosion. The problem is that the flame arrestor can plug up and thereby render the PCV system inoperative.*

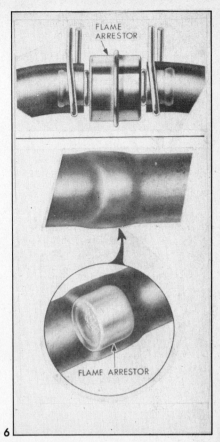

When the Type 4 system is under zero vacuum, there is no suction on the crankcase, just as in Type 1, but the gases go from the rocker cover through the hose into the air cleaner, where they are drawn into the engine. If an engine has a lot of blowby, some gases will go into the air cleaner at all times. This can ruin a dry paper element in a short time, because of the oil fumes. The remedy is to fix the engine so it doesn't have as much blowby, or change to an oil-wetted cleaner element.

So there you have the four types of crankcase devices. They really aren't hard to understand, and it's amazing that something so simple could cause such an uproar among mechanics and car owners. In 1961, Type 1 devices were installed by the car factories on new California cars only. Problems came up on these early models because few people understood how the things worked, and there were some cases of poor design. The carmakers cleared that up, however, and smog valves settled down to do their job.

In 1964 the uproar began all over again because the new cars were now equipped with Type 4 instead of Type 1, and devices were required on some used cars. The used car scene gave a lot of trouble, simply because mechanics and car owners did not follow instructions when installing the devices.

One source of trouble was the installation of a crankcase device on a worn-out engine. If an engine is really bad, a crankcase device may not handle the smoke. The device may also cause plug fouling and other problems if installed on a worn engine. The law says a man has to put a device on his car, but if he does, the car will not operate correctly. The only solution is to junk the car or do a ring and valve job, which can cost more than the car is worth.

In fairness to the smog authorities, however, we must point out that if an engine is worn so badly that it will not accept any crankcase device, then the engine must really be in terrible condition. There is no such thing in California as an exemption for worn engines. The car must comply with the law or it can't be operated on public streets.

This may seem unfair, but there are many states where a cracked windshield or bald tires or a brake pedal that goes down too far will result in our being unable to drive the car until it is fixed. And fixing it may cost more than the car is worth.

Sometimes a smog device is installed and the car runs rough, or a smog valve is changed and the car won't idle without shaking you out of the seat. This can be caused by installation of the wrong valve or system for that particular engine. A smog device must never be "made up" out of tubing, hose, and individual parts. The whole device must be designed to fit and approved for that particular engine, and it must be installed exactly as instructed. Also, the tune-up items on the engine must be according to specifications, or the engine will not perform—whether it has a smog device or not.

Do smog devices do any good? Yes. They do a better job of crankcase ventilation than any road draft tube ever did. This results in less oil contamination and a longer-lasting engine. Crankcase systems do cause slightly increased intake valve and intake manifold deposits, but the increase is so slight that the authorities claim it won't hurt an engine.

One definite benefit of the crankcase system is better gas mileage. California smog authorities not only claim 3% better gas mileage, but they can prove it.

If you put on custom equipment, such as rocker covers or intake manifolds or carburetors, you must not remove the smog valve, in California. Most speed equipment manufacturers provide the proper holes so that the smog equipment can remain in the original position.

Maintenance of the crankcase device is important. If the valve or hoses are allowed to plug up, then damage to the engine can result. Some carmakers say the system should be checked at every oil change. Others say clean or replace the valve once a year or 12,000 miles. Checking the valve is simple. The valve should be clean, and the plunger should be free so it rattles, or if it is the fixed-orifice type the hole should be clear. All hoses should be checked for obstructions, and any flashback screens in the hoses should be cleaned. The Type 2 valve is never cleaned, but a simple test of mouth suction will tell if it's okay.

Different systems are found on different year models. There are exceptions, but usually the following are what you will find: California models 1961-63½ have factory-installed Type 1 systems. California models 1963½ and later have factory-installed Type 4 systems. Before 1963, cars sold outside of California had no crankcase system; 1963-67 cars manufactured for sale outside of California have Type 1 systems; 1968 models nationwide have Type 4 systems.

If your car came with a crankcase device, then under California law you must not remove it, unless for the purpose of putting a used car device in its place. If your car did not come with a device, there are certain situations that will require installation of one. It depends on the year model of the car and where it is registered, in most cases. Crankcase devices are required on all 1963 and later models. Models from 1955 to 1962 must have a crankcase device if they are transferred to an owner who lives in a county that requires it. This doesn't mean that the new owner can remove the device after he has the car registered. Once a crankcase device is installed, it is illegal to remove it.

Exceptions are provided in the law for certain types of engines. Motorcycles are also excepted. We won't go into all the technical details of the California law here. This is only to give you a general idea of the situation in California, and what you might expect in your own state. Now let's get into exhaust controls and find out how they work.

The smog authorities tell us that hydrocarbons from automobile exhaust are a major cause of smog. If hydrocarbons are mostly unburned gasoline, then it follows that the automobile engine must be running with a rich mixture when it is putting out hydrocarbons. If we could make an engine run on lean mixtures, then it wouldn't cause nearly as much smog as it does with rich mixtures.

The problem is to find out whether a particular engine is running rich or lean, and this is done with an exhaust gas analyzer. These analyzers have been around for many years. They are made by manufacturers of tune-up equipment, and come in all shapes and sizes. Basically, they are all the same. They measure the thermal conductivity of the exhaust gas, which is directly related to how rich the engine is running.

The meter on the analyzer gives a reading in air/fuel ratio, which may be anywhere from 11:1 up to 15:1. If the meter read 12.5:1 it would mean that the engine was running on a mixture with an air/fuel ratio of 12½ lbs. of air to 1 lb. of fuel. A rich mixture is one that has an excess amount of fuel, and a lean mixture, of course, is just the other way around. Any reading near the 15:1 end of the scale is lean, and a reading on the 11:1 end of the scale is rich. An engine can run as rich as 8:1, but only if the distance between gas stations is very short. The leanest the analyzer will measure is 15:1.

At idle, most engines without exhaust emissions controls run about 12:1 At cruising speed they usually lean out to somewhere around 14:1 The richer mixture at idle is necessary because the combustion chamber has some exhaust gas left in it at idle speed. Another time engines run rich is on deceleration. Under most other operating conditions, an engine will run lean enough that it doesn't overly pollute the air.

So the problem narrows down to eliminating the rich mixtures during idle and deceleration. There are two ways to do this—with an air injection system or with an ignition-induction system.

AIR INJECTION SYSTEM

The air injection system is nothing more than an engine-driven pump

1. Smog pumps may be mounted in many different positions at the front of the engine. This is on a Chevy Nova 4-cylinder.

2. If the engine doesn't idle right, don't be quick to blame the carburetor. Maybe the smog valve needs cleaning. On a Cadillac it is plugged into the right rocker cover.

3. Ford Thermactor air pump system on a 1968 302 engine. The present system is pretty much the same as shown here.

4. A slide hammer is used to remove the relief valve on the pump. The relief valve is merely a safety factor to keep the pressure from going too high.

5. Installing the relief valve. The tool numbers are from Ford. In most instances the pump is replaced in case anything goes wrong with it.

2

3

fold. Chevrolet V-8's have the injection tubes entering the exhaust manifold, and from there they go up the passageway to the exhaust valve.

All air injection systems have check valves to keep the exhaust gas from going into the system and back up to the pump. A relief valve in the pump

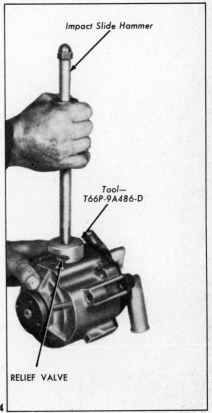

Impact Slide Hammer

Tool—
T66P-9A486-D

RELIEF VALVE

4

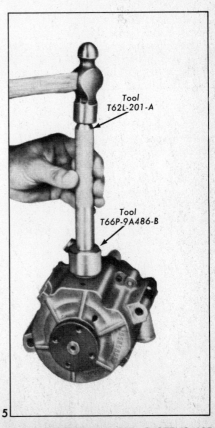

Tool
T62L-201-A

Tool
T66P-9A486-B

5

that pumps air into the exhaust passage close to the exhaust valve. As the unburned fuel comes out the exhaust valve, it combines with the fresh air from the pump and actually burns in the exhaust passage. This means that the exhaust system is going to get considerably warmer than usual, and it also means that there has to be a lot more tubing and hose cluttering up the already cluttered engine compartment.

A warmer exhaust system may have a benefit, because it may eliminate condensation in the muffler, which is the major cause of mufflers falling to pieces. Not enough statistics are in to tell about this yet. The cluttered mess in the engine compartment is something we just have to

live with in this system, so let's take a look at how it works:

The air injection pump is mounted at the front of the engine and is driven by a belt off the front pulley. The pump gets its air from the engine compartment. Some pumps have a filter on their air intake, and others take air from the clean side of the carburetor air cleaner.

From the pump, the air goes under pressure of about 1 psi to a manifold on each cylinder head. Then the air goes into the injection tubes, which direct the air to the underside of each exhaust valve. Various methods are used to get the air from the pump to the exhaust valve. Some engines use a passageway cast into the cylinder head instead of an external mani-

prevents excessive pressure in the system. An anti-backfire valve (pressure relief valve) keeps the engine from backfiring when the driver lifts his foot off the throttle.

The anti-backfire valve works by sending the air output from the pump directly into the intake manifold instead of the injector tubes. This leans out the excessively rich mixture that occurs just after the driver lifts his foot off the gas. If this mixture were not leaned out, it would explode in the exhaust system, causing a loud noise out the tailpipe.

Some anti-backfire valves dump atmospheric air into the intake manifold instead of pump air. Other types don't dump air into the manifold. Instead, they allow the pump air to exhaust into the carburetor air cleaner, which effectively cancels any airflow through the injector tubes and silences the sound of the exhausting air. Design of the backfire valve depends on whatever is necessary to stop the engine from backfiring.

The backfire valve only operates to eliminate backfire just after the driver lifts his foot from the gas. After that, the air injection system returns to normal operation whether the driver puts his foot back on the gas or leaves it off. These anti-backfire valves can cause some funny things to happen when the car is started. Since the valve is controlled by engine vacuum, it takes a couple of seconds for the vacuum to build up. Until it does, the type of valve that dumps air into the manifold is wide open, allowing outside air to enter. Some engines will shake like jelly on a plate until the vacuum builds up enough to close the valve. This doesn't do any harm to the engine or anything else, but it sure makes the driver wonder what in the world is going on under the hood.

If the air injection system consisted of only the pump and all its plumbing, things would be fine, but it also includes changes in the carburetor, distributor, cooling system and many internal changes in the engine. This means that it is impossible to take an air injection system off one engine and transfer it to another. It might be possible to design an air injection system that could be installed on an engine that did not originally come with it. But the cost would be fantastically high, and probably would involve changing everything on the engine except for the crankshaft, the block and the rods.

When the air injection system was originally installed by the carmakers, it seemed to be an emergency system, as nothing else was available to

"A.I.R." SYSTEM

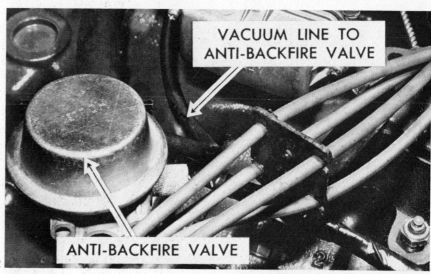

VACUUM LINE TO ANTI-BACKFIRE VALVE

ANTI-BACKFIRE VALVE

do the job. Some even thought that the ignition-induction system (described below) would eventually replace air injection completely. But manufacturers like Ford—which dropped its Thermactor system for a few years only to return to it in 1974—found the increasingly stringent emissions levels imposed by legislation more and more difficult to meet. With the advent of catalytic converters on 1975 models, the air injection system found a new lease on life.

IGNITION-INDUCTION SYSTEM

The ignition-induction system was pioneered by Chrysler Corp. In the 1963 model year, Chrysler installed its Clean Air Package on 2000 Plymouths. The cars were sold in the Los Angeles area to fleet accounts only. A careful check was kept on

1. The pump system can be a pain in the neck, because it adds so much plumbing to the engine.

2. The anti-backfire valve is controlled by engine vacuum. When the engine is decelerating at high vacuum, the anti-backfire valve is actuated and relieves the pump pressure so that no air is pumped into the exhaust manifold.

3. Corvair's smog pump looked a little different, but did the same job as all the rest of them.

4. Air pumps can make gurgles when they are running, so the filter is often made large in an attempt to muffle it.

5. Inside the smog pump. If you ever had occasion to take one of these things apart, the chances are excellent that you would never get it back together. It's not really difficult, but because of the eccentric action of the vanes they are rather tricky to get in the right place.

6. Chevrolet's air pump system. The air is not really pumped into the cylinder, but into the exhaust manifold.

AIR PUMP AND FILTER

4

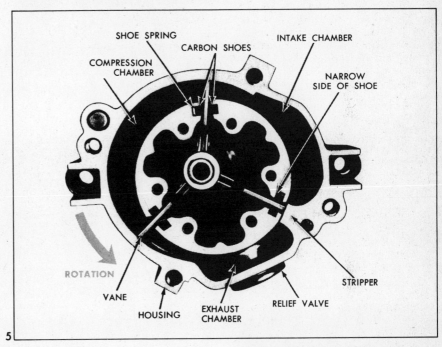

5

how they performed, and in November 1964, the CAP system was given a clean bill of health.

The CAP exhaust emissions system worked so well that similar systems were adopted by the other auto manufacturers. Some variations of ignition-induction have appeared on many late-model cars.

The ignition-induction system (sometimes called "engine modification system") reduces emissions at idle by using a carburetor that is set lean. On some cars the idle mixture screws are installed with a pin in the throttle body which prevents anyone from backing the screws out and obtaining a rich mixture. If the screws are backed out forcefully, they will break, which means that the carburetor must be removed from the engine and the pins and screws replaced with parts from a special kit.

Other cars have idle mixture screws with special limiter caps which butt against the carburetor so that the screws can't be unscrewed past a certain point. Also, some carburetors are designed so that the mixture will not richen excessively even if the screws are backed out a lot. Those carburetors don't use limiters on the idle mixture needles.

If a lean mixture is all that is required to reduce emissions at idle, then it ought to be possible to adjust any carburetor on the lean side. The only trouble is that when you do this the engine won't run. Exhaust dilution of the mixture at idle requires an air/fuel ratio of about 12:1. The mixture is very thin, also, because it is under a high vacuum. Both of these problems can be overcome by opening the throttle wide enough to get a denser mixture and more flow to

scavenge some of the exhaust gases from the cylinder, so that the engine will run at 14:1. The result is fewer emissions but an engine that is idling so fast you can't hold it down. Without touching the idle speed or mixture adjustments there is only one other way to get the engine down to a normal idle: retard the spark.

This is what the Chrysler engineers did, and it worked. All CAP engines have an initial spark setting that is retarded as much as 15° from normal. This is accomplished by using ported spark. When the throttle is closed, the spark port is above the throttle plate. Thus, there isn't any vacuum on the advance diaphragm and the distributor goes into full retard. When the throttle plate is opened, the spark port is uncovered, and the vacuum diaphragm advances the spark all the way up to a conventional setting.

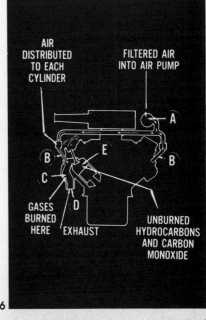

6

SMOG CONTROL

With this system, the spark will be retarded during deceleration, because the throttle plate is closed at that time. The designers found out that the only way to reduce emissions during deceleration was to advance the spark. To accomplish this, they put a little spark valve in the line between the carburetor and the vacuum advance diaphragm, and connected it to manifold vacuum. Whenever the driver lifts his foot, this spark valve sends full manifold vacuum to the distributor advance diaphragm, which advances the spark. The spark valve will hold the distributor in full advance position as long as the deceleration continues, even if the car is going down a hill from here to eternity. As soon as manifold vacuum drops below about 21 ins. the spark valve changes the distributor back to carburetor vacuum and the distributor works normally.

1. Design of this later system on a Ford V-8 is much cleaner, but there is still quite a bit of plumbing and parts cluttering up the top of the engine.

2. Here's one of Ford's later air pump systems, which doesn't look bad at all. The pressure relief valve takes the place of the old backfire suppressor valve and shuts off air to the exhaust manifolds to prevent backfire.

3. This is approximately the position of the air pump tube—right next to the exhaust valve in almost all air pump systems. The tube itself is super-tough, so that it can withstand the exhaust heat without burning up.

4. American Motors has this system on some of their cars, with heated air supplied to the air cleaner. Tubes in the exhaust manifold connect to the pump.

5. A conventional spark advance system using ported spark has no vacuum applied to the advance unit during deceleration. At that time the spring in the unit pushes the breaker plate to the fully retarded position, which is usually a few degrees in advance of top dead center

6. When an engine with the spark valve system decelerates, the spark valve switches from the spark port to full manifold vacuum, which advances the breaker plate to full advance position.

7. In the spark valve system on new cars, there are a few things done to cut down on emissions. The most important element here is the retarded initial spark setting.

8. The new car spark valve system at idle. Because the initial spark is retarded, the distributor vacuum advance mechanism has to be specially designed so that it pulls the distributor up to what would be a normal spark setting as soon as the throttle opens enough to apply vacuum to the spark port. From that point up to as fast as the engine goes, the spark advance is normal.

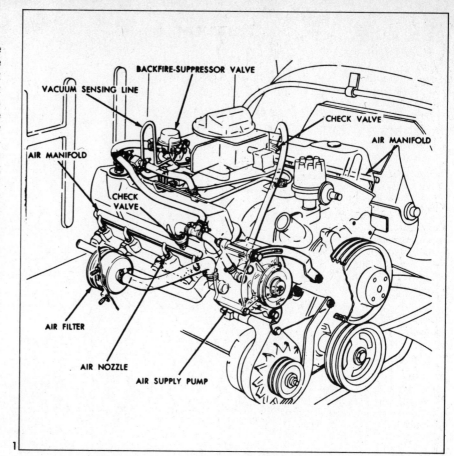

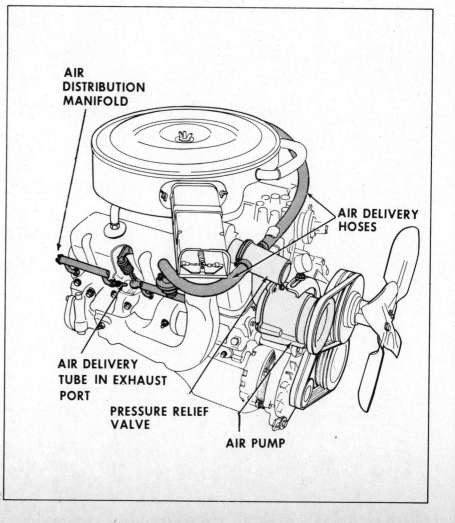

Chrysler's CAP system has been modified by other carmakers so that it works a little differently, but still accomplishes the same thing. Some designs do not use the spark valve to advance the timing during deceleration. They get away with this because their carburetors do not go rich during deceleration. Other designs use the spark valve, but for the purpose of eliminating exhaust popping rather than lowering emissions.

The Chrysler distributor has one vacuum diaphragm to advance the spark all the way from the retard position to full advance. Some Ford engines use a dual diaphragm with two hose connections, while Pontiacs use a single diaphragm with two hose connections. One of the hoses goes to carburetor vacuum and the other to manifold vacuum. The hose to carburetor vacuum controls the distributor in the normal way, but the hose to manifold vacuum pulls the breaker plate to the retard position during idle and deceleration.

This, of course, is exactly opposite to the CAP system, which goes to full advance during deceleration. Ford and Pontiac were able to get away with this on some engines because of changes in combustion chambers, cam timing, stroke length, manifolding and other areas. It didn't work on all engines, so you will find some that

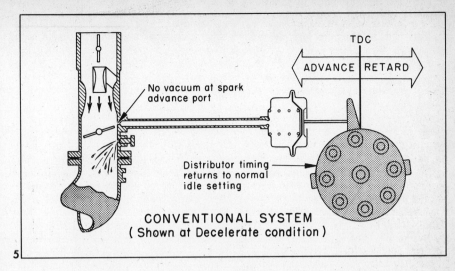

5

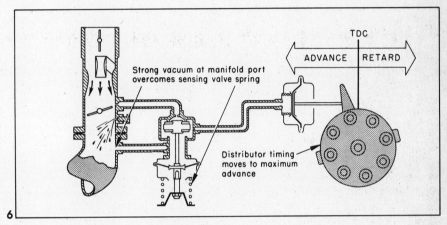

6

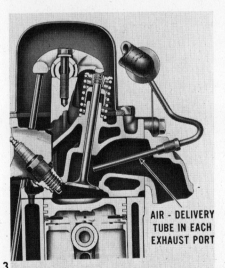

AIR - DELIVERY TUBE IN EACH EXHAUST PORT

3

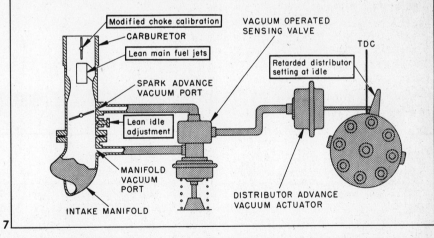

7

4

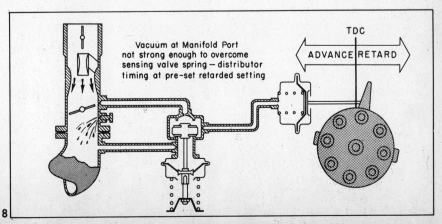

8

SMOG CONTROL

still require the spark advance valve. The same situation exists on late-model Chrysler Corp. cars. Some engines use the spark advance valve and some don't. A tune-up man has to be sure he has the exact specifications for the engine he is repairing.

Late-model Chrysler product carburetors have an idle-speed adjusting screw that seats against a little metal contact on the side of the carburetor. A wire runs from the contact to a solenoid mounted on the side of the distributor. When the throttle is in the curb-idle position, the idle-speed screw touches the contact and retards the spark. If the carburetor also happens to be equipped with an anti-dieseling solenoid, then the contact for the screw is located at the end of the solenoid plunger.

All that the solenoid retard does is bring the spark to a retarded position to slow the engine down so that the idle is at a reasonable speed. The solenoid itself is a little electromagnet, mounted on the distributor vacuum-advance chamber, so that it can exert a small amount of pull on the rod that links the vacuum diaphragm with the breaker plate.

The old system of ported spark and a long throw on the single-vacuum diaphragm worked very well for Chrysler, but the solenoid retard does an even better job, because it allows advanced timing during a cold start. When cold-starting an engine, the fast-idle cam holds the idle-speed screw away from the retard solenoid contact. A cold engine needs all the help it can get, and the slight spark advance, about 5.5°, is a good rule for quicker starting. As soon as the engine warms up, the choke opens and the fast-idle cam goes off. Then whenever the throttle is let down to the idle position, the solenoid is energized and retards the spark to keep the idle speed at a reasonable level.

The solenoid is not strong enough to overcome any vacuum applied to the advance unit. Let's suppose that the initial spark setting is incorrectly set to the retarded side. This would result in a slow-running engine. To overcome the slow running, somebody who didn't know any better might open the throttle further to get the idle speed up to where it should be. However, when the throttle is opened further to increase the idle speed, it uncovers the spark-advance port, applying vacuum to the vacuum-advance unit and overriding the distributor-retard solenoid. The engine would probably idle fine with this kind of a mix-up, but because the initial spark setting is retarded, it would have loss of power in all driving **2**

ranges. There is no such thing nowadays as just setting the idle speed and letting it go at that; you must check the timing and idle speed and mixture to be sure that the engine is going to run right.

Chrysler's original CAP system evolved into the CAS or Cleaner Air System. The changes involved were subtle—many of them inside the engine where they made a big difference in emissions—but there was very little change in servicing procedures. Strange things were done with the controls on some of the carburetors: there are 4-bbl.'s with single idle mixture screws similar to some older Holley designs, and a nonadjustable bypass air slot was used in others to direct air below the throttle valve to break up raw fuel. Now the latest-model carburetors used with automatic transmissions incorporate an idle enrichment system. Further modifications in Chrysler's application of its ignition-induction system and the addition of air injection on 1975 California engines have caused the company to drop its CAP/CAS designation.

If you think Chrysler Corp.'s solenoid retard is complicated, take a look at Ford's electronic distributor-control module. This gadget is hooked into the speedometer cable and controls the spark advance according to the speed of the car. There is no spark advance at all until the engine reaches about 23 mph on acceleration. From that point up, spark advance works normally. On

deceleration, spark advance is present until the vehicle speed drops to approximately 18 mph. Then the electronic control module shuts off the vacuum to the advance unit and the spark is allowed to retard. The electronic module works in conjunction with the usual dual-diaphragm Ford vacuum-advance unit. The diaphragm closest to the distributor is for retard and is connected to manifold vacuum. The other diaphragm connects to the spark port in the carburetor above the throttle plate. The electronic distributor modulator is entirely

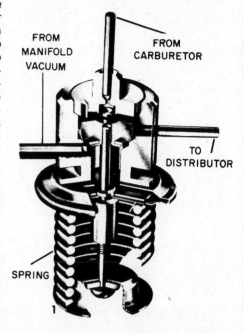

FROM MANIFOLD VACUUM
FROM CARBURETOR
TO DISTRIBUTOR
SPRING
1

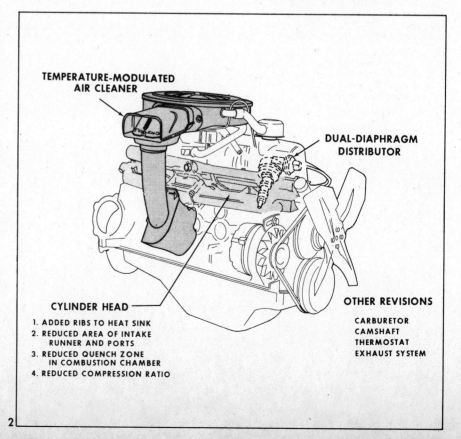

TEMPERATURE-MODULATED AIR CLEANER

DUAL-DIAPHRAGM DISTRIBUTOR

CYLINDER HEAD
1. ADDED RIBS TO HEAT SINK
2. REDUCED AREA OF INTAKE RUNNER AND PORTS
3. REDUCED QUENCH ZONE IN COMBUSTION CHAMBER
4. REDUCED COMPRESSION RATIO

OTHER REVISIONS
CARBURETOR
CAMSHAFT
THERMOSTAT
EXHAUST SYSTEM

separate from the electronic rpm limiter that appears on some Ford products. The two units have no connection and could appear on the same engine if the factory wanted to install them that way.

General Motors and Chrysler Corp. also have spark control systems. The GM system is called Transmission Controlled Spark (TCS). A switch in the transmission connects to a solenoid which controls the vacuum applied to the distributor diaphragm. The result is that vacuum spark advance is eliminated in all lower gears, on both manual and automatic transmissions. On a 4-speed box you will get vacuum spark advance in both 3rd and 4th gears, but in all other transmissions, vacuum spark advance is permitted in top gear only.

In a GM Turbo Hydra-Matic the transmission switch is actuated by pressure from the direct clutch circuit, which is pressurized in 3rd gear. But the direct clutch is also pressurized in reverse, which means you not only get vacuum spark advance in 3rd gear, but in reverse, too. When you shift into reverse from neutral, the engine will speed up, an indica-

1. The spark valve that advances the spark on deceleration. These valves can be noisy at idle. The cure is to insert an inline fuel filter between the valve and the intake manifold. It dampens the pulsations to quiet the valve.

2. Whenever they could, manufacturers have tried to incorporate design changes into the engine that would make it emissions free, without the necessity of adding the smog pump. On this Ford 6, you can see that there have been many changes to engine to reduce emissions.

3. Even something as simple as an air duct is redesigned from year to year. This shows the difference between the 1968 Olds (left) and the '69, with a shorter path for the heated air.

tion that the system is working the way it is supposed to.

A temperature-sensitive vacuum control valve located in the water jacket and connected between the distributor, carburetor and the intake manifold is not really a new idea; it's been used in the past. But with the advent of the catalytic converter on 1975 models, this temperature-controlled vacuum advance has replaced the Transmission Controled Spark system on many GM and Ford engines. The source for the distributor vacuum advance unit is the port above the throttle plate, which results in no spark advance at idle. Because of the retarded spark at idle, an engine may overheat in heavy traffic. The thermal vacuum switch (TVS) senses this excessive heat and changes vacuum source from the spark port in the carburetor to full intake manifold vacuum. This causes the spark to advance and speeds up the engine to help control the overheating condition.

Pontiac uses a variation in which distributor vacuum is received directly from manifold vacuum until the engine warms up. Reaching a given temperature, the manifold vacuum is then shut off and vacuum is sent to the distributor through a spark delay valve. The application of the thermal switch in a temperature-controlled vacuum advance system is not really much different from the old air conditioning idle speed-up solenoid on many early air-conditioned engines. Chrysler uses no spark control at all on its '75 engines; only AMC has retained TCS on a few of its 6-cylinder applications.

Ford's Cold Start Spark Advance (CSSA) system operates in much the same way as the GM versions, but uses twin ported vacuum switches.

When a cold engine is started, vacuum is allowed to pass through one ported vacuum switch (PVS) and a check valve enroute to the distributor. The check valve is inserted into the system to retain vacuum in the distributor's vacuum advance unit should you decide to floor the throttle; thus the spark stays advanced. Once the engine has reached its normal operating temperature, vacuum is then routed through the other PVS and the spark delay valve. You'll find this particular system only on the 460-cu.-in. V-8.

A variation of this, the combined vacuum, or COVAC, system blends the EGR and spark port vacuum signals, sending a combined signal to both the EGR valve and distributor advance diaphragm through a ported vacuum switch. Both CSSA and COVAC are 1975 innovations.

COMBINATION EMISSION CONTROL VALVE

In 1971 many of the GM divisions continued to use TCS, except Chevrolet. Chevy eliminated the TCS solenoid in favor of a vacuum-electric gadget called a Combination Emission Control (CEC) valve. This was used that year only on the Chevrolet V-8 engines, but retained through 1973 on the 6-cylinders. Beginning in 1974, the Chevy 6's used the vacuum solenoid, the same as on the V-8 engines.

The CEC valve looks very much like an anti-dieseling solenoid, but it doesn't do the same job. Unfortunately, it occupies the same space on the carburetor, so many mechanics will probably use the CEC valve plunger to set curb idle. Let's get that clear right now: Never use a CEC valve plunger to set curb idle. You must set curb idle with the normal throttle-

SMOG CONTROL

cracking screw on the carburetor.

Now let's see how the CEC valve works. First, it does exactly the same job on vacuum spark advance that the TCS system did. There is no vacuum spark advance available until the transmission is in top gear, or in 3rd and 4th on a 4-speed manual.

An additional function of the CEC valve is that it opens the throttle on deceleration. If the throttle is allowed to close down to the curb idle position during deceleration, a high vacuum results, which pulls in great gobs of fuel through the carburetor idle system. Keeping the throttle at a slightly greater opening reduces the vacuum and creates fewer emissions because the mixture is not so rich.

The CEC valve does both jobs at once, so that anytime you have vacuum spark elimination, you also have a greater throttle opening on deceleration. The CEC valve can do two things at once because it has a long plunger. One end of the plunger shuts off vacuum to the distributor while the other end moves away from the throttle linkage. The CEC valve is normally in that position, with the plunger shutting off vacuum and not affecting the throttle opening.

When the transmission goes into top gear, electricity flows to the solenoid coil that is in the CEC valve, and the plunger moves out. This movement of the plunger uncovers a hole to allow vacuum to the distributor, and at the same time the end of

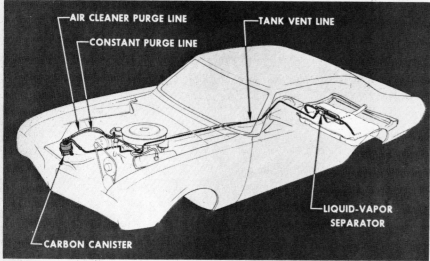

AIR CLEANER PURGE LINE
CONSTANT PURGE LINE
TANK VENT LINE
CARBON CANISTER
LIQUID-VAPOR SEPARATOR

1

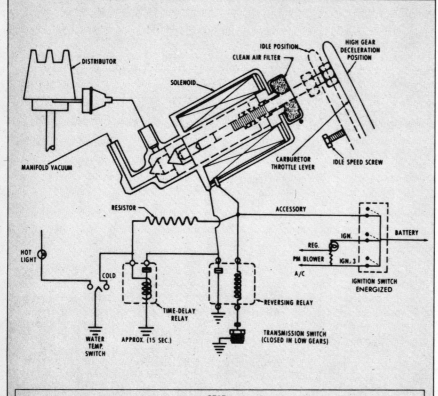

DISTRIBUTOR
SOLENOID
IDLE POSITION
CLEAN AIR FILTER
HIGH GEAR DECELERATION POSITION
MANIFOLD VACUUM
CARBURETOR THROTTLE LEVER
IDLE SPEED SCREW
RESISTOR
ACCESSORY
HOT LIGHT
COLD
REG.
IGN.
BATTERY
PM BLOWER
IGN. 3
A/C
IGNITION SWITCH ENERGIZED
TIME-DELAY RELAY
APPROX. (15 SEC.)
REVERSING RELAY
WATER TEMP. SWITCH
TRANSMISSION SWITCH (CLOSED IN LOW GEARS)

	GEAR						
Transmission	Park	Neutral	Reverse	1st.	2nd.	3rd.	4th.
3 Speed	-	-	-	-	-	Vac.	-
4 Speed	-	-	-	-	-	Vac.	Vac.
Torque Drive	-	-	-	-	Vac.	-	-
Powerglide	-	-	-	-	Vac.	-	-
Turbo Hydra-Matic 350	-	-	Vac.	-	-	Vac.	-
Turbo Hydra-Matic 400	-	-	Vac.	-	-	Vac.	-

2

1. Vapor control systems consist mainly of a separator, lines and the carbon storage canister, where used.

2. CEC (Combination Emission Control) valve is a complicated arrangement because it does so many different things. Using a combination of electricity and engine vacuum, the valve controls spark advance and throttle opening. The valve is normally closed, which shuts off vacuum to the distributor and eliminates all spark advance. When the transmission is in a position labeled "Vac" on the chart, the transmission switch opens, which operates the reversing relay to energize the valve. This opens the vacuum line to the distributor, giving normal vacuum advance, and also extends the plunger to the high gear deceleration position, which gives a larger throttle opening on deceleration so there will be fewer emissions.

3. Vapor control went nationwide in 1971. The carbon storage system uses activated carbon in a canister to trap the vapors.

4. Crankcase vapor storage is used on many cars. You may not like the idea of diluting your engine oil with gasoline vapors, but that's the way they do it. Actually, dilution of engine oil would not occur unless the vehicle were allowed to stand through several days of hot sun and cool nights. Under those conditions it would be theoretically possible to end up with a considerable amount of gasoline in the oil pan. But the chances of this situation occurring are extremely rare.

5. The Combination Emission Control Valve is used mostly on Chevrolet cars, but also appears on some other GM makes. Curb idle is set with the normal throttle-cracking screw, not the CEC plunger screw. There is a specification in rpm for the plunger screw, but setting it is not necessary unless you disturb the original setting. CEC valve rpm setting varies as much as 300 rpm above normal curb idle. If you set curb idle with the CEC valve plunger by mistake, engine braking on deceleration will be greatly reduced, which can be dangerous.

6. Ford has added a Cold Start Spark Advance (CSSA) to its '75 460 V-8. The Check valve (1) keeps vacuum in the advance when the engine is cold. Once it warms up, vacuum is then routed through the spark delay valve (2).

the plunger moves out so that the throttle will not be allowed to close completely. The plunger does not normally have enough force to push the throttle open, only to keep it from closing. The result is a goofy situation in reverse gear on a Turbo Hydra-Matic in which you may get two different idle speeds, depending on whether you step on the gas after you put the transmission in reverse.

Additional controls complicate the CEC valve situation even further. A temperature switch cancels the whole operation, allowing vacuum advance below 82° F. A time-delay relay cancels the CEC valve for 15 secs. after the ignition switch is turned on, allowing vacuum advance for easier drive-away and fewer stall-after-start problems.

Curb idle on CEC-valve carburetors is set with the ordinary throttle cracking screw. Deceleration idle setting (considerably higher) is set with the CEC valve plunger in the energized position. If curb idle is set with the CEC valve plunger, the throttle will be held open too far on deceleration, which can be quite a surprise when you take your foot off the gas and the car keeps going. The CEC valve is easily recognizable because it has

a vacuum hose connected to it. An ordinary anti-dieseling solenoid has no hose.

Because the throttle is automatically held open on deceleration, it isn't necessary to idle the '71 cars as fast as earlier models. Idle speed specs dropped about 50 rpm. The lower idle speeds made anti-dieseling solenoids unnecessary. But air-conditioned cars posed a problem, because the car has to idle faster with air conditioning. The faster idle leads to dieseling. Chevrolet solved this by putting a solid-state time device on air-conditioned cars that turns the compressor on for 3 secs. after the engine is turned off. The added load of the compressor slows the engine down to keep it from dieseling.

NOx CONTROL SYSTEMS

We also mentioned a Chrysler Corp. spark control system. Installed on all California cars in 1971 (and nationwide in 1972); Chrysler's nitrogen oxide (NOx) system took the place of the solenoid-controlled spark advance previously used. As initial emissions control efforts had concentrated on hydrocarbons, little attention was paid to NOx emissions—resulting in a less-

ening of hydrocarbons, but an increase in NOx.

Chrysler's approach to NOx control was quite sophisticated: it used a special camshaft with increased overlap. This overlap produces more exhaust gas contamination in the cylinder, which reduces peak combustion chamber temperatures, the primary cause of NOx emissions. Along with a camshaft, the engines are equipped with a 185° ± thermostat, a move directly opposite to that made to reduce hydrocarbons, which resulted in the use of a 195° ± thermostat. Because of the many other changes made, this doesn't mean that hydrocarbon emissions will increase, but you can see a rather complicated interplay of forces at work here. The lean mixtures necessary to bring hydrocarbons under control resulted in higher combustion chamber temperatures, and so an increase in NOx emissions.

Until the 1973 model year, the heart of Chrysler's NOx system was a solenoid vacuum valve that controlled vacuum spark advance. On manual transmission cars, this valve is connected to a transmission switch to eliminate vacuum advance in all but top gear. In any other gear position,

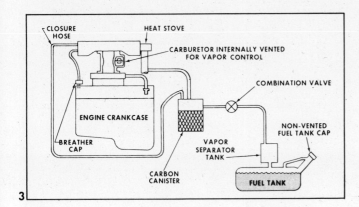

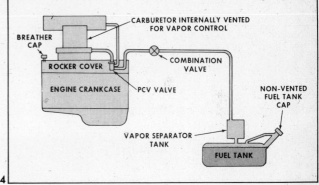

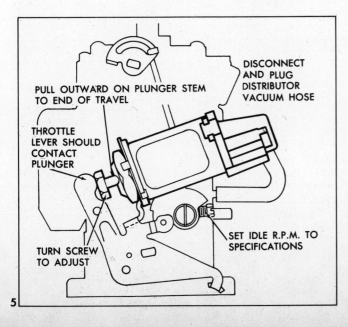

SMOG CONTROL

the valve is energized, shutting off vacuum to the distributor. In high gear, the transmission switch breaks the electrical circuit to the solenoid, the spring in the valve opens the passageway and vacuum is allowed to advance the spark. The only additional control on manual transmission cars is a thermal switch mounted on the firewall to sense the temperature in the fresh air cowl inlet. Below 70° ± F., the thermal switch breaks the circuit to the solenoid valve, which allows normal vacuum spark advance; above that temperature, the thermal switch makes the connection and allows the NOx system to operate as described above.

Automatic transmission cars are different—they have an increased-overlap cam, a 185° F. thermostat and a solenoid vacuum valve, but the control mode is different. A control module, vacuum switch, thermal switch and speed switch all work together to tell the solenoid when to turn distributor vacuum on or off.

Chrysler's NOx control on the '73 and later line is handled by the combination of a temperature-actuated Orifice Spark Advance Control (OSAC) and Exhaust Gas Recirculation (EGR) system, replacing the solenoid vacuum valve. When going from idle to partial throttle, a small opening in the OSAC valve delays the change in ported vacuum to the distributor by about 17 secs., but when reversing the sequence (part throttle to idle), the change is instantaneous. As vacuum is provided by a tap just above the carburetor throttle plates, manifold vacuum is not present under idle conditions, but as soon as the throttle plates open slightly, the system kicks into operation, provided the temperature is 58° F. or higher.

EGR first appeared on 1972 Buicks, and variations of the system are now in use on all domestic and foreign cars sold in the U.S. The theory behind EGR operation is quite simple: We know that high combustion temperatures cause nitrogen and oxygen to combine, forming nitrogen oxides which pass through the system into the air as a pollutant. EGR simply recirculates exhaust gases through the engine intake manifold and into the cylinders, where they combine with the air/fuel mixture for combustion. Since exhaust gases are relatively inert and burn at a considerably lower temperature than the air/fuel mixture in the cylinder at the moment of peak combustion, they dilute the combustion chamber charge, slowing the process of combustion and thus reducing the combustion temperature to a level where forma-

1

2

tion of nitrogen oxides is inhibited.

A vacuum-operated recirculation control valve, generally mounted on the engine manifold near the carburetor, is connected to an inline temperature control valve whenever the underhood temperatures are below 55° F. When the throttle valves are opened beyond the idle position, vacuum is applied against the EGR valve actuating diaphragm. As the diaphragm moves up against spring pressure, it opens the exhaust gas intake valve, allowing exhaust gases from the manifold exhaust crossover

channels to be drawn back into the engine intake. The valve remains closed during idle and deceleration conditions, when excessive exhaust gases added to the air/fuel mixture would cause rough engine idling.

EGR is handled on Chrysler Corp. cars by either a ported vacuum control, a venturi vacuum control or a floor jet system, depending upon the engine involved. However, the end result is the same—a predetermined amount of hot exhaust gas is recirculated to dilute the incoming air/fuel mixture and thus lower the combus-

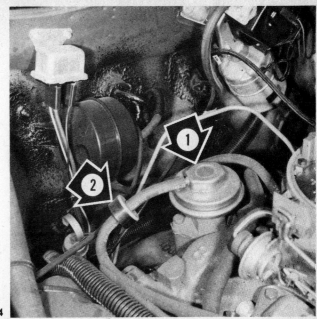

3

4

5

1. *Orifice Spark Advance Control, or OSAC (1), is Chrysler Corp. device to delay vacuum during acceleration. Delay is accomplished by restricting airflow from distributor advance chamber to carb port. A thermal cutoff device in OSAC valve assures good drivability when ambient temperature is under 58° F. EGR temperature control valve (2) blocks vacuum from carb whenever underhood temperatures are below 55°.*

2. *Chrysler EGR valve location differs from engine to engine. Valve is not repairable and must be replaced if bad. Six-cylinder engines have the unit mounted on intake manifold, where valve stem action is easily seen.*

3. *Most Ford EGR valves are mounted on the rear of an internally chambered spacer plate which fits between the carburetor and manifold. In 1974, Ford used a floor entry system on some V-8 engines, but dropped it in favor of the spacer plate for '75.*

4. *EGR valve (1) on '73 Buick was mounted at rear of manifold. Exhaust gas intake port connects to intake manifold exhaust crossover channel, where it picks up exhaust gases. Valve is operated by vacuum from the carburetor and is controlled by the inline temperature control valve (2).*

5. *Chrysler now uses a coolant-actuated temperature switch to control EGR valve operation on some '75 models.*

tion temperatures and resulting NOx formation.

Ford's approach to EGR is tied into the engine coolant temperature as the actuating device, instead of the air temperature used at first by GM and Chrysler cars. (During '74-'75, both GM and Chrysler introduced coolant control.) The Ford system has varied with each succeeding model year and is rather complicated in that several different coolant temperatures are used (depending upon the engine application involved) to activate the system. Ford has also used three dif-

ferent types of EGR valves: a poppet, a modulating type and a tapered-stem, again dependent upon the type of application.

The temperature control device used to activate the Ford EGR system is a ported vacuum switch similar to the distributor vacuum control valve used in 1972. To eliminate the add-on piping system used in other EGR designs, exhaust gases are picked up from the exhaust crossover passage in the intake manifold and routed through a thick carburetor spacer to the EGR valve, which meters the gases back through another passage in the spacer. This means that the exhaust gases are directed to the primary bores, where they dilute the incoming air/fuel mixture headed for the combustion chambers. As vacuum for EGR operation comes from the carburetor's primary bore in this system, you'll find twin vacuum ports on the carburetor, one for EGR con-

trol and one for the distributor spark advance.

Ford further confused the EGR issue in 1974 by using a Floor Entry System on some V-8 engines, in which the valve was mounted on the intake manifold instead of the spacer. Passages in the manifold were used to transmit exhaust gas to the engine through the manifold floor after being passed through the EGR valve. A venturi vacuum amplifier replaced the ported vacuum system on some 6-cylinder engines as a means of opening/closing the EGR valve This amplifier was connected to the EGR valve and to the intake manifold. Airflow of a certain speed through the venturi caused vacuum to open the amplifier, which used manifold vacuum in this manner to open the EGR valve. With venturi vacuum high and manifold vacuum low at wide open throttle, the amplifier dumps the air trapped between it and the EGR

SMOG CONTROL

valve, which closes. On 1975 systems, Ford has abandoned the floor entry method in favor of its original spacer design and revamped the vacuum amplifier into three different versions; the one used in 1974 malfunctioned far too frequently.

Since EGR systems made their appearance, numerous problems have developed with their functioning, partially because the driver did not pay enough attention to proper operation of the system. If the valve stem becomes covered with deposits, it won't work properly and causes problems. To help overcome this, Chrysler Corp. has added an EGR Maintenance Warning System for 1975. When the speedometer has recorded 15,000 miles, a nice bright light comes on in the instrument panel—and it's going to stay on until you either do something about it or the bulb burns out from old age. Chrysler Corp. is betting that you'll get darned tired of seeing that light and, as a result, you'll go back to the dealer to have the EGR system inspected and cleaned and the warning system's mechanism reset, turning off the light.

The system itself consists of a digital counter mechanism and switch assembly inserted in series in the speedometer cable. The device contains a set of gears and electrical contacts, which close to activate the reminder light at the specified 15,000-mile intervals. On 6-cylinder cars, the mechanism is located below the master brake cylinder; on V-8's, you'll find it along the toe-board area of the floorpan, just to the rear of the engine compartment. When you locate it, the switch will be covered by a rubber boot attached to the upper speedometer cable.

To reset the mechanism, you'll have to hoist the car up in the air. The boot is slipped up the speedometer cable to expose the switch, which is then disconnected from the cable. A reset screw on the switch is given a one-quarter turn with a screwdriver and the unit is replaced. Of course, while you're doing this, Chrysler means to have you inspect the EGR system and either clean out the carbon from the passageways or replace the EGR valve, the timer or the solenoid if necessary. Look for similar devices to appear on GM and Ford vehicles soon.

VAPOR CONTROL SYSTEMS

Beginning with 1970 California cars, and extended nationwide the following year, there's an additional system, entirely separate from the exhaust and crankcase-emissions controls, to take care of any gasoline va-

pors that might escape from the fuel tank or the carburetor. The fuel tank is sealed, except for a line that goes to the engine crankcase. Vapors move along the line and are stored in the crankcase until the engine is started; then they are sucked into the intake manifold and burned. To keep liquid fuel from getting up to the crankcase, a vapor separator on top of the gas tank sends all the liquid fuel back to the tank.

Some vapor control systems use a canister filled with activated carbon to trap the vapors, instead of letting them go into the crankcase. The carburetor float bowl also connects to the crankcase or the carbon canister, whichever is used, so that vapor from the float bowl will not escape into the atmosphere.

CATALYTIC CONVERTERS

Introduced on many 1975 model cars, the catalytic converter is the newest emissions control device. This is nothing more than a can or container which holds a chemical substance through which exhaust gases are passed enroute to the muffler. The catalytic material acts chemically on the hydrocarbons and the carbon monoxide gases in the exhaust to change or "convert" them into harmless water and carbon dioxide by promoting a further burning or oxidization of the pollutants. To provide sufficient fresh air for this conversion process to take place, catalytic converter-equipped California cars use an air pump system in conjunc-

tion with the converter; non-California cars are not required to meet such a stringent emissions level and converters are used in most applications without the air pump (but some non-California cars are equipped with an air pump and no converter).

There are two different types of converters presently in use—the GM/AMC unit, which contains pellets coated with platinum and palladium, and the Ford/Chrysler units which use a ceramic "honeycomb" core coated with the same catalytic agents. Because leaded gasoline will contaminate the catalytic agents, all converter-equipped engines are designed to run on unleaded fuel. To protect against using the wrong fuel, catalyst-equipped cars are fitted with a smaller than normal fuel tank filler tube that will only accept the smaller nozzles used to pump unleaded fuel.

A combustion-type reaction takes place as exhaust gases pass through the converter, raising the heat level in the exhaust system by several hundred degrees. The greater temperatures created have meant that special heat shields must be used to protect the car's underbody. In addition, the Ford and Chrysler converters are fitted with special sieve-type shields to help in dissipating the high temperatures as well as in protecting the converter unit itself from road damage.

Those who thought that equipping a car with the catalytic converter system would end the problem of emissions control were wrong—they're simply not that foolproof. While the

use of leaded fuel can destroy the catalytic agent, so can excessive richness in the exhaust. The amount of unburned hydrocarbons in the exhaust increases considerably under conditions of high-speed deceleration, temporarily overloading the converter to a point where it may overheat and thus melt the catalytic material. Because of this possibility, each Ford and Chrysler converter application uses a catalyst protection system; one is not required with the pellet-type unit used by GM.

Ford has incorporated its converter protection system in the Thermactor air pump operation. When you decelerate, a vacuum differential valve (VDV) momentarily dumps vacuum to the bypass valve, which in turn diverts air pump output to the atmosphere. The bypass valve also dumps the pump output when a cold engine is started, or when the engine overheats. This lockout/overheat function uses a solenoid vacuum valve (SVV) to control the bypass valve, getting its lockout signal from a temperature-sensitive switch in the air cleaner and its overheat signal from an electric PVS on trucks and a floor-mounted sensor switch on passenger cars.

The 1975 Fords use two different types of systems: In Type 1, the air cleaner switch opens when the engine is cold. This causes the PVS switch to open, de-energizing the solenoid vacuum valve. This blocks vacuum from the differential valve and causes the bypass valve to dump. Once the engine has warmed up, the PVS and air cleaner switches both close, and pump air then flows through the bypass valve to the exhaust manifold.

Type 2 operates the same way, but in reverse modes. The air cleaner and ported vacuum switches are open in normal operation, with the solenoid de-energized. A cold-start or overheat condition will close the switches and energize the solenoid to block vacuum from the differential valve. This causes the bypass valve

1. Ford uses a fuel vapor return system with certain engines to reduce amount of vapor entering carburetor. On '73 Gran Torino, it's difficult to get at unless car is on a hoist.

2. The '75 GM vapor canister has a third nipple to accommodate the mechanical bowl vent feature on the new Rochester carburetors.

3. Chrysler's newest EGR system incorporates a delay timer (arrow) on the firewall. When the ignition is switched on to start the engine, the delay timer prevents the EGR valve from opening for a specified interval (early versions used a 35-sec. delay; 60 secs. after December 12, '73) to give better drivability during initial engine operation.

to dump the air pump output. The Type 2 system is a carryover from 1974 models, while Type 1 is a new system. You can tell which one your car is equipped with by examining the air cleaner temperature switch connector: Type 1 uses a flat connector while Type 2 has a round one.

The Chrysler Catalyst Overheat Protection System (COPS) consists of an electronic speed switch that's connected between a throttle position solenoid—mounted on the side of the carburetor—and the electronic control

unit—on the firewall. When engine speed drops to 2000 rpm, the control unit signals the speed switch to energize the solenoid; this holds the throttle open slightly during deceleration only. The slightly open throttle increases airflow to the engine in order to burn the hydrocarbons *before* they reach the catalyst. As engine speed falls below 2000 rpm, the speed switch turns off the solenoid, allowing the throttle to return to its normal idle stop position, and the engine continues to decelerate to idle speed.

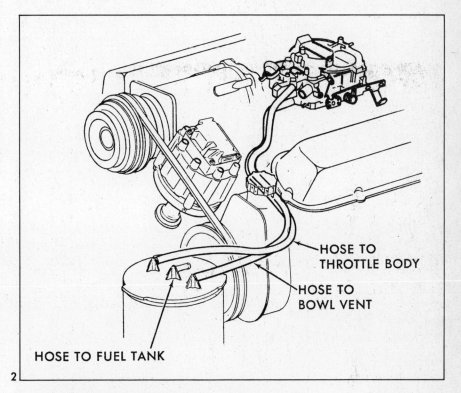

HOSE TO THROTTLE BODY

HOSE TO BOWL VENT

HOSE TO FUEL TANK

2

3

SMOG CONTROL

The throttle position solenoid used looks a good deal like the anti-dieseling solenoid previously used on Chrysler cars—but it isn't. If you have a carburetor-mounted solenoid on a '75 Chrysler Corp. car, it's a part of the COPS and should not be adjusted. There is one exception to this statement: the 318-cu.-in. non-California engine without the converter retains the anti-dieseling solenoid.

We mentioned above that excessive richness in the exhaust, as well as the use of leaded gasoline, can damage and ultimately ruin the converter's effectiveness. As much as possible, the manufacturers have taken steps to protect the converter from accidental damage, but there are some problems that are simply beyond their ability to control. For example, any engine condition—such as misfiring—which leads to excessively rich exhaust will damage the catalyst. This means that regular tuning and servicing of the engine is even more important than it was in the past; just because your car is equipped with a converter, you can't run it to death before a tune-up.

You should also avoid running out of gas; if you can't, shut off the ignition just as soon as the engine begins to sputter, indicating it's going to quit on you. Shift into neutral and coast over to the side of the road where you can stop safely. This prevents any damage to the converter and leaves sufficient fuel in the system so that you won't have to prime it when you refill the tank and try to start the car.

If you try to run the car just as far as possible before you quit, you're apt to be in for a costly surprise. Pumping the pedal while the engine is sputtering will push unburned gasoline through to the converter. As if this isn't bad enough by itself, the problem is further complicated when you try to restart the engine. You'll either have to pump the pedal to work enough fuel up into the carburetor or prime it by pouring gas into the carburetor bowl. In either case, some of the gas will pass on to the converter in the form of excessively rich exhaust, and that may well be enough to damage or destroy the catalytic agents. This situation will require the installation of a new converter, in the case of Ford/Chrysler cars, or the replacement of the pellets in the GM/AMC systems.

The catalytic converter concept has been a storm of controversy since it was first proposed; some consider it to be the only answer, while others feel that as a cure, it's worse than the problem. Despite some misgivings, the federal government sanctioned the converter's use on 1975 models, but has since concluded that perhaps the critics had a better case. It seems that in the course of doing their job destroying hydrocarbon and carbon monoxide pollutants, the catalysts release an equally dangerous (if not more so) substance into the air in the form of sulfur. How long the converter will remain in favor cannot be predicted at this time, but it's a safe bet we'll have them with us through the 1977 models.

HEAT RISER VALVES

Heat risers have been operated by

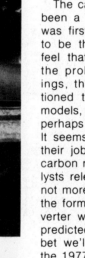

1. The GM catalytic converter is a pan-shaped device containing pellets coated with a catalytic agent and can be "recharged" by changing the pellets via the fill plug. AMC uses the same converter unit.

2. Ford and Chrysler converters are nonrechargeable, require a sieve-like protective shield that also helps dissipate increased exhaust gas heat.

3. Ford's Thermactor (air pump) system contains a vacuum differential valve (1) and a bypass valve (2) as part of its converter protection system. To prevent converter overheating on deceleration, the VDV dumps vacuum to the bypass valve, which then dumps air pump output to engine compartment.

4. To determine which type of converter protection system your Ford is equipped with, check the air cleaner temperature sensor connection. This flat connector indicates a Type 1 system; a round one indicates a Type 2.

thermostatic coils for the most part until the 1975 models appeared. Most of us tended to ignore its operation in the past, but the heat riser managed to work fairly well without pampering. About the worst that usually happened was a stuck valve, and that could ordinarily be freed with an application or two of Liquid Wrench. But in the car makers' drive to provide better evaporation and distribution of the air/fuel mixture, the heat riser valve has now gone vacuum on GM and Ford cars.

By its name you'd never know that GM's Early Fuel Evaporation (EFE) valve was really that lowly heat riser in disguise. Applications of the EFE system vary from one engine to another. Some use a vacuum solenoid controlled by a temperature switch to operate the valve, while others use a thermal vacuum switch (TVS) actuated by coolant temperature. A few even combine functions with other systems: The same TVS that controls vacuum to the distributor also operates the EFE valve, and Pontiac combines EFE operation with EGR operation on its 350X engine series vehicles.

Ford's version has a vacuum diaphragm mounted on the exhaust manifold and mechanically linked to the heat riser shaft. A ported vacuum switch allows vacuum to reach the diaphragm during start-up, when coolant temperature is low. The diaphragm pulls the lever, closing the heat riser valve. As the engine warms up, the coolant temperature closes the PVS, blocking vacuum passage to the diaphragm, which now returns to normal and pulls the heat riser valve open to let exhaust gas flow through.

In spite of the sophisticated control of the heat riser's action by temperature and vacuum, the same old problems remain. Those hot exhaust gases flowing through will continue to affect the heat riser's shaft in the same way, and unless you keep it lubricated, the butterfly is going to hang up one of these days. While there's no doubt that heat riser operation is bound to be more efficient, bringing vacuum and temperature controls into the picture just adds more links in an already complex chain of emission controls that require periodic servicing. Who said cars were getting back to the basics?

LEAN BURN

Since the advent of the catalytic converter, the only new emissions control device or system that has appeared on American cars is Chrysler's Lean-Burn system.

Catalytic converters have little effect on NOx emissions, since oxides of nitrogen are not rendered harmless by further oxidation. To control NOx, Chrysler had to continue playing with EGR, OSAC and special camshafts, whereas all the time its engineers felt that the way to really control emissions was with a more sophisticated version of the old original Chrysler Clean Air Package: Burn lean air/fuel mixtures and control the ignition advance accordingly. Chrysler's adoption of the no-points electronic ignition system in 1973 paved the way for Lean Burn, which was introduced in 1976.

An industry first, Lean Burn is a fully electronic control system for the ignition. Its heart is a book-size spark control analog computer located near the carburetor. This computer receives signals from sensors located throughout the engine, integrates the data, determines when the exact moment of combustion ought to be and triggers the distributor to fire the plugs. By comparison, the old mechanical systems using spark ports and solenoids are very crude. So successful is this system that Lean-Burn engines operate on air/fuel ratios of 18:1 to 20:1—mixtures so rarefied that ordinary engines could not run at all on them. The happy result is that not only are Lean-Burn engines very clean, they are obviously also very economical. That in itself is quite an accomplishment. Lean Burn is the first emissions control system which simultaneously boosts gas mileage and improves drivability and reliability.

3

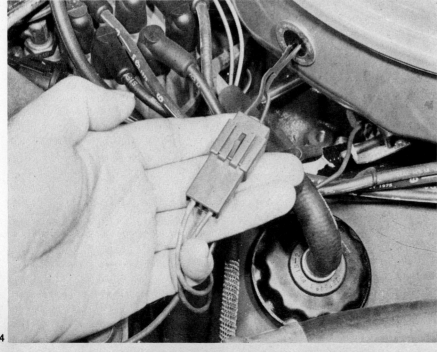

4

SMOG CONTROL

For 1976 Chrysler offered Lean Burn only on its 400-cu.-in. federal engine with 4-bbl. carburetion, of which 109,000 were built. So clean was the system that no catalytic converter or EGR was required.

For '77, however, the federal standards for allowable NOx emissions were cut almost in half (from 3.1 to 2.0 grams per mile), and to meet this level Chrysler added a converter to Lean Burn. Availability was also widened, however, and Lean Burn was offered on Chrysler's 360 and 440 4-bbl. engines and the 318 2-bbl., as well as the 400 4-bbl. Of these, only the 440 4-bbl. also met California emissions laws and was offered there as well as in the other 49 states. The new midsize Chrysler LeBaron and Dodge Diplomat have a Lean-Burn 318 V-8 engine as standard equipment, with no options. Chrysler expected to produce about 400,000 Lean-Burn engines for the 1977 model year, a very substantial fraction of its total engine production. Lean Burn is obviously scheduled for practically all of the company's engines in the near future.

Even such an advanced system could be improved, however. The spark control computer was changed so much for the '77 cars from the '76 version that Chrysler referred to it as a second-generation control computer. It had only one circuit board instead of two, only one distributor pickup point instead of two, and the electronic circuitry was so rearranged

1. *The carburetor-mounted solenoid on '75 Chrysler Corp. cars was part of the COPS system and acted as a throttle positioner instead of an anti-dieseling solenoid. The sole exception to this was the non-California 318 engine.*

2. *With the increased use of thermal vacuum switches on cars, you must be very careful to replace all lines exactly. The placement of these three PVS units on the '75 Ford V-6 engine points up how confusing the issue has actually become these days.*

3. *GM calls its vacuum heat riser an Early Fuel Evaporation (EFE) system; this is mechanically linked to valve shaft. Chrysler has retained older thermostatic coil operation.*

4. *Buried under this mess of hoses and lines on the '75 Buick is a thermal vacuum switch (arrow) which operates EFE valve. GM use is not quite as confusing as that of Ford—so far.*

5. *Chrysler's Electronic Lean-Burn system, seen here on a '76 Cordoba, is best emissions control system yet. Spark control computer (arrow) senses six different engine functions and calculates the best ignition time, then fires the distributor.*

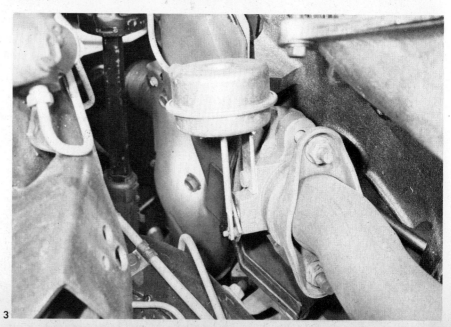

and simplified that the computer's size was reduced by 30%. If Chrysler keeps it up, pretty soon the control computer will be some space-age chip the size of your fingernail (don't laugh).

An interesting sidelight to Lean Burn is that Chrysler has developed a diagnostic tester specifically for it and is selling these testers to Dodge dealers. This tester contains the auto industry's first microprocessor computer, a handy device which prevents the tester from becoming outdated. It uses tiny, replaceable modular data banks for each engine. If the dealer wants to test a 318 instead of a 440 or a '78 instead of a '77, he simply inserts the proper memory cartridge, and the computer is then programmed for that engine. Since it is a solid-state electronic system, the Lean-Burn control is very reliable, but these testers make sure that it will stay in tip-top shape. ♛ 4

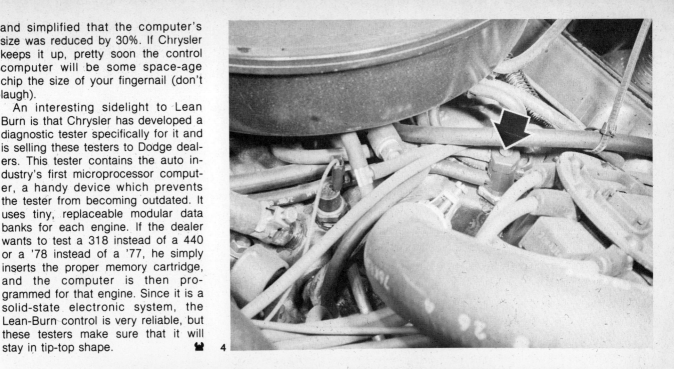

5

REBUILDING CARBURETORS

So you've never taken a carburetor apart and put it back together again? Well, don't let that little matter stand in your way—rebuilding a carburetor (any carburetor) isn't quite the job it might seem to be, especially if you tackle it in an orderly manner. Before you get the yen to yank the carburetor though, we suggest that you make certain that it's *really* the problem. In many cases, a simple adjustment somewhere else in the system will solve your dilemma.

But once you've satisfied yourself that the carburetor is indeed at fault, the first thing you must do is find out exactly *which* carburetor you're dealing with. To do so you'll need the model number and part number—then you can purchase the proper carburetor kit. For most carburetors, you can buy one of three kits—a gasket set, a light repair kit or an overhaul kit. Which one you'll need will depend upon what's wrong and exactly what you're going to do; if you've worked on the carburetor before and your past experience has told you that its parts will not need to be replaced, you can probably get by with just the gasket set.

A light repair kit will contain the complete gasket set, in addition to all the parts that usually require replacement, such as the needle and seat, accelerator pump and any rubber parts. This is the kit most often used. The complete overhaul kit contains almost every part on the carburetor that can wear out or be left out—except the throttle shaft—and is probably the best bet if you've been having lots of trouble with the carburetor.

When you have the rebuild kit, you can think about removing the carburetor from the engine. Once a simple bolt-on unit, the carburetor has become a complicated piece of machinery in its own right these days, and you'll find all kinds of hoses, lines and fittings that must be disconnected on late-model cars. Unless you're absolutely familiar with each and know what it does (as well as where it goes), it's a good idea to wrap a piece of masking tape around the hose when you remove it and jot some form of identification on the tape with a felt-tip pen. Taking the cue, Rochester has initiated the practice of identifying each such fitting on its '75 line of carburetors with a code letter. This makes it easy for the home rebuilder, who merely writes the code letter on the masking tape.

Reassembling a carburetor should be an orderly process and the reverse of the disassembly procedure. Work slowly; avoid forcing/bending parts.

You'll need a small container into which you can put the reusable parts that you'll remove during disassembly; this will prevent that inevitable search on the floor for a missing check ball or spring. You'll also want a quantity of good carburetor cleaner at hand. There are all kinds of cleaners and solvents available. A good one is quite powerful and will virtually eat dirt and grease from the carburetor when it's fresh. However, it's something you won't want to get your hands into, nor will you want to splash it in your eyes. Treat the cleaner with respect. If you don't have a small mesh basket for lowering parts into the solution's container, a small tea strainer—available at most department stores—will serve the purpose; this will hold those small parts. You can use a metal clothes hanger hooked around the main body and air horn to lower them into the cleaner.

Carburetor disassembly is a matter of good judgment; there are any number of ways to approach the task. Of course, if all you plan to do is to pull off the air horn and replace a gasket, there's no need to remove the carburetor from the engine, but once you have, approach the disassembly sequence in an orderly and logical manner. There's no rule book that states A must come off before B. True, in some cases it may have to—but you can start almost anyplace on the unit you wish. Solenoids and dashpots should come off, as carburetor cleaner will make short work of them. While the fastidious may insist on removing the main jets, it really isn't necessary in most cases, and some carburetors are made with non-removable jets.

Once you've stripped the carburetor down, gather up the parts and dunk them in the cleaning solution. Let the stuff do its job for at least 30 mins. If the carburetor is really filthy and the cleaner isn't fresh, it may take up to an hour or two to do a thorough job. When the parts look clean and bright, the cleaner has done its work and you can remove them from the container. Let the parts drain and then dunk them into a second solution of fresh cleaner for a few minutes, giving the solvent time to work its way into all the passages. Then remove the parts and blow them dry, one by one.

You'll find a specification sheet included with each rebuild kit—this will give you the necessary data for making required adjustments when you begin reassembly. If you bought one of the "bargain" kits, the spec sheet may not be included; in that case, you'll have to turn to the factory shop manual, the carburetor spec books published by the manufacturer, or Petersen's *How To Tune Your Car*. The most important adjustment, and usually the only one required inside the carburetor, is the float level. Surging, dying, hesitation, rich or lean running—all can be caused by an improper float level; other engines will die on turns if the float level is not correctly set. Above all, work carefully to avoid bending or otherwise damaging any parts, and never force anything into place.

If you've disassembled the carburetor in an orderly, logical sequence, you found it easy going. Reassemble it in a similar manner (last thing out is first thing in) and you'll be surprised at how well the entire job goes. And the best part of all is that you don't have to completely understand the theory of carburetion to do the job. Of course, if you do know and understand the theory, so much the better.

To help you along, we've provided four how-to sequences on the following pages: a 1-bbl., two 2-bbl.'s and a 4-bbl. They're typical of most of the factory-provided carbs and quite similar in design to many of the older ones still in use on cars of the late '50's and early '60's. These will give you an idea of the degree of complexity involved, as well as help you should you get stuck somewhere in the middle of the job. So, if your carburetor needs some attention and you've been putting it off because of the cost involved, here's your chance to do-it-yourself.

1. Chrysler Corp. cars use the Holley 1945 as factory equipment. Begin rebuild of this 1-bbl. carburetor by removing the screws holding the choke actuator in place.

2. Lift choke actuator up and angle connecting linkage off choke lever; remove throttle position solenoid, if so equipped. Neither should be placed in solvent.

3. Remove bowl cover screws. To free the bowl and cover, tap gently with a rubber mallet or a screwdriver handle to break the seal—do not pry apart.

4. Now remove "E" clip holding fast idle cam in place. Leave throttle lever intact with fast idle and curb idle screws in place—these need not come off for cleaning.

5. Slip fast idle cam from its shaft and off choke lever connecting linkage, then remove the link from the choke lever. Choke lever stays in place also.

6. Note position of connecting link in accelerator pump rocker arm; remove nut and lock washer holding arm in place and take it off, angling arm to free it of linkage.

HOW-TO: HOLLEY 1945

7. You can now lift bowl cover off. Pull straight up and off. The accelerator pump is attached to the cover, along with the vacuum piston assembly.

8. Take off the old gasket and discard it. Remove screw holding pump rod retainer in place before attempting to disconnect accelerator pump from pump rod.

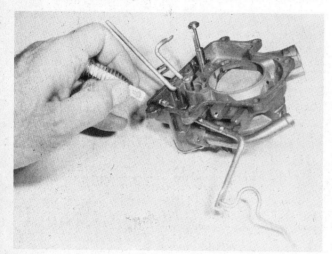

9. Pull up on pump drive spring; rotate pump operating rod slightly and pump assembly will slip off. Note two tangs on end of rod; pump arm fits between for reassembly.

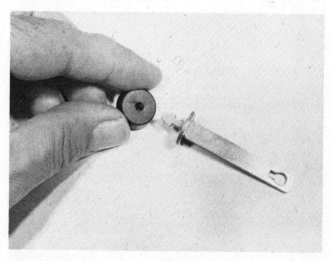

10. Remove pump drive spring and pull off old pump cap. Replace cap with new one furnished in rebuild kit. Install carefully, making sure it fits properly over "arrowhead."

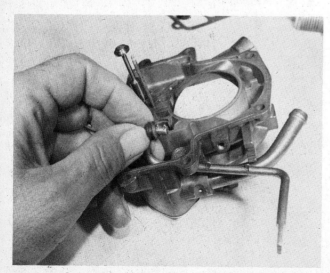

11. Before you can remove pump operating rod, you must rotate it to free the rubber cover grommet, which must come out before cover is dunked in cleaner.

12. Turn cover over and remove bowl vent cap. Under the cap, you'll find a spring over the vent adjusting screw. Vent device is held in place by a retaining screw.

13. Loosen or remove retaining screw and lift plastic vent device out. Don't touch adjusting screw, as this is factory set and should not require adjustment.

14. You'll find a tiny pump discharge check ball under this weight. Remove both and set to one side. Normally, a new check ball is included in rebuild kit—weight is reused.

15. A wire float shaft retainer is fitted to hold the dual-lung nitrophyl float in place. This lifts out easily to allow access for float removal.

16. Lift the dual float assembly and the float shaft up and out of the carburetor body. Be careful not to bend the wire arms attached to the two floats.

17. Unscrew the fuel inlet fitting and valve. A "vitron"-tipped fuel inlet needle in fitting is held in place by a cap which allows fuel to flow out its sides.

18. The power valve assembly can be removed with a screwdriver blade, but due to the close quarters it's better to use a deep socket to prevent valve stem damage.

HOW-TO: HOLLEY 1945

19. The power valve is a 1-piece assembly in some 1945 carburetors; a 3-piece assembly in others. Don't lose or overlook tiny spring on valve stem end of 3-piece unit.

20. The same removal procedure holds for the main jet. If it must come out, a wide, square-point screwdriver can be used—but a jet wrench is best protection against damage.

21. This completes carburetor body disassembly. Turn body over and remove three throttle body screws, then tap gently to separate the carburetor and throttle body units.

22. Lift the throttle body up and off, then remove old gasket and discard. Always install new gaskets when reassembling any carburetor—old ones are prone to leak.

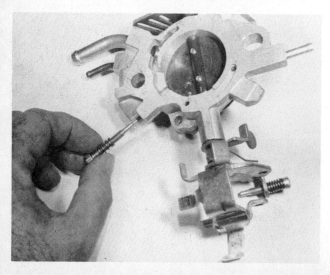

23. Remove the idle limiter cap and turn mixture screw clockwise until it seats, counting number of turns required. Then turn screw counterclockwise to remove.

24. Once cleaning is completed, blow carburetor body dry with compressed air and install main jet, power valve and float assembly. Seat float shaft and fit retainer in place.

25. Reinstall pump rod and grommet; reconnect pump to pump rod and check action of the pump by working rod. Vacuum piston is staked in place and not normally removed.

26. Drop vent valve and shaft into place; tighten the retaining screw, then set the spring over the adjustment screw before replacing the vent cover.

27. Install new gasket on bowl cover and fit to carburetor body. Make sure accelerator pump goes into pump well and vacuum piston actuating rod rides under piston flange.

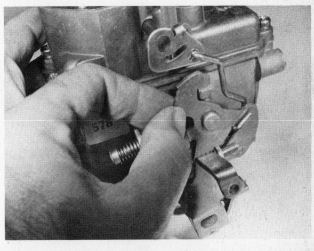

28. Fit fast idle cam linkage to choke lever, then slip cam over shaft as shown. After this has been done you can go ahead and replace the large retaining E clip.

29. Reattach the throttle position solenoid, then connect the choke actuator linkage arm to the choke lever and fasten the actuator bracket to the carburetor bowl.

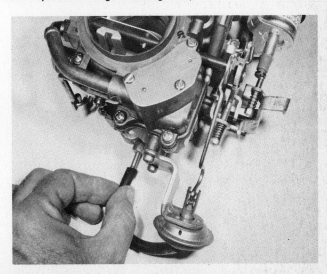

30. Connect vacuum hose to carb body fitting and rebuild is complete. This model 1945 fits standard transmission cars, and is not equipped with idle enrichment valve.

HOW-TO: HOLLEY 2245

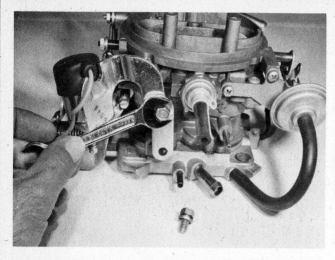

1. Disassembly of Holley 2245 begins with removal of throttle positioner solenoid. You'll need a couple of small wrenches to work on this one, in addition to usual tools.

2. Remove choke pulldown diaphragm and angle unit to free connecting linkage from choke lever. The solenoid and diaphragm should not be placed in solvent.

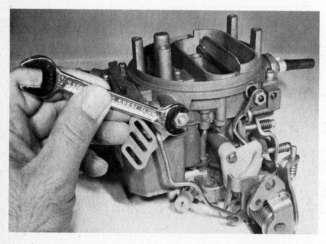

3. Remove nut and washer holding rocker arm in place, then pull arm from pump shaft. Disconnect linkage from rocker arm (after noting slot it's in) and throttle lever.

4. Take off the nut and washer that holds the choke lever to the choke shaft. Disconnect the fast idle rod from the choke lever and the fast idle cam.

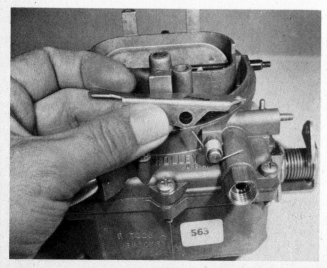

5. Examine bowl vent lever, noting position of spring ends inside which control lever action. Remove "E" clip and carefully slide the lever/spring off the shaft.

6. Air horn attaching screws come next; note position of long screw in center. Lift air horn straight up to prevent damage to main well tubes. Do not pry air horn off.

7. To disengage accelerator pump from pump shaft, push up on pump while angling it to one side. This allows pump end to slip off shaft for removal; a washer comes with it.

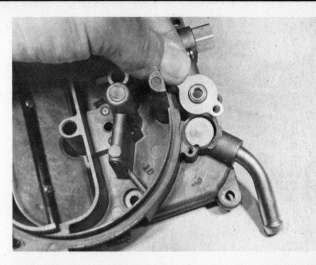

8. Two screws hold the bowl vent cover in place. Beneath the cover, you'll find the plastic vent device with a small spring and seal underneath it.

9. Remove the screw holding the float retaining plate in place, then slide the float shaft to one side and lift the float up and out of the air horn.

10. Fuel inlet needle comes out next. If you're not familiar with carburetors, take care not to mix this up with the discharge check needle, which is similar size/shape.

11. Fuel inlet seat and gasket can be removed with a wide-blade screwdriver. Work carefully in order to avoid damage to the soft metal seat flanges.

12. Model 2245 carburetors used with automatic transmission cars are equipped with an idle enrichment circuit and vacuum valve; the valve should be removed.

HOW-TO: HOLLEY 2245

13. Power valve seat is a 3-piece unit. Use a wide-blade screwdriver and work carefully to avoid damage to either the seat or power valve needle when removing.

14. If you remove the main jets, be sure to note where each one goes, as the two jets may be of different sizes, depending upon the carburetor application.

15. The discharge check needle is positioned here. This carburetor doesn't happen to use a check ball, so don't panic right away if you can't find one.

16. Remove attaching screws holding throttle body to main body and separate the two. As gasket is very thick, it will probably pull apart. Clean it off and discard.

17. To remove idle mixture needles, pry off limiter caps and turn screws in until they seat, counting the number of turns required; then back screws out all the way.

18. After cleaning in solvent, blow pieces dry with air. Reinstall and seat idle mixture screws. Back out exact number of turns counted above. Reattach main and throttle body.

19. Turn the air horn over carefully to prevent bending the main well tubes and replace vent valve seat, spring and valve. Fit cover into place and tighten screws.

20. Install float assembly, then replace pump cover, compress spring and fit through slot in air horn, tilting to one side to reconnect pump to pump shaft lever.

21. Install new gasket on air horn. Gasket should fit over this pin for proper positioning; pin also keeps it from slipping when the air horn is inverted.

22. Invert air horn and fit to main body, making sure that main well tubes and accelerator pump fit into respective places in main body. Replace attaching screws and tighten.

23. Fit spring inside the vent lever and slip the unit onto shaft. Check the lever action and replace the "E" clip. Reinstall the idle enrichment valve.

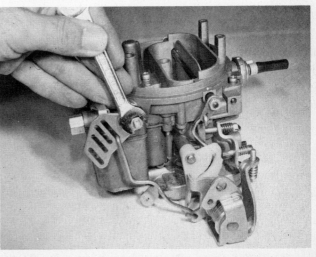

24. Reconnect choke lever and linkage, then install rocker arm and linkage. Replace the throttle positioner solenoid and choke vacuum diaphragm . . . rebuild is now complete.

HOW-TO: MOTORCRAFT 2150

1. Motorcraft 2150 2-bbl. carburetor rebuild begins with removal from the car. The 1975 version has more lines and hoses to be disconnected, so you'll do well to mark each with masking tape if you're not sure where they go.

2. With the carburetor off the car, begin disassembly on a clean part of the workbench by removing the screws holding the upper body or air horn to the main body. A power screwdriver is handy but not necessary.

3. With the upper body attaching screws removed, disconnect the choke plate rod (arrow) as you gently break the gasket seal; then you're ready to lift the upper body straight up and off the main body.

4. After removing the gasket and pouring out the gas in the fuel bowl, we set the air h⎯ ⎯ck in place while we finish working on the outside. While you don't have to do it, it's a habit we like.

5. Now turn the carburetor over and place it on top of an empty 3-lb. coffee can. Remove the four screws holding the enrichment valve cover and lift the cover off. You'll have to replace this gasket when you put it back.

6. Loosen and remove the enrichment valve; this used to be called the power valve and was a weak point in Motorcraft carbs. It still performs the same function and is still a weak point—it has a tendency to leak.

7. Counting the number of turns, screw the idle mixture needles all the way in until they stop, then unscrew and remove them. Break off the limiter caps by tapping them sharply with a hammer.

8. Four screws also hold the accelerator pump cover in place. Remove them and the large return spring will pop the cover off in your hand. Separate the diaphragm from the cover and check it for ruptures.

9. The 2150's accelerator pump return spring, shown at left, has far too much tension and should be replaced by the one shown at the right in order to prevent a premature failure of the diaphragm.

10. Three retaining screws hold the choke cap with thermostatic coil in place. Because the use of any sort of carburetor cleaner will destroy the plastic cap, remove it from the housing and lift off the gasket.

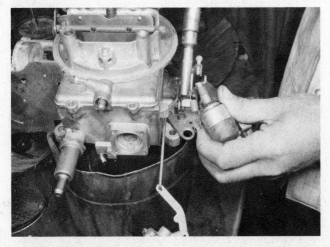

11. Unhook the throttle solenoid positioner spring and remove the two screws holding it to the main body. Don't touch the adjustment of the TSP screw on the lever assembly and you'll have no problems when you reassemble it.

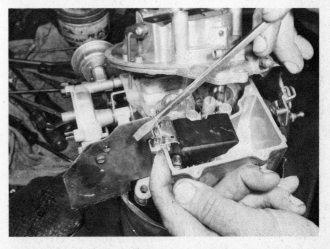

12. The float is lifted out of the fuel bowl by its shaft retainer. Watch the fuel inlet needle and screen which comes with it—and don't let it drop off onto the floor. Fuel inlet has been a problem on the 2150.

HOW-TO: MOTORCRAFT 2150

13. Now that we're finally ready to get at the heart of the matter, the choke plate rod is disconnected again and the upper body removed. Don't let the little plastic dust shield on the rod drop off and get lost.

14. Loosen and remove the booster venturi screw and its gasket. Booster venturi and nozzle bar design is just about the same as in the past, but on the 2150 it accommodates the new mechanical metering rods.

15. Under the booster venturi screw, you'll find a small weight and discharge check ball. Once these are removed, you can then lift the nozzle bar—with the metering rods still intact—out of the main body.

16. But before removing the nozzle bar, it's a good idea to check this capscrew holding the metering rods in place. Unless you suspect malfunctioning rods, there's no need to remove them from the unit.

17. The metering rods are quite fragile and should be left intact unless replacement is indicated. Replace the gasket at the bottom of the nozzle bar and make sure that it fits over the booster venturi lips.

18. Fuel inlet needle seat is removed as last step inside. Too-loose installation of seat by factory on some units has led to all kinds of problems with the 2150—in some cases, they weren't even installed.

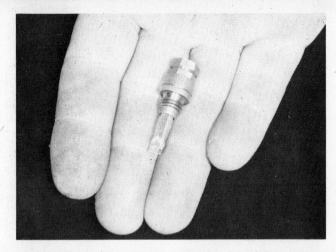

19. Main jets are not removed for routine cleaning/overhaul. Insert new filter in fuel inlet nozzle seat for replacement in main body. As screen fits seat snugly, make sure it's all the way in before installing.

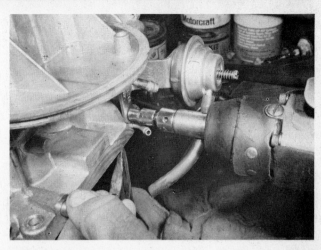

20. Before dunking the carb in cleaner, remove the choke pulldown assembly—one screw and a connecting link does it. Don't touch adjusting screw on rear of pulldown and you'll have no problems after it's replaced.

21. Begin reassembly by installing a new gasket on the enrichment valve and screwing valve into seat. Tighten very snugly with a wrench ... but, despite your best efforts, it'll probably still leak in use.

22. Carefully fit booster venturi and metering rod assembly into place and seat properly, then install the discharge check ball and drop the weight in on top of it. If you overlook this step, you're in trouble.

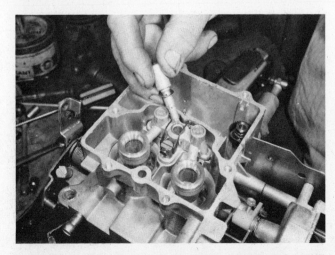

23. Fit the gasket to the booster venturi screw and install, making sure that the gasket is properly seated before you tighten the screw. Gasket seat is tapered and gasket will only fit in place one way.

24. Hang the fuel inlet needle on the float arm and drop into place; the inlet needle should fit into its seat and the float shaft into the main body cutouts. You may have to wiggle shaft into position.

HOW-TO: MOTORCRAFT 2150

25. Use a small screwdriver, as shown, to depress the float shaft retainer around the fuel inlet seat. This will hook the float in position for adjustment. Don't despair if it takes you a couple of tries to do this.

26. Dick Ward of Chaffee Motors in Hawthorne, Calif., does this for a living, so he can eyeball the float level without difficulty. Unless you're as proficient, we suggest that you take the trouble to measure it.

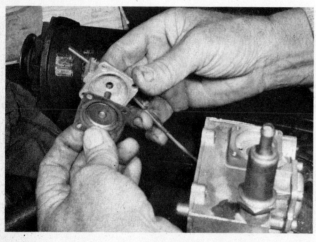

27. Install the accelerator pump diaphragm in the pump cover. Take pains to reinstall this carefully as it's easy to end up puncturing the diaphragm—and if you do that you're really going to be in for some problems.

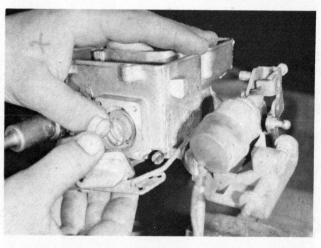

28. Seat a new elastomer valve in center hole of pump housing, then install shorter return spring, diaphragm and cover. Hold pump lever against case while tightening cover to prevent incorrect diaphragm seating.

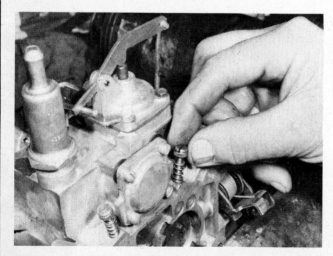

29. Install idle mixture screws with springs and turn inward until they touch seat. Back off the number of turns you counted in step 7 for preliminary adjustment. Limiter stops on valve cover provide positive stop for cap tabs.

30. Never try to reuse an old gasket. Place a new one in position on the main body. Correct gasket and proper fit are absolutely essential if the carburetor rebuild is to last any length of time.

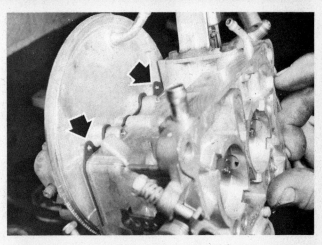

31. When you're ready to replace the air horn, position it so that the choke plate rod fits through the plastic dust seal and opening in main body. Be careful not to bend the velocity fuel feed pickup in the process, however.

32. Once the air horn is in place, turn the carburetor over on its side and check these two pins, which should engage holes in the gasket. If they don't, the air horn is not on correctly . . . try again.

33. If pins engage the gasket, replace the air horn attaching screws and tighten them down. Be sure to replace identification tag, as it contains information you'll need if parts must be ordered for a later rebuild.

34. Replace the choke gasket, then position the choke cap so that the tang on the end of the thermostatic coil engages the connecting arm slot. Line up the index marks and tighten the cap retaining screws.

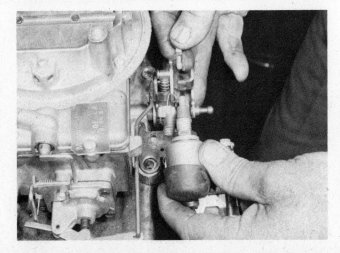

35. Set the throttle positioner solenoid in place and reconnect its spring to the linkage; then replace the two attaching screws that hold it to the carburetor body. Be certain that the assembly is tightened down securely.

36. Install a new gasket on the manifold and you're ready to drop the rebuilt 2150 carburetor back in place. Bolt down and reconnect the fuel line and all vacuum lines/hoses and you're ready to "fire it up."

HOW-TO: ROCHESTER QUADRAJET

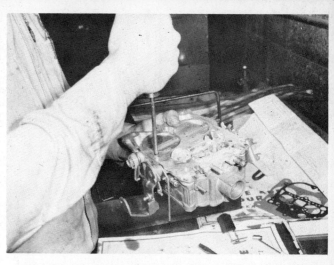

1. After cleaning, Quadrajet rebuild begins by fitting new gasket between fuel bowl assembly and throttle body. Two locating dowels on fuel bowl help to position it.

2. Throttle body screws are easy to find; they are the only Phillips-head screws used in the Rochester 4MV-4MC. Tighten evenly to secure the two units together properly.

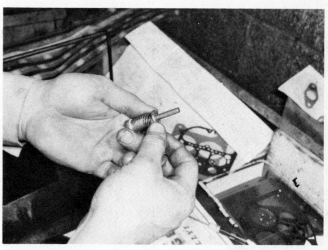

3. Install the power piston spring as shown. Some first-time enthusiasts attempt to fit the spring over the top of the accelerator pump piston and end up with a mess.

4. Compress spring and remove end clip on accelerator pump piston; remove old piston and replace it with the new one furnished in the rebuild kit.

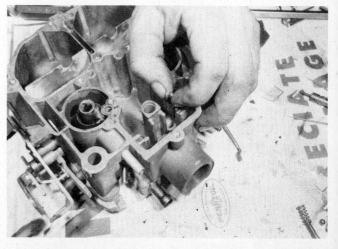

5. Install piston here. A spring goes in first—and here's where some first-timers make another error; they fit one spring right, but this one on top instead of underneath.

6. Now drop the pump discharge check ball in the little hole shown beneath it. This ball is also easy to lose, forget or misplace, so let's do it right—now.

7. Screw the pump discharge check ball's retaining plug in place and tighten down snugly. Unless you removed main jets for cleaning, you've finished the odds and ends.

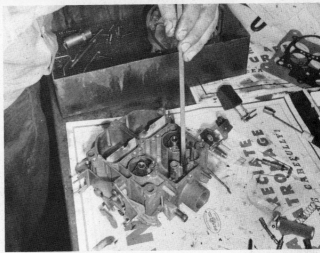

8. If you did remove the main jets, replace them now. Use the correct size screwdriver blade to fit into the slotted top, and be sure to screw in snugly.

9. Here's how the inside should look now: main jets (1), power piston spring (2), check ball and retaining plug (3) and accelerator pump piston and spring (4).

10. Float needle pull clip is not included in many rebuild kits; the old one is carefully removed and then installed in the new float needle.

11. Hang float hinge pin from float lever and position float needle pull clip, then slip the needle/diaphragm assembly into position. Set into needle seat in bowl.

12. Install power piston assembly in well with metering rods properly positioned in metering jets. Press down firmly to ensure that retainer is flush with top of bore.

HOW-TO: ROCHESTER QUADRAJET

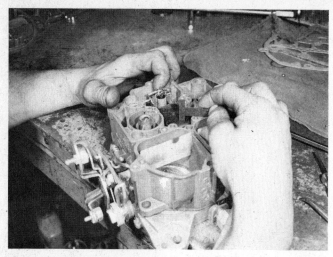

13. Use float level measuring device provided in rebuild kit and refer to adjustment chart (also included) for correct level. To bend float arm, push on pontoon.

14. Now fit the float retainer in place and gently push down to seat in position. Check to make sure everything has been installed before proceeding.

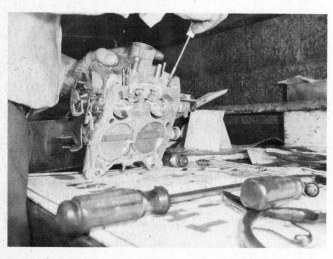

15. Install the idle mixture adjusting needles and springs. Turn in all the way until they seat, then back off the number of turns counted when you removed them.

16. Position new air horn gasket. As more than one is furnished in kit, make certain you use the correct one—and make sure it's positioned properly.

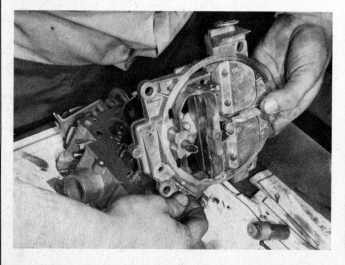

17. Before setting air horn in place, you'll have to angle it to slip connecting linkage into accelerator pump lever as shown—there's no other way to make the hookup.

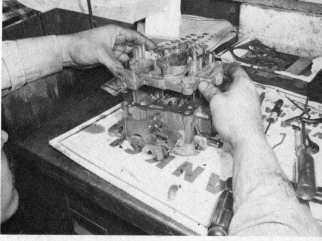

18. You'll find it easier to fit the air horn to the bowl without the metering rods attached; make sure that vent tubes and well tubes fit through gasket properly.

19. Install the two countersunk screws in primary venturi area, then drop metering rods and air valve arm in place and fit screw, checking valve action before tightening.

20. Insert choke plate rod and hook it at the bottom, then slip top end into slotted lever controlling butterfly and replace the small retaining clip to hold in position.

21. Slip rear vacuum break into attachment lever and press all the way in by hand, then connect linkage in place and check for proper operation.

22. Install front vacuum break in the same manner; connect linkage and control hose on both units. Bend the attachment arms slightly to secure the units.

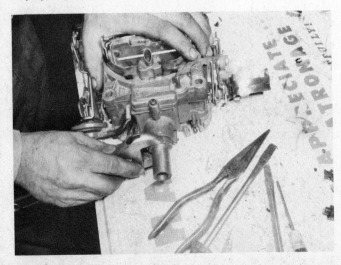

23. Fuel filter on newer models is longer, but still the same configuration. A spring goes in first, then the filter (gasket end first). Tighten securely.

24. Rebuild is now complete; you can replace the carburetor on intake manifold (use a new gasket), hook up lines/hoses and make the necessary idle adjustments.

HOW-TO: MOTORCRAFT 5200

1. The 5200 series 1971-73 Holley/Weber carbs utilize hot water to actuate the choke. The '74 and later 2300cc engines use both water and electrical heat to control choke. Vacuum-controlled valve on the manifold leans the air/fuel ratio.

2. Jerry Spotts of Bonneville fame removes the Pinto carb for this overhaul story. Note: If you haven't found it out yet, Pintos are all metric. You will need a complete set of metric tools. Jerry used an 11mm swivel socket here.

3. Close-up reveals the hot water choke control (center), the vacuum-operated acceleration boost pump (left) and the vacuum-operated automatic choke hold-off valve (right). Deceleration valve connection is above boost pump.

4. Remove the hot water chamber from the choke control. It will have to be cleaned thoroughly to remove rust and sediment. Later units have a bimetal electrical heater that operates to open choke before radiator water is hot.

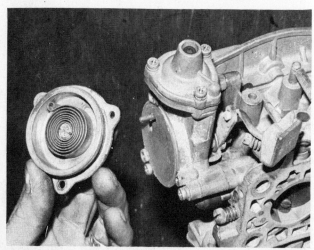

5. Hot water actuates the old, familiar, thermostatic choke control spring. Three screws retain this assembly, as in the past. Electric heater unit in later models complicates the disassembly procedure only slightly from that shown.

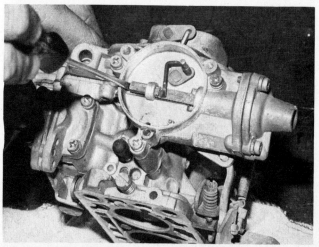

6. Screwdriver actuates choke hold-off slide here. Test for freedom of movement. This unit opens butterfly valves via vacuum when engine starts. It avoids flooding and allows the engine to run at a fast idle. Travel adjustment is at right.

7. Remove screws holding the choke hold-off assembly to carburetor. Engine vibration often loosens these screws, so be sure to use a drop of blue Loctite on threads during reassembly. Always use proper size screwdrivers.

8. Careful twisting and maneuvering is required to disconnect the linkage. Make a note of how linkage is fitted. Better yet, make a sketch. Needless to say, linkage must always go back in the correct position or trouble will ensue.

9. Removal of choke hold-off reveals fast idle control screw at rear of hold-off assembly. Main idle control screw is just behind throttle control arm. Note tiny O-ring (arrow) that seals vacuum passage to hold-off valve.

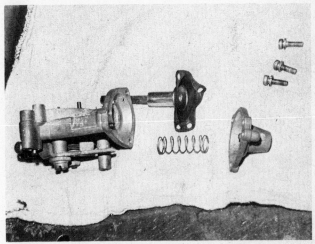

10. Disassembly of choke hold-off unit reveals piston and diaphragm assembly. Rebuild kit (Motorcraft No. CT-858A) provides a new assembly. Don't let the spring fly out when removing cover. The screw in the cover adjusts hold-off travel.

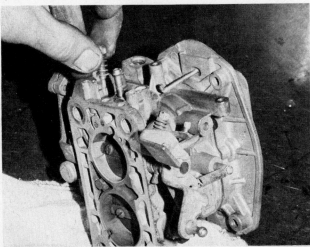

11. Here Jerry removes the idle air adjusting needle. The smaller bore is the primary side of the carb, while the larger bore is the secondary system. Keep this in mind as you take things apart; don't mix parts from different sides.

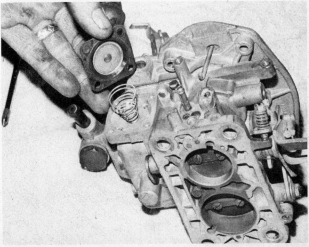

12. Remove the vacuum-controlled acceleration booster pump cover and diaphram. Watch for spring and note that it goes in with the large end outboard. Rebuild kit supplies a new diaphragm. Vacuum control simplifies design and operation.

HOW-TO: MOTORCRAFT 5200

13. Remove cover screws and lift cover off, straight up. Here again, be sure to use the proper size screwdrivers. The blade must fit the screw slot exactly, because screws are steel, but jets are brass and can be ruined very easily.

14. Primary and secondary bores are the same size at the top. Primary and secondary are linked mechanically. The secondary begins to open after primary is ⅓-open, and both reach full open together. Carb flows about 290 cfm.

15. To remove floats and needle valve, slip pivot pin out with needle-nose pliers. For larger engines (or racing), the primary can be bored to size of secondary. Parts swapping will produce a 312-cfm carb that can really get with it.

16. The needle valve lifts out of its housing along with the floats. Note that these floats are molded foam blocks. Occasionally they soak up fuel and become heavy, thus negating float level setting. Floats should be very light.

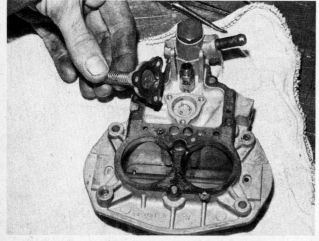

17. Remove three screws that secure power valve to carb cover. Repair kit will have a new diaphragm. Spring-wound plunger reaches to bottom of carb bowl, actuating metering jet to supply additional fuel under heavy acceleration.

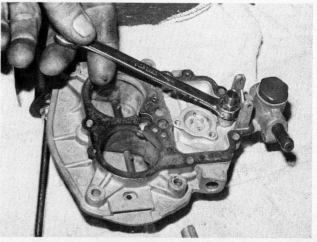

18. Use a box-end wrench to remove needle valve housing from carb cover. Note .160-in. fuel inlet opening in brass hose nipple. Pre-'72 carbs had full .250-in. fuel inlet. Fitting can be twisted out; drill to .250-in. for competition.

19. Brass plug covers internal fuel strainer screen. Remove screen and wash thoroughly. Jets are very small, so even a tiny particle of dirt will affect performance. Hose nipple is a press fit; it can be twisted out with vise-grip pliers.

20. Power jet has a tiny needle valve actuated by vacuum-controlled plunger from carb cover. Depress needle and remove jet from bottom of bowl. This jet transfers fuel from primary to secondary circuit when throttle nears wide open.

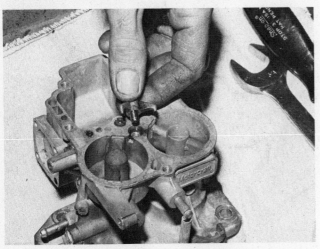

21. Remove the acceleration pump fuel nozzle cluster. One screw secures the little cluster. A new gasket is in the kit. Note how tiny the orifices are. Everything must be kept scrupulously clean on assembly; this is critical.

22. Be careful—after nozzle cluster is removed, invert the carb body and catch the two tiny ball checks. It is essential that these get put back upon reassembly. These are the smallest parts you will have to keep track of, and no problem.

23. There is a pair of air-bleed jets, one on each side of the carb bowl near the top. Unscrew the jets. Note that the jet itself slips out of the end of the screw. Don't mix up the jets from different sides; primary is slightly larger.

24. The two small jets on top of carb bowl are high-speed air jets and emulsifier tubes, one primary and one secondary. Don't get them mixed up. Tag them if you have to. All jets and passages are very small, so compressed air is a must.

HOW-TO: MOTORCRAFT 5200

25. Use a fine-mesh basket to lower the disassembled carb parts into the carb cleaning solution. Don't put floats or any rubber or plastic parts in cleaner. If carb is very dirty, clean parts with solvent first to save cleaning solution.

26. While carb parts soak in solution for about an hour, remove and inspect the decelerator valve. Hold fitting with a wrench and tap valve with rubber mallet to unscrew from intake manifold. Most rough idle problems are due to this valve.

27. Decelerator valve opens by vacuum when throttle is closed as engine decelerates. Valve bleeds fresh air into intake manifold to lean air/fuel ratio, thus reducing emissions. Bottom diaphragm is prone to rupture; always check it first.

28. Remove parts from carb cleaner and wash thoroughly with high-pressure water. Next, use compressed air to blow out all the jets and passages. Once reassembled, even a trace of water in carb will cause rough engine operation.

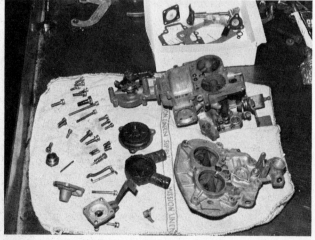

29. Be neat! Lay out all the parts and pieces on a very clean surface when ready to reassemble. All flanges must be clean; linkages and shafts must move freely. Note that carb rebuild kit in background has all new gaskets and needles.

30. Check venturi ring assemblies with fingertips. They are often loose in bore, resulting in leaks and poor fuel atomization. That little 4-banger vibrates a lot. The two jets in bottom of bowl are primary/secondary mains.

31. If venturi rings are loose, they can be restaked with a sharp center punch. Be careful—that carb body is only pot metal. Stake both ends carefully to lock the rings in place. Fuel is atomized into the airstream via these rings.

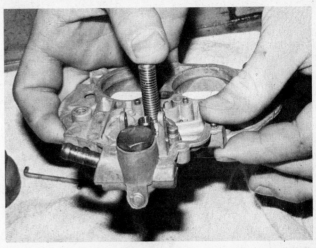

32. After new power valve diaphragm assembly is installed, check by pressing plunger down and covering vacuum hole at edge of cover with tip of thumb. Plunger should remain depressed until thumb is removed from vacuum passage.

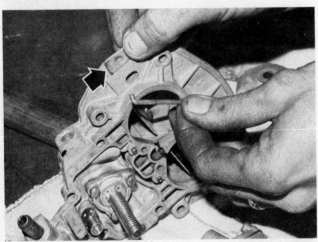

33. Now is the time to refer to your sketches. You are ready to install the linkage. Note the tiny plastic guide (arrow) that must be installed in cover flange. The double-staked end of this short link goes to the carburetor body.

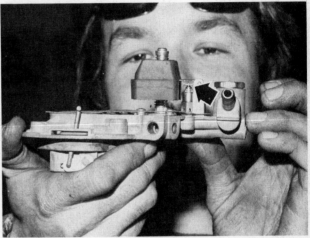

34. Jerry relies on eyeball engineering when setting the float level. Floats must be set so that the top of the float is parallel with the carb cover flange. Invert cover and eyeball the setting. Bend tab over needle valve to adjust.

35. Use a sharp-edged tool to carefully scrape the flanges of the hot water thermostatic choke cover. Flanges must be smooth, clean and seat perfectly with thermostat spring housing to prevent leaks. Kit provides new gaskets.

36. Adjust choke butterfly tension by rotating thermostat cover in the usual manner. Jerry uses a .040-in. drill bit between butterfly and air horn. Release tension slowly until bit falls free. You can use a piece of thin cardboard.

TUNING YOUR CARBURETOR

Ever since carburetors appeared on automobiles, mechanics have been following a standard procedure for adjusting and repairing them. There have been some changes because of exhaust gas analyzers and tachometers, but basically the carburetor repairman relies on the same two tools as the earliest mechanics, a screwdriver and knowledge.

The screwdriver is easy; the knowledge something else. So let's go through the procedure on carburetors, from the time it is running, through the repairs, to the time when it's ready to go again. This won't make a carburetor expert out of you, but it will show you how a carburetor man works on carbs, and that's a real good place to start.

Usually, nobody pays much attention to the engine in their car until it gives trouble. This is not a good idea, but since this is the way most people have their cars repaired, let's assume that our car is acting up. The carburetor may be the easiest thing on the engine to reach and fiddle with, but actually the carburetor should be the last part suspected of causing trouble.

Ignition and compression should be checked first. When you are sure that the plugs, wires, and distributor are in good shape, and the compression is reasonably even between all cylinders, then it's time to take a look at the carburetor.

Before changing anything, or even removing the air cleaner, an exhaust gas analyzer should be hooked up to the tail pipe and a tachometer hooked to the engine. Suppose you get a reading of 11-to-1 air/fuel ratio. Most engines idle at 12-to-1, so you would assume that this carburetor is running rich and the gas mileage is bad. You don't need an exhaust gas analyzer to tell you the mileage is bad, so why use it? Let's suppose that you overhaul the carb, put it all back together and the engine still runs at 11-to-1. This would tell you instantly that whatever is wrong still isn't fixed.

Of course, you could drive the car until you used up a tank of gas, and that would tell you if the mileage problem was cured. The modern mechanic hasn't the time for that, so he uses instruments that get the answers quicker and make his work just a little more accurate than the man who uses only hand tools. This doesn't mean that you have to have a lot of fancy and expensive instruments to work on your own carbu-

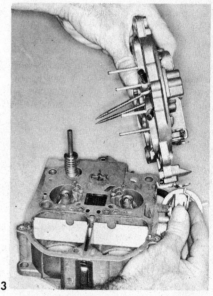

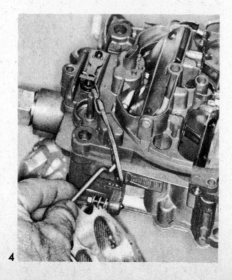

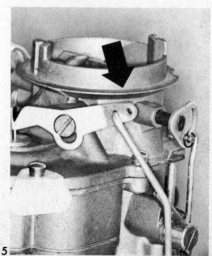

retor. Most of the time simple hand tools will be good enough, but you should know about the instruments so that if you get in trouble you can hunt up someone who has them.

In California an automobile repair shop cannot be licensed as an official pollution control device station unless the shop has a specified number of instruments and a man who knows how to use them.

ADJUSTING THE IDLE

The tachometer is hooked up before starting work on the carburetor so that you have a basis for change. Suppose you adjust the idle to 550 rpm, which is correct for your car. But the engine keeps dying, which it never did before. If the tachometer had been hooked up before adjust-

1. Part of carburetor overhaul is checking the filters. In this selection of Rochester carbs we find a filter at each carburetor inlet. Some are paper and some are bronze. Don't attempt to clean any of them. Even the bronze ones must be replaced, because the pores fill up with dirt. Lower quadrajet with solenoid throttle has late-style filter that is really just a screen, and not a very fine one at that.

2. The choke rod on a 4MV is hooked up after everything is assembled by fishing down into the little dark hole underneath the choke lever. If done right, rod will slip into place easily without force.

3. Hooking up the rods on a 4MV carburetor can sometimes be difficult to figure out. To hook up the rod between the vacuum break and the air valve, you have to tip the bowl cover sideways like this, and then lower the cover onto the carburetor after rod has been hooked up.

4. Getting the accelerating pump rod hooked up on a 4MV can be tricky. The bowl cover and bowl assembly must be tipped to the side, so that the rod can be hooked up before the throttle body is attached.

5. Accelerating pumps are adjustable by bending the rod or moving to a second hole, as on this Carter BBS.

6. When replacing choke coils, be certain the hook on the coil is on the correct side of the lever. If it isn't hooked over the lever properly, the choke won't work at all. If the coil is removed from the cover, it must be replaced the same way, or the coil will work backwards, and you won't have any choke action.

7. This Carter YF is adjusted one notch rich. If the two long marks coincide, the setting is called "on the index."

8. A well-type choke is being used on many makes of cars now whereas formerly it appeared only on Chrysler products. If the nut is loosened, the choke coil can be adjusted rich or lean, according to the marks. Most factories recommend that you leave the coil alone and make any needed adjustment by bending the rod as required.

ing the idle, you might have found that the engine was idling at 600 rpm. It was probably set that high because the engine was dying at 550.

This doesn't mean that the manufacturer's specifications should be ignored. It does mean that all engines are not alike. Some require a slightly different adjustment than others. Anybody can read a specification sheet and set idle with a tach. A good carburetor man will also read the spec sheet, but he will use that only as a starting point. Then he will make the settings as they are needed on the particular engine he is fixing. This applies to any part of the car, the engine, the front end, or even the deck lid.

If the engine is idling at a reasonable curb idle, the first thing to check is the idle mixture needle sensitivity. Screw each needle in, one at a time, until they bottom. This must be done gently so that the needles are not damaged, preferably with the fingers. If it can be done with the air cleaner on, that's good.

On most cars it will be necessary to remove the cleaner before you can even find the carburetor.

As the needles are screwed in, the engine will start running very rough or may even die. This is a good indication, because it means that particular idle passage was doing its job. If there is no effect when any one of the mixture needles is turned in, it means that the passage is evidently blocked by dirt and the carburetor will have to be cleaned.

The same thing applies when the needles are screwed out, although it does not have as marked an effect. Some carburetors cause very little change when the needle is unscrewed. Late-model carburetors with exhaust emission control do funny things when the needles are unscrewed. On some there is a stop so that the needle breaks off if unscrewed forcefully. On others the needle just falls out of the carburetor, and there are others that won't richen the mixture no matter how far the needle is backed out.

6

7

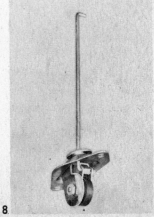

8

TUNING YOUR CARBURETOR

When you turn the needle in, you are leaning the mixture. Turning it out richens the mixture. Each needle should be turned in, then out, to check for sensitivity. Then the needle should be adjusted to give the highest and smoothest engine rpm. This will usually be somewhere in the middle, between the lean fall-off point and the rich falloff point, if there is one.

Each car manufacturer makes slightly different recommendations for adjusting idle mixture, but they are all similar. The thing to remember is that the leaner you make it, the better gas mileage you will get, but the engine also will have a tendency to die. If the mixture screw is left out ¼ turn or less from the high-rpm point, gas mileage will suffer slightly, but the idle will be much more dependable.

One mixture screw should be adjusted, and then another one until all are done. Then you should repeat the process for a finer adjustment. If the engine speed becomes too high or low as a result of adjusting the mixture screws, then the idle-speed screw should be reset to the

speed you want. After that, go over the mixture screws again. Repeat as many times as necessary to get a smooth idle at the right speed.

On cars with ignition-induction exhaust smog controls, the situation is slightly different. Instead of 12-to-1, these engines idle at about 14-to-1. Idle is still adjusted to the midpoint between lean and rich, but the correct air/fuel ratio must be maintained at the same time. The idle needles have an extremely fine thread. A movement as small as 1/16 of a turn will affect the air/fuel ratio. On Chrysler Corporation cars with Clean Air Package exhaust control, the idle air/fuel ratio must be kept between 14.0-to-1 and 14.2-to-1.

Many late model cars have special instructions for idle setting so the engines will comply with emission regulations. In many cases, following the instructions results in a poor idle, but that is necessary to prevent poisoning our atmosphere. All 1971 Rochester carburetors used on GM cars are set by computer at the factory. Then a limiter cap is put on the idle mixture needles so they cannot

be adjusted. Chrysler Corp. has used limiter caps for years, but they allowed about 3/4 of a turn so that the mixture could be adjusted enough to take care of the slight differences between engines. The Rochester limiter caps on '71 carbs do not allow any adjustment.

Because the limiter caps do not allow any adjustment, many dealer mechanics are scared to death to touch the car. They think there is some law that will get them 20 years in Sing Sing if they attempt adjustments. Let's squelch that rumor right now. The law says (if your state has any laws at all about emissions) that the car must be adjusted according to the *manufacturer's recommendations*. If these mechanics that are so afraid to touch the '71 cars would read their official Chevrolet or other GM division service manual, they would find that there is a definite procedure for adjusting the carburetor. It involves breaking off the limiter caps (without bending the mixture needles, we hope) adjusting the needles, and then installing new limiter caps.

In the Chevrolet manual, two pro-

1. The vacuum break pulls the choke open when the engine starts. How much it pulls it open is determined on this Carter BBS by varying the angle of the "U" in the link, which can be adjusted by bending gently.

2. Some chokes can really be complicated, as on this Carter YF. You must have the Carter specification sheet if you are going to do the job correctly.

3. In an ordinary carb cleaning or overhaul, it isn't necessary to remove the throttle plates. If you do remove them to install a new throttle shaft, be sure they are marked so you can get them back in the same holes.

4. You may not like air cleaners, but they won't do you any harm if they are clean. Hold a light behind the filter element to see if it is clean or not.

5. Removing this cap on the bottom of your Autolite 2100 2-barrel reveals the power valve.

6. Idle settings should be done with a tachometer if you want to get them right. Idle may not seem important, but it has to be correct or you will get a stumble.

7. Autolite and Holley use a similar power valve. Holes in side don't meter fuel; they just allow it to pass through.

8. These two holes underneath an Autolite or Holley power valve meter the fuel when the power valve is open.

9. The proper tool makes all the difference—like this Proto wrench made expressly for removing main jets. You'll save ruining a lot of jets by using this handy gizmo.

cedures are given, one if you have a carbon monoxide (CO) meter, and another if you don't. Without the CO meter, you should follow the instructions on the tune-up sticker to be sure the ignition system is in good shape. Remove and plug the distributor vacuum hose and fuel tank vapor hose. Then the mixture needles should be unscrewed four turns from the seated position. Idle speed is then adjusted with the throttle cracking screw to an "initial idle speed." After that, the mixture needles are screwed in (leaner) to reach a "final idle speed." Then new limiter caps are pushed onto the mixture screws, the hoses hooked up, and the job is done. If you are tempted to leave the limiter caps off, remember that your car may not pass state inspection if the inspector notices the caps are missing.

Setting idle speed and mixture on late model cars is a science in itself. The days when a man with nothing but a good ear could make an engine idle smooth are gone forever. A tune-up man still needs the good ear, but he also needs the written procedure for the car he is working on, and some accurate tune-up test instruments. Following are some of the things that must be considered when setting idle on late model cars.

1. Engine must be at operating temperature. This usually means at least a 20 minute warmup at fast idle or on the road.
2. Ignition timing must be right, including initial timing, vacuum advance, and centrifugal advance.
3. Choke must be open.
4. Hot idle compensator must be closed.
5. Headlights must be on when setting some models with alternators. This loads the engine with the charging alternator.
6. Air conditioners usually must be on, but some models require that it be off.
7. A new or rebuilt engine with less than 50 miles on it may loosen up and increase idle speed in the next 100 miles.
8. Do specifications apply with air cleaner on or off car?
9. Are specifications up to date, including any late changes?
10. Does engine have correct stock equipment, or have some things been changed which would require a different idle speed?
11. Some automatic transmissions with variable pitch require the blades be moved to a different angle while setting idle. This is done by operating the kickdown switch on the carburetor.
12. Should engine be in drive or neutral?

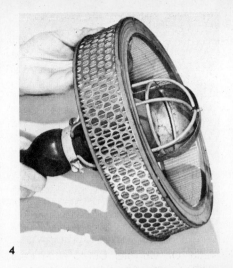

4

5

6

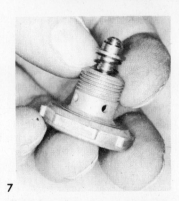

7

8

9

TUNING YOUR CARBURETOR

13. Idle vent valve may require re-setting after idle is set.

14. Air/fuel ratio must be set to specifications, but smooth idle must also be maintained.

15. Tune-up equipment must be accurate. It should be checked periodically at a laboratory.

16. Vacuum release parking brakes must be disconnected from engine vacuum when setting idle in drive range. If this is not done, the mechanic may have great difficulty making accurate settings because he has to run alongside the car while it drives down the street by itself.

17. For a true reading on exhaust gas analyzers, any exhaust emission air pump must be disconnected, and the air cleaner must be on the carburetor. On dual exhaust cars, analyzer must take samples from side opposite heat riser valve.

18. Hot idle speed-up mechanisms must be off. One of these may be in the cooling system. It increases idle speed by advancing distributor when engine is hot.

You can see that idle speed and mixture settings are not to be taken lightly, and certainly cannot be done correctly by just anybody stabbing around with a screwdriver.

A vacuum gauge is valuable in adjusting idle, probably just as valuable as a tachometer as far as sensitivity goes. When using a vacuum gauge the idle should be adjusted to give the highest vacuum reading.

The problem with modern cars is that most of them don't have any place to hook up a vacuum gauge. It can take as long as 10 minutes just to take fittings off the engine so the vacuum gauge can be used. For this reason, very little tuning is done today with a vacuum gauge.

If the idle mixture needles lack sensitivity, then it will be difficult to get a satisfactory idle. The only remedy is cleaning the carburetor. If the problem is an accumulation of deposits around the throttle valve, then you can pour special cleaning solvents through the carburetor while the engine is running at a fast idle. However, this method will definitely not clean deposits out of the air bleeds, and that is usually where most of the trouble is.

If you do clean the carburetor on the car, there is a simple test you can make to tell if the solvent you have chosen will really do the job. Select a space on the outside of the carburetor that is covered with that typical brown or red gasoline stain, and pour some of the solvent on the stain. If the solvent is really high-powered, it will dissolve the stain instantly, leaving clean metal as it runs off. Some of these chemicals will do the same thing to the car paint, if you are unlucky enough to spill them.

Pouring solvent through the carburetor has its place. Every time a car is tuned up, one of those high-powered chemicals should be poured through the air horn to give

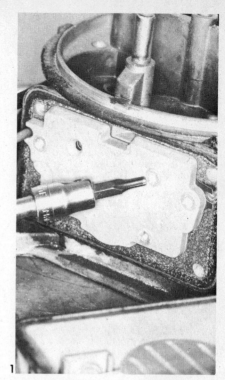

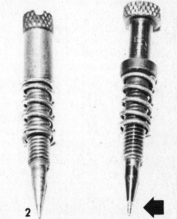

1. *Clutch-type screws hold the secondary metering body onto the Holley's main housing—which necessitates the purchase of a special headed screwdriver.*

2. *Turn the idle-mixture needles in too tight and you'll dig a groove in them that makes adjustments difficult.*

3. *Some car owners go around looking for hot rod modifications, when all they really need is a good tune-up. A little of this juice poured down the carburetor while the engine is running will do wonders to clean the carbuncles out of the combustion chamber.*

4. *Before trying to modify your carburetor, make sure your fuel system is in good shape. If this filter has seen lots of miles, it could be partially plugged.*

5. *Oldsmobile 2GC for '71 has the plastic caps that don't allow any adjustment of the mixture screws.*

6. *Closeup of the '71 Rochester cap shows the double tang that prevents movement of the screw.*

7. *Limiter caps on the idle-mixture needles (arrows) are supposed to prevent anyone from unscrewing them far enough to get the mixture too rich. This is a 4MV quadrajet model.*

8. *To check float level on this Holley 1920, you invert the carburetor and measure from the top of the float to the top of the bowl, with just the weight of the float resting on the needle.*

5

6

7

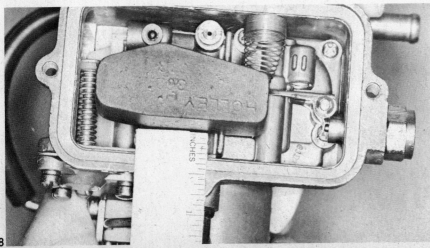

8

the carburetor and engine a good physic. But if the carburetor is dirty and insensitive to adjustment, then there is only one way to clean it, and that is by removing it, taking it apart, and putting the pieces in the "soup."

Before you take the carburetor off the engine, be sure that parts are available. If you buy the parts from a general store, chances are that all they will want to know is the year and model of the car. In turn, they will supply you with a kit that will have all the parts you need to put the carburetor back together. The only problem you might have is that the carburetor on your car might have been changed, or you may own a car that had as many as four different original equipment carburetors on the same engine in one year.

CARBURETOR IDENTIFICATION

If you have this kind of problem, you should identify the carburetor by its part number, then go to an automotive parts house which will be able to get the right kit direct from the manufacturer of the carburetor. In some instances a parts house will be able to supply a kit even though they don't handle your make of carburetor. This has been true only in recent years, because of the tremendous competition in parts merchandising. Some carburetor manufacturers make more parts for other makes of carburetors than they do for their own.

To identify the carburetor, you find the number on it. The number you are looking for is the part number, not the model number. The model number is just a designation of the type of carburetor. For example, Carter makes the AFB, BBS, and BBD carbs. Rochester makes the BV, 2GV, and 4MV carbs. In Holley we have the 1920, 2300, and 4160 models. Stromberg makes the WW, and WWC. Ford puts out the 1100, 2100, 4100, and 4300. These are all model numbers. What you need to buy parts is the part number, and that is sometimes a little tricky to find.

Carter carbs usually have the part number stamped on a tag attached by one bowl cover screw. Sometimes the number is stamped into the edge of the throttle body flange. The number usually has four digits, followed by an "S" and maybe some additional letters, such as 4325S, 4211SA, or 4135SB. The "S" stands for assembly. If there is no additional letter following the "S" it means the carburetor is the original design. An "A" or "B" following the "S" means that slight improvements have been

TUNING YOUR CARBURETOR

made in succeeding designs of the same carburetor.

If the tag is gone, and there is no number on the carburetor, it can be identified by casting number or by the sizes of the various parts. It's not easy, but it can be done. Authorized Carter outlets have the information you need in this case.

Rochester carburetors have the number either on a tag or stamped on the carburetor. The tag usually has the complete number, but if the number is on the carburetor it may have only the last four or five digits. One-barrel models such as B, BC, or BV models have the numbers stamped into the mounting gasket surface of the throttle body. If the tag is missing, the carburetor must be removed from the manifold to identify it.

4GC models have the number stamped on the bowl cover, as wel as on the tag. Two-barrels and 4MC or 4MV models can be identified only by tag. If the tag is gone, some carburetor men can identify the carburetor because they are familiar with the designs used in certain years. Rochester numbers run seven digits long, such as 7037058, or 7027101.

Holley uses combinations of letters and numbers on early carbs. Examples are R3489AAS, R-1864-1AAS, or R-3575A. However, only the numbers will appear on the carburetor. Single-barrels usually have it on the fuel inlet. Two-barrels have the number on a tag, on the throttle body, on the air horn or on the bowl cover. Four-barrels have it on the throttle body or air horn. Holley calls this the list number, and the word "List" will be stamped in front of the numbers.

Recently, Holley has made a change in their numbering system. All carburetor numbers are now a combination of "1-" followed by a number. For example, the R-3130AAS carburetor is now the 1-81. Either number can be used to identify the carburetor.

Stromberg carburetors used on the old flathead Fords had a large number cast into the side of the main body, such as 97, 48, or 81. Things were simpler in those days. All you needed to know was that the carburetor was a "97" and you could get parts for it. The "97" actually was the size of the venturi in hundredths of an inch, but all the parts men knew what you meant, and they would look up the carburetor by the actual part number. The situation is different with Stromberg these days.

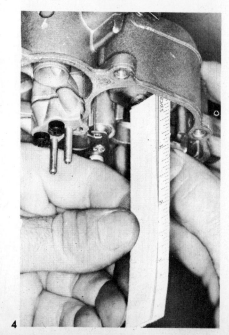

1. Checking float level can be done with a scale or with a gauge. When the float is this wide, as on the Autolite 4300, the gauge is a necessity.

2. On this Carter AFB, the float level is measured with the bowl cover inverted and the gasket in place.

3. Checking float drop is usually done with a scale. It's important that the needle drop enough so fuel can enter.

4. Carter BBD float level is measured from the top of the float to the top edge of the bowl with the carburetor inverted, so that the float rests on the closed needle. You have to hold the float pin with your thumb in order to obtain an accurate measurement.

5. This small tang on the float arm can be easily bent to change the float level. On this model Holley, the float has to be set dry because there is no external adjustment.

6. Little "E" ring must be removed from this Holley float pin in order to take the float out of the primary bowl.

7. Float in the secondary bowl is removed the same way. Note the spring attached to the float. It is designed to seat in the little channel built into the bowl.

8. Float level adjustment is usually achieved through bending a float arm or tang. This 4-barrel carburetor features both methods. On the left is the bending point for setting the level, and on the right is the adjustment for float drop.

9. We don't recommend this on a stock carburetor, but we took the choke plate out so that you could get a clear view of the accelerating pump on this Holley 4-barrel model.

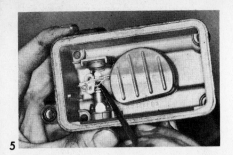

5   6   7

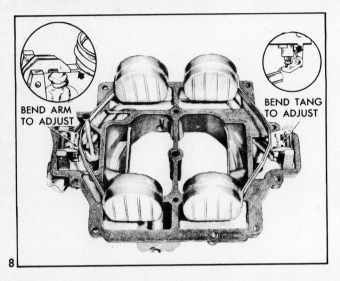

BEND ARM TO ADJUST

BEND TANG TO ADJUST

8

9

Now Stromberg's are identified by a code number stamped into the bowl cover near the fuel inlet or on a tag. The number usually looks something like this: 3-150, 15-24, 6-130, or 7-114A. The first digit indicates the make of car. The rest of the code is used to look up the actual part number of the carburetor, and all the things that wear out inside it.

Ford puts carburetor numbers either on a tag or on the bowl cover or throttle body. A typical Ford number might be C7AF-9510-AD. The 9510 means "carburetor," so that is left out when the number is put on the carb. It ends up looking like this: C7AF-AD. Late model Ford carburetors are also known as Autolite carburetors, because they are made by the Autolite-Ford Parts Division of Ford Motor Company.

The numbers discussed so far are put on the carburetor by the manufacturer. You may also find other numbers which are put there by the car maker. If Chevrolet uses Carter carbs, then the Chevrolet part number may also appear on the carb, and if you go into a Chevrolet dealer to get parts you should identify the carb by the Chevrolet number, not the Carter number. The same is true of Ford, Plymouth, or any other car maker. However, many of the new car dealer parts men will work with you on this and translate the numbers back and forth into whatever is needed.

So now that you know what carburetor you have, the decision must be made about what parts to buy. For most carburetors there are three choices, a gasket set, a light repair kit, or an overhaul kit. If you have been into the carburetor before, and you know from experience that the parts do not require replacement, then use the gasket set.

Most popular today is the light repair kit, known as a Zip Kit, Pep Tune-Up Kit, or other names, depending on the manufacturer. It includes a complete gasket set, and all the parts that usually require replacement, such as needle and seat, accelerating pump, and any rubber parts.

If you are having lots of trouble with a carburetor, and you suspect that someone has drilled the jets or installed the wrong parts, then use the complete overhaul kit, if available. It has virtually every part on the carburetor that can wear out or be left out except the throttle shaft.

Parts are also available individually. In fact, you can buy every part in every carburetor except one. In some, this unobtainable part is the throttle body, in some the float bowl or main body. I think the object is to keep somebody from assembling carburetors in his backyard in competition with the manufacturer. The manufacturers give other reasons, such as the necessity of flow testing the parts as an assembled carburetor and then disassembling it in

order to sell the pieces. Whatever the reason, this policy will not hamper your work on carburetors. A much bigger problem is finding a parts house that keeps a good supply of the parts that are available. You may have to place an order and wait.

REMOVING THE CARBURETOR

Now that you have the parts you can remove the carburetor, disassemble it, and drop it in the "soup." There are practical limits to this disassembly business. If all you are going to do is take the bowl cover off, then you would do better to leave the carburetor on the engine. Disassemble the carburetor as completely as is necessary for the replacement of all gaskets and rubber parts. It's also a good idea to remove the jets so the cleaning solution can readily enter all cavities, and so those same cavities can be blown dry before reassembly.

There are all kinds of cleaning solutions on the market. Some are available in a 3-gallon can, with a mesh basket included, which makes it easy to dunk the parts without letting the solution eat up your hands. A good solution is very powerful. Never put your hands in it, and don't under any circumstances allow it to splash into your eyes.

Leave the parts in the solution long enough to clean them. This may be only half an hour or 3 hours, depending on how dirty the carburetor is and how strong the solution. If the parts look bright and clean when you lift them out, then they are ready.

Let the cleaning solution drain off, and then submerge the basket in a bucket of clean solvent. Give the solvent a couple of minutes to get into all the nooks and crannies, and then remove each part and blow everything dry with compressed air. You can rinse the carburetor with a stream of water from a garden hose, but very hot or boiling water is better. Some mechanics have been doing this for years, but since there is a chance that some water may be left in a small passageway, it's better to use solvent. Gasoline and water don't mix very well.

At this point you need the specification sheet so the adjustments can be made as you assemble the carburetor. If you bought a Zip Kit or an overhaul kit, the spec sheet should have been in the box. Other than that, the specifications are available in many publications. Each carburetor maker puts out a book with the specifications of all his carburetors. Many repair manuals published by independent firms also have carb specs. If the specs are unobtainable, assemble the carburetor very carefully without bending anything, and the chances are it will run okay. This is definitely not recommended, but if the adjustments are not known, then it is the best you can do.

The most important adjustment, and usually the only one that is made inside the carburetor, is the float level. Some engines will die on turns if the float level is not set exactly as specified. Surging, dying, running rich, running lean, or hesitating can all be caused by improper float level. Sometimes a change is made to cure one or more of these complaints. In this case it is best to have the latest information from the car maker or carburetor manufacturer.

ADJUSTING THE REASSEMBLED CABURETOR

After the carburetor is completely assembled there are many adjustments that make it work right. Follow the spec sheet and make the adjustments in sequence. If anything is badly out of adjustment, there may be a good reason for it. Suppose the accelerating pump is set for an extremely long stroke. This may have been done to cure a flat spot. Changing the pump to the short stroke called for in the specifications may just cause the flat spot to reap-

pear, so be ready and willing to change it back.

Some spec sheets give an initial adjustment for the idle mixture needles and idle speed screw. If not, it's a good idea to check the position before tearing down the carburetor so they can be put back in the same place. If possible, start the engine cold so you can watch the action of the choke. The fast idle speed should be checked too. However, if you are going to adjust the fast idle speed to specifications, do it only when the engine is at operating temperature. As soon as the engine is warmed up, make the idle mixture and idle speed adjustments described in the beginning of this chapter.

At this time you should use the

1

2

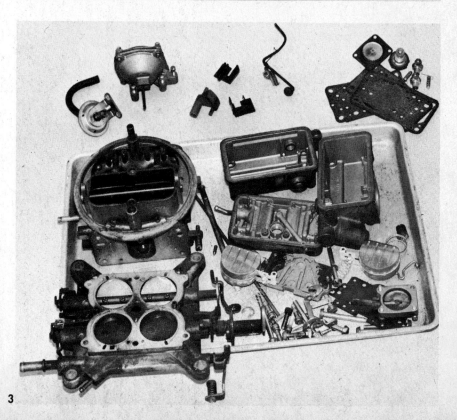

3

4

5

6

7

8

9

1. If you have a Rochester 4MV with stripped threads where the fuel inlet nut screws in, this self-threading steel fitting will save the carb.

2. Screw the fitting in part way by hand, and do the final tightening with a wrench. Many companies make these replacement fittings. On some, the threads are not long enough to get a good, safe bite. The replacement fitting should have several more threads than the old fitting.

3. To get a carburetor cleaned, strip it down far enough so that you can remove all gaskets and rubber parts. It isn't necessary to remove the throttle shafts or the choke shafts.

4. These two plugs on the bottom of Rochester 4MV's are famous for leaking. They make the car hard to start, because the fuel drains out of the bowl. To remove the old plugs, drive a nail into them enough to make a hole.

5. Thread a sheet metal screw into the hole and use a screwdriver to pry the plug and screw out of the hole.

6. If you work carefully, the plug will come right out of the hole.

7. Once the old plugs are out, the installation of this repair kit is easy.

8. The new aluminum plug, with an O-ring around it, slips into the hole and stops the leak. Do not drive the plug in. It's a slip fit. Hole at right is still stock.

9. The foam gasket fits in the cavity in the throttle body. When the carb is assembled, the foam presses against the plugs to prevent them from falling out. Result: no more leaks or hard starting.

exhaust gas analyzer and the tachometer. If the engine is not equipped with exhaust emission controls, it should idle at about 12.5-to-1, and at 2000 rpm in neutral the needle should swing over to approximately 14-to-1. Whenever the gas pedal is pushed down and released, the needle should swing to the rich side. This shows that the accelerating pump is working.

Some engines run rich, some lean. Experience is the best teacher when using an exhaust gas analyzer. If you work with one for any length of time you will discover all kinds of interesting facts. An analyzer can even be used to detect the need for a valve job, because leaky valves result in incomplete combustion which shows up as a rich mixture.

If you put an analyzer on a car with factory dual pipes, and get no reading, try the other pipe. Only one pipe works at low speeds because of the heat riser valve.

With a tachometer you can set idle speed a lot easier and more accurately. But don't expect to get fine readings from an instrument panel tach. They are intended to show shift points only. For tune-up work you need a sensitive garage-type instrument with an expanded scale. For good tune-up work you will be better off without any instruments than with cheap ones that are inaccurate and insensitive.

When synchronizing multiple carburetor installations the best and easiest way to get the mixture screws right is to unscrew them all the same distance from the fully seated position. If there are only four screws, as on a dual 4 barrel installation, then you can vary the setting of each screw to get a better idle. But if the installation has six screws, as on a flathead Ford with triplet manifold and simultaneous linkage, then a lot of trouble can be avoided by keeping all screws the same distance from the seated position.

When synchronizing throttle plates on multiple carbs with progressive mechanical linkage, the only necessary move is to be sure that the secondary carbs are wide open when the primary is. If the linkage is simultaneous, it's a different story. Then you must back off the idle speed screws and be sure each throttle plate closes fully in its bore. With the throttle plates held closed, hook up the rods between the carbs so they just slip into place without moving the plates. Then it is only necessary to use the idle speed screw on one carburetor to control all of them. You can use the speed screws on all carbs if you want, but this shouldn't be necessary unless the linkage is sloppy.

HOLLEY OPTIMIZING

Carburetor application and calibration is becoming an increasingly important factor in attaining optimum performance from contemporary engine designs. And though it may seem strange, up to a point the same basic approach to carburetor tuning may be used for either performance or economy.

Holley Carburetor Division of Colt Industries has been moving ahead in leaps and bounds for the last few years in order to offer the most efficient equipment for optimizing calibrations for your particular needs. Their complete line is much too extensive to cover here, but let's touch on some of the more important features of their various models, and investigate what may be done to mate these units to your engine.

Holley's unique modular construction is probably its greatest asset. With it, basic metering components can be applied to a variety of carb sizes, ranging from the 350-cfm model 2300 to the 1150-cfm R-4575 Though there are a number of different carburetors manufactured by Holley for O.E.M. and small-car applications, we're going to concentrate on four of their basic assemblies—the model R-2300 2-bbl., the 4160-4150 4-bbl.'s, the 3160 3-bbl., the 4500

''Dominator,'' and the latest 4165-4175 ''spread bore'' 4-bbl.'s.

For all practical purposes the above models are identical in operation, except for minor engineering differences. In fact, the ''modular'' component concept is responsible for the extended flexibility of application. In effect, components from models 2300, 3160, 4160, 4150 and 4500 are interchangeable—up to, but not including, the carb body and throttle assembly. The 4165-4175 models, on the other hand, are completely different designs, so fewer components can be swapped from the former models. However, this does not mean that the spread bore series can't be calibrated just as effectively as the earlier types.

If carburetor tuning is new to you, and you're planning to employ a Holley aftermarket model (or a rebuilt production model for that matter) on your engine, a good source of detailed tuning data is Holley's High Performance Parts catalog. Armed with this handbook, and the tuning tips we are about to outline, you should be able to get maximum performance and efficiency from your installation. It should be kept in mind, however, that the following data is aimed at improving *efficiency* of oper-

ation, which, when applied sensibly, will provide optimum performance *and* economy—within limits. So, before we delve into any actual tuning theory, let's consider carburetor capacity limitations.

CFM VS. ENGINE SIZE

The fact that Holley ''rates'' their carburetors in terms of airflow capacity at a given depression (3.0 and 1.5 ins. of mercury—Hg—for 2-bbl. and 4-bbl., respectively) in cubic feet per minute (cfm) is a great aid in applying a specific carburetor—but it can also be a hindrance. And numbers bare this out, as Holley's best-selling model is the 800-cfm, model 4150 double-pumper (list No. R-4780). What's so strange about that? Well, consider that for a small engine to flow that much air it must be in close to racing tune, yet the small-block Chevy is a favorite resting place for the 800! The following will give you some idea of the revs which are necessary to flow 800 cfm with various engines *at 100% volumetric efficiency (VE)*.

CU. INS.		RPM
262	=	10,550
283	=	9770
302	=	9150
327	=	8450

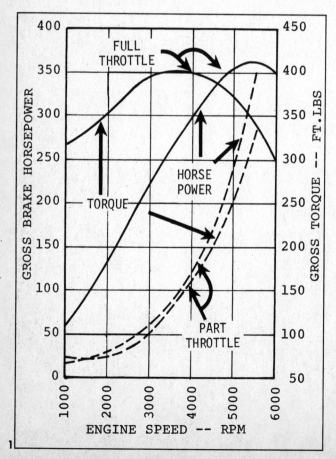

350	= 7900
373	= 7410
400	= 6910
427	= 6470
454	= 6090

From the above calculations it's obvious that the 800-cfm model would be a more practical big-block application. So, take heed! If you're looking for economy through efficient performance, you can't simply add a "high-performance" carburetor.

We also mentioned "100% VE," which equates to an engine inhaling air at a rate equal to its displacement. However, 100% efficiency is seldom attained, except in all-out racing engines. Typical values go something like this:

2-bbl. stocker	70-75%
4-bbl. stocker	75-80%
Hi-Po stocker	80-85%
4-bbl. semi-race	85-90%
4-bbl. racer	88-92%
8-bbl. all-out	90-95%
8-bbl. hi-ram	90-105%

Of course, there are many variables from engine to engine, since some just breathe better than others, but the above estimates can be used reliably in most situations.

1. These typical high-performance torque and horsepower curves illustrate the main difference between the amount of engine performance available vs. that which is actually needed during part-throttle operation.

2. This carburetor top view more clearly illustrates the use of smaller primary venturis (left) in the new emissions carbs. Note also that different booster venturis are employed for an improved main signal, along with the "new" butterfly accelerator pump shooters that first appeared in the spread-bore series.

3. Holley's latest 4150/4160 emissions series carburetors (left) have taken on a new look. Like the spread-bore, but less radical, the primary venturis and throttle bores are smaller than the secondaries. The reason for this is to improve emissions values and fuel economy without sacrificing overall performance. Thus, the full-power calibrations are similar, with the rear throttles handling most of the air/fuel mixing chores under full throttle.

4. Most Holley aftermarket carburetors are supplied with linkage that is compatible with OEM equipment. For example, the only adjustment required on this 4175 Blazer installation was the choke actuating rod and the transmission kickdown link.

5. For hot summer months, a special "phenolic" heat barrier spacer is available to insulate the carb from the hot intake manifold (arrow).

6. Probably the most impressive setup for a carbureted race car is dual 4500's. Though it may seem that this would be too much carburetion for even big-inch motors, more horsepower is actually attainable because there is less airflow restriction.

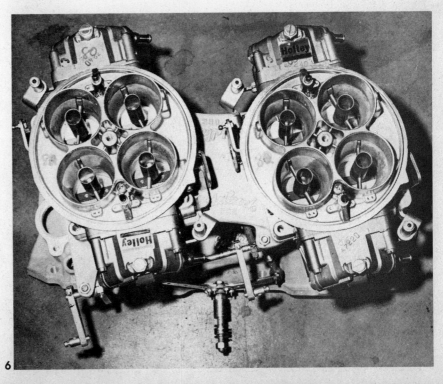

HOLLEY

A basic formula you can use for estimating the cfm airflow rate of your engine is as follows:

$$cfm = \frac{cid \times rpm \times VE}{3456}$$

VE can usually be plotted against the engine's torque curve (if available), since torque and VE are proportional. Thus, peak volumetric efficiency will be reached at the peak torque engine speed, and will fall off with torque production as engine speed increases or decreases.

As an example of the above, let's consider Chevy's pre-EGR Z-28 engine (330 hp) at an assumed 83% VE factor.

RPM	TORQUE	VE%
800	230	53
1200	260	60
1600	287	66
2000	308	71
2400	326	75
2800	340	78
3200	351	81
3600	357	82
4000	360	83
4400	356	82
4800	347	80
5200	333	77
5600	312	72
6000	285	66
6400	250	58
6800	210	48

These estimated VE values are for full throttle conditions, but you'll note that the engine's peak power VE (@5600) has fallen off to a lowly 72%. Thus, utilizing the previous cfm formula, we have:

$$\frac{350 \times 5600 \times .72}{3456} = 408.3 \text{ cfm}$$

This simple formula illustrates the impracticality of applying an 800-cfm carb to the 350-cu.-in. Z-28 engine, though a 780-cfm version was factory stock! Even at peak efficiency (4000 rpm), the flow rate would only be 336 cfm, and at 6800 rpm the value falls off to a mere 330!

For high-performance applications, since torque and/or VE curves are seldom available to the average tuner, it's been customary to apply a carburetor with a flow capacity equal to that of the engine when producing 100% VE at peak power—so the above-mentioned Z-28 would be nominally fitted with a 600-cfm carb. Or if the engine were recammed to peak at, say, 6500 rpm, a 650-cfm version would be applicable.

The above technique may seem to be simplicity in itself—and it *does* work—but the balance of your components, such as manifold, headers and ignition, as well as compression, also have an effect on carb capacity. For example, a well-tuned 350 will perform best for racing with an 850-cfm carb when mated to a Tarantula or Scorpion type manifold! The only catch is that in order to use that kind of high-rpm horsepower you need

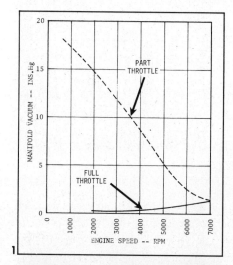

1. A vacuum gauge inside vehicle is handy for monitoring engine load vs. rpm. Note that the higher your engine speed climbs, the lower vacuum will be. Typically, small carb will give higher reading than larger one.

2. Unlike their more contemporary models, Holley's 4500 series employs a one-piece throttle and venturi body casting. Also, the primary-to-secondary linkage is hidden away underneath the carburetor between the throttle bores. However, most other parts are readily interchangeable with 4150/4160 items.

3. Several late-model Holleys use a "backwards" idle system (right) for emissions purposes. Fuel flows from main well (1) through idle feed restriction (2), and is mixed with air (3) entering through idle air bleed (4). This air/fuel goes to both curb idle port (5) and transfer slot (10); but more air can be bled into system via a venturi air bleed (6) by turning idle adjustment needle (7) counterclockwise to decrease restriction at (8). Normal system (left) is similar, except that curb idle mixture is only one affected, and the needle must be turned clockwise to lean mixture.

4. Secondary idle circuit operates much like primary, but no adjustment needle is provided. Fuel flows through main jet (1) into idle well (2), where it is pulled up through idle feed restriction (3) by vacuum supplied by idle air bleed (4); it's then discharged at curb idle port (5) until secondary throttles begin to open, uncovering idle transfer slot (6).

5. Fuel flows from the float bowl through the main jet (1) into the main well (2), where it is mixed with air entering through the high-speed bleed (3). A high vacuum signal provided by the booster venturi (4) pulls the air/fuel mix up from the main well, until it enters the airstream through the main nozzle (5).

6. Holley jets are numbered according to flow rate, not size of drilled restriction. As can be seen, more than one jet size may be listed under same drill diameter, while numbers indicate from lean to rich, respectively.

7. In some situations in which a small carb is used on a large engine, you may find that it's impossible to set the idle speed properly, since the throttles have to be opened to a point where the idle transfer slot is partially uncovered. One solution to this problem is to reset the secondary throttle idle position by turning the stop screw (arrow) in ¼-turn from a fully closed position.

8. Special bowl vent "whistles" and main jet slosh tubes are very helpful in preventing fuel spill-over from bowl during hard acceleration or braking, or for off-road. Slosh tubes are normally only used in secondary jets when metering block is employed, while vent whistles are applicable to both primary, secondary bowls, as long as metering block is used for attachment.

9. Models 4160/4175 do away with use of a metering block by using drilled metering plate. Thus, idle and main fuel-feed restrictions are part of the plate—so any metering changes in secondary system necessitate replacement of entire plate.

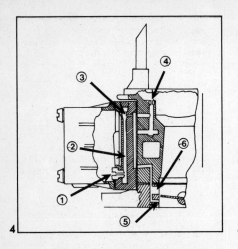

4

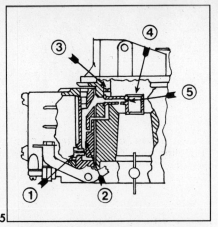

5

DRILL SIZE	JET #	DRILL SIZE	JET #	DRILL SIZE	JET #	DRILL SIZE	JET #
.045	45	.055	56	.066	66	.093	80
	452		562		662		81
.046	462	.056	57	.068	67		82
.047	47		572		672	.094	83
	472	.057	58	.069	68	.099	84
.048	48		582		682	.100	85
	482	.058	59	.070	69	.101	86
	49		592		692	.103	87
	492	.060	60	.073	70	.104	88
.049	50		602		702		89
	502		61	.076	71		90
.050	51		612	.079	72	.105	91
	512	.061	62		722		92
.052	52		622		73		93
	522	.062	63	.081	74	.108	94
	53		632		742	.118	95
	532	.064	64	.082	75		96
.053	54		642	.084	76	.125	97
	542	.065	65	.086	77		98
.054	55		652	.089	78		99
	552			.091	79	.128	100

6

super-low rear axle gears, a light chassis and, it would seem, a service station, too, considering the rate of fuel consumption under normal driving conditions. Just how much carburetor capacity you will need for your particular requirements will depend on engine tune, so it's wise to have two carburetors for your dual-purpose engine—one for weekend racing, another for everyday driving.

Economical operation can be very important in these times of inflation and high fuel prices, so selecting the proper street carb can be doubly rewarding. We made a comparison of fuel consumption not too long ago that really opened our eyes. The base machine was a 1967 Corvette with 350-hp 327, close-ratio 4-speed and 3.36:1 axle ratio. With an 800-cfm double-pumper (R-4780), early-model Tarantula, 46-in. headers and electronic ignition as the only modifications, we recorded an average consumption rate of 12.5 mpg. However, simply bolting on a 600-cfm vacuum secondary model (R-6619) raised this figure to an average of 16.5, with only a slight sacrifice in throttle response and acceleration!

You might think that employing a smaller carb for street use will starve or hurt your engine, particularly if you've modified it to any extent; but if ignition and compression are compatible with on-the-street operation, you shouldn't have any trouble with a swap of this sort. Look at it this way: If you were to install a large carburetor on an engine equipped with a mild, stock cam, you might gain a slight amount of horsepower in the upper speed ranges. However, on the other hand, if you install a wild camshaft—even utilizing a 2-bbl. carb—the engine will rev right up into the higher speed ranges and give a substantial increase in power—though more power could undoubtedly be had by using a larger carburetor.

A good example of a small carb installation is reflected by NASCAR's handicap rules for the 426 Mopar Hemi. When these new rules were

7

8

9

first adopted, a 340-cfm double-pumper with 1.063-in. venturis was used to "limit" horsepower potential. The 426 would still rev to 7000 rpm on the racetrack, and would breathe close to 800 cfm (91% VE) at that speed! Horsepower was no doubt lessened because of pumping losses, but that was NASCAR's objective.

Considering the above factors, it is obviously a bit difficult choosing just what size or type carb you should use; however, there is no set rule to use as a guideline, so some sort of compromise must be made. To this end, Holley devised the vacuum-actuated secondary throttle linkage. Though not new—Holley has used

this system since the mid-'50's—the vacuum secondary setup actually limits its airflow in proportion to engine demand. Thus, if the engine will only breathe 400 cfm of air, the secondary throttles of a 600-cfm carburetor will not open completely, even at peak engine speed.

Another point to consider is air velocity through the carburetor. The larger the carburetor is in proportion to engine size, the slower the air will move through the venturis. Relatively high air speeds are important for two reasons: (1) a higher state of vacuum is obtainable—and the functioning of most of the carb's metering circuits is proportional to a strong vacuum "signal,'' and (2) high air speed also improves fuel particle breakup. This point alone is worth extra horsepower from improved distribution inside the intake manifold. So, for street use, the vacuum secondary feature is the optimum—though not necessarily mandatory—setup.

WHICH CARB DESIGN?

The various controls that have been applied to late-model engines to reduce exhaust emissions have stimulated much research and development at Holley to improve on O.E.M. offerings. In some instances the results have been dramatic, with reduced emissions being accompanied by increases in fuel economy of up to 25%. Though we're not going to claim that this will be the result in all cases, it does give you some idea of what is *possible* if the engine and carb are properly matched.

In effect, Holley now offers two different types of carburetor. They classify them as either Competition/ Off-Road or Emission Design/Street models. Thus—unless you're building a racer—if you own a late-model machine, by all means opt for the emissions-type carb. Just because they are termed ''emissions'' designs doesn't mean that they will not perform effectively compared to the

''pre-emissions'' types. The truth of the matter is that they have full-power fuel calibrations similar to those used in factory-installed Holleys of the super-car era. The only difference is that they incorporate special vacuum signal controls that engage or disengage the emissions devices installed at the factory. The off-road types are calibrated slightly richer to conform with the metering requirements of pre-emissions-control engines.

In 1974, Holley introduced a whole new series of carbs aimed at the emissions engines, and though they are based on previous designs (components will interchange), there have been substantial changes. The greatest alteration was to modify the 4160-4150 models to a semi spreadbore configuration. That is, the carbs are now proportioned with secondary venturis that are substantially larger than the primaries. These changes resulted in two distinct advantages: improved emissions values, and increased low-speed torque and throttle response.

If you're tuning a pre-emissions engine without controls, the off-road type carburetor should suit your needs, while the newer models should be used with emissions controls. However, if you're planning to race your machine, you will undoubtedly deactivate the emissions controls, so the off-road carb would also be best suited for an installation of this type. Usually, when a new Holley carburetor is purchased, it will be jetted properly for optimum performance and/or emissions right out of the box, so only a minimum of fine tuning is necessary. However, it is possible to get the most from your specific combination of components by optimizing the calibration of the various fuel circuits in the carburetor. Yet, there are many variables involved, so each of the carb's metering circuits will have to be tuned individually. They are: the idle, main, power and accelerator pump circuits, and the secondary throttle opening period.

IDLE SYSTEM

The idle system actually has two functions: to meter fuel under standstill and no-load conditions, and to act as a low-speed metering device

until the transition from idle to main metering (or high-speed) system has taken place. Proper calibration of the idle system is very important for fuel economy because of the low-speed metering chores. However, Holley employs nonreplaceable metering orifices in the idle system, pressed-in, brass air bleeds in the air horn, and similar fuel-flow restrictors in the carburetor's metering block(s). They may be carefully drilled—the air bleed to lean the idle mixture, the idle feed restriction to richen it—but care must be taken, since the brass restrictors are not replaceable! And if you have an emissions engine, any tampering with the factory idle mixture calibration will undoubtedly make it harder for you to pass those impromptu roadside pollution checks.

Two different idle systems have been applied to Holley carburetors. The earlier type is similar to that used in most conventional carbs, whereby the curb-idle fuel is calibrated by an adjustment needle on the side of the primary metering block. The newest system, which is gradually being incorporated into all of Holley's emissions carbs, is similar, but instead of metering fuel by means of the adjustment screw, the amount of *air* entering the idle circuit is controlled with the idle adjustment needle, not unlike an adjustable air bleed. Thus, mixture adjustments are made in reverse: thread in to richen and out to lean. All carbs so equipped are

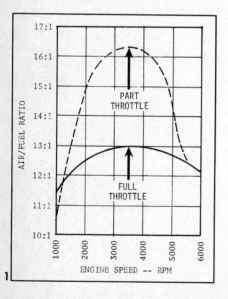

1. *Though this graph illustrates a mixture curve that would be too lean for a modern emissions engine at cruise (broken line), it does typify the differential in air/fuel ratios required in a high-performance engine during full- and part-throttle runs.*

2. *Here is a listing of the various single calibration plates offered by Holley. Note that there are a variety of idle restrictions used with the same main restriction. Be sure to match this idle "jet" with your carburetor when changing plates.*

3. *Holley doesn't offer them, but there are special conversion metering plates available to allow the use of removable secondary main jets in the 4160/4175 type carburetors. This Rocket plate (left) comes complete with .055-in. main jets that are numbered by size; they can be drilled to the proper dimension, but it's best to check Holley's catalog for the best starting jet size for your particular size carb. Also, check the idle feed restrictions (arrows) to ascertain whether they're compatible with your carburetor.*

4. *Holley power valves are numbered to indicate their opening point; i.e., a #85 opens at 8.5 ins. Hg of manifold vacuum. Also, the "window" type valve (left) has sufficient capacity to feed a .098-in. power valve channel restriction, while the standard hole-type will only handle a restriction of up to .067-in.*

DRILL SIZE	PLATE #	IDLE RSTN.	DRILL SIZE	PLATE #	IDLE RSTN.	DRILL SIZE	PLATE #	IDLE RSTN.	DRILL SIZE	PLATE #	IDLE RSTN.
.052	7	.026	.067	8	.026	.073	39	.029	.081	21	.040
	34	.029		23	.028		37	.031		31	.052
.055	3	.026		16	.029		17	.040		29	.063
.059	4	.026		9	.031	.076	10	.026	.086	25	.043
	32	.029		36	.035		22	.028	.089	27	.040
	40	.035	.070	6	.026		12	.031		26	.043
.063	5	.026		19	.028		28	.040	.094	15	.070
.064	18	.028		20	.031	.078	38	.029	.098	14	.070
	30	.029		41	.053	.079	11	.031	.113	42	.026
	13	.031	.071	35	.029		24	.035			
	33	.043		(prefix part number = 34BP-2007-x)								

Graph labels (Figure 1): AIR/FUEL RATIO (vertical axis, 10:1 to 17:1); ENGINE SPEED -- RPM (horizontal axis, 1000–6000); PART THROTTLE; FULL THROTTLE.

marked with arrows at the adjustment screws.

Another factor to consider when tuning the idle system is the actual throttle opening at idle. In some instances—especially when a small carburetor is used on a large engine, or when a radical cam dictates a high idle speed to maintain manifold vacuum—it may be necessary to readjust the throttle position to ensure its alignment with the idle transfer slot, or hole, in the carb throat. Some sources recommend drilling holes in the primary throttle plate—but this should only be done as a last resort, and some sanctioning organizations have even outlawed such a modification. One adjustment that sometimes works is to reposition the *secondary* throttle in relation to the transfer slot. With the carb removed from the engine and inverted, you'll find a small adjustment screw below the secondary linkage. This is the secondary throttle stop, and should be threaded out until the secondaries close completely, then threaded in one-quarter turn. If this doesn't work, then, as a last resort, the throttle plates may be drilled through with a 3/32-in. (or smaller) drill.

For racing purposes it is sometimes advantageous to richen the idle mixture—but this would only be in isolated cases, or when an automatic transmission is used. For street use the idle system should really be left alone, particularly if you're working with an emissions carb. The possible performance gains, when compared to the loss in fuel economy from richening the idle circuit, just aren't worth the risk of tampering with this factory-calibrated system. In most competition situations it's possible to rev the engine substantially before launching the vehicle, so the main metering system is usually already flowing fuel anyway.

MAIN METERING SYSTEM

When you buy a new Holley carburetor it is usually jetted for optimum efficiency, as far as the main metering system is concerned. In fact, you'll probably find that no main jet change will be necessary—except for racing applications—since the size of the jet is proportionate to venturi size rather than engine displacement. Thus, a 600-cfm carb with No. 62 main jets will meter fuel effectively on either a large or small engine, since fuel flow is relative to airflow through the carburetor.

Holley jets are broached and flow tested, then stamped according to their flow rate, so the number "62" is a flow factor, not an indication of jet diameter or any drill size (a No. 62 jet is actually .061-in. in diameter). These jets should never be drilled to

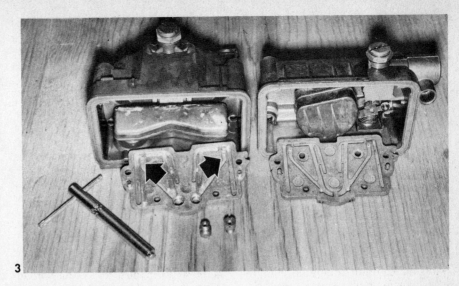

3

richen the fuel mixture, as this will cause an unbalanced condition between throats in the carburetor. For racing it will seldom be necessary to increase the flow of the main system by more than four "numbers" from an out-of-the-box calibration; the only exception being when a large-volume, plenum-ram manifold is used. In fact, when employing some of the new emissions manifolds—such as the Torker and Streetmaster—older, rebuilt carbs may require *leaning* by a couple of sizes to obtain an optimum calibration.

The main metering jet—as with the idle feed restriction—operates in conjunction with a main, or high-speed air bleed located in the carb's air horn. In most instances these should be left untouched, since it is very difficult to drill all four bleeds to similar diameters. In any case, increasing the size of the main air bleeds will *lean* the mixture calibration. And remember that any increase in bleed size requires a recalibration of the main jets—and if they're drilled incorrectly you'll ruin the carburetor body, since Holley does not supply replacement air bleeds!

The best procedure for determining whether or not you've found a good calibration is by "reading" the spark plugs. A white insulator indicates a lean condition, as do small beads of shiny metal on the insulator. This latter condition should be watched for, even if plug coloration looks good, as it indicates that the pistons are "melting" from excessive combustion temperature. A tan to light brown coloring indicates the proper mixture, while a dark brown, black or sooty appearance indicates a rich mixture—and though it won't hurt your engine, fuel economy will suffer considerably.

POWER SYSTEM

Under heavy loads, and during acceleration, some sort of mixture enrichment is necessary to provide a

4

compatible air/fuel ratio. The power system takes care of this chore, and consists of removable, vacuum-operated valves. The 4160 and 4175 vacuum-secondary models employ only one valve—on the primary side—while the other 4-bbl. models use both a primary and secondary power valve. A variety of valve opening values are available, and their calibration is relative to manifold vacuum. For example, a typical high-performance power valve part number is 25BP-591A-65, where the number "65" indicates the opening value—or 6.5 ins. Hg of manifold vacuum. The only exception is when a two-stage power valve is specified, but we'll touch on that in a moment.

Power valve tuning isn't difficult, but it does require a vacuum gauge installation in the vehicle's passenger compartment. With the gauge installed you will note that the pressure drop (vacuum) decreases as the throttle is opened. If the throttle is slammed open, such as during a passing maneuver, you'll note that vacuum will drop from a nominal 15-18 ins. Hg (except where a hot cam is used, since idle vacuum seldom exceeds 6-10 ins. Hg) to between 0 and 8 ins. High-compression engines tend to allow less of a drop, giving a reading of 5-8 ins. Hg, while low-compression engines will usually drop considerably lower, or even to zero. The actual drop in vacuum is relative to a number of factors, such as carb size, manifold design, compression ratio, camshaft timing, axle gearing, vehicle weight, etc.

An optimum power valve calibration for the primary side of the carburetor would be one that is full open at a point about 1 in. *above* the vacuum gauge reading obtained as outlined above. Thus, if your vacuum reading drops to, say, 5 ins. Hg when the throttle is opened quickly, you will need a No. 65 power valve. However, care must be taken when selecting the correct power valve, because there will be certain situations, such as when climbing long grades, in which power enrichment will be needed, but vacuum will not drop off sufficiently to open the power valve. The best method for preventing a lean condition such as this is to watch the

vacuum gauge for a few days and see how it reacts under a variety of load conditions—then select a power valve that will provide you with the optimum opening time.

Performance applications can be treated a bit differently, depending on the type of racing you will be doing, but such calibrations should not be used in a street driven vehicle. In fact, for racing, the power valves may even be replaced with plugs; but when this is done it is necessary to compensate by increasing the main jet size by about four or five steps. Just how much main jet enrichment you will need depends on the size of the original power valve restriction.

The power valve restrictions are located in the metering body(s) behind the power valve. Some sources recommend drilling these holes for added enrichment, but do so only in

steps of about .002-in. at a time as a fine tuning measure. Carbs using four and six-hole valves should never have the power valve restrictions increased to larger than .060-in., since these valves are limited to feeding restrictions of up to .067-in. The newer window-type, on the other hand, have a restriction of .095-in., thus the power valve restrictions in the metering body can be opened up to a maximum of .090-in.

Idle speed and camshaft timing can also affect manifold vacuum—and in some performance applications for street use as little as 6 ins. Hg is available at idle. Of course, it's obvious that a standard valve (8.5 ins. Hg) would already be open at this depression, so it's necessary to employ one that opens later, say at 3.5 ins. Hg. For this reason Holley will supply valves with opening values of

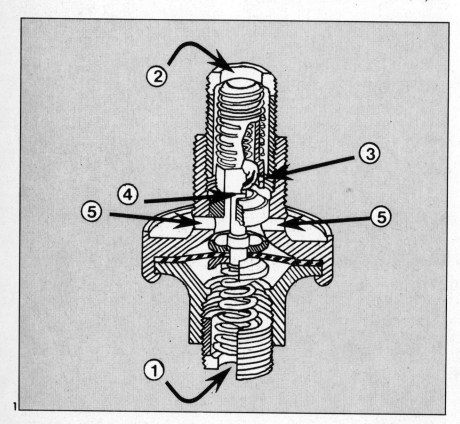

1

2

1. As manifold vacuum is applied at point (1) the first stage valve opens, allowing fuel to flow into the valve at (2) and through the first-stage restriction (3). As the vacuum signal decreases, the plunger uncovers the second-stage opening (4), which increases the flow of fuel through restriction (5).

2. There are actually four different types of Holley power valves—from left to right: a two-stage type; latest high-flow window configuration; the original six-hole high-performance type; and the standard production four-hole valve.

3. It's also possible to richen the power circuit when a power valve is used by increasing the size of the power valve channel restriction. However, since the power valves are of limited flow value, the restriction should be a maximum of .065-in. with hole-type valves, and .095-in. with window valves.

4. Though the "Rio" type 5cc accelerator pump is acceptable for use on the primary side of the carburetor in racing applications, it is seldom needed on a street machine. Its use is mandatory, however, on double-pumper secondaries, since its function is to "cover up" the flat spot, or lean condition, caused by the secondaries opening mechanically before the main nozzles have had a chance to function.

5. Here you can see the physical difference between the new butterfly-type accelerator pump shooter and the original 4150/4160 type. The former is employed in conjunction with a special ball-check in the main metering block, which prevents premature fuel pull-over from the shooters under high manifold vacuum.

6. Before the double-pumper was developed, racing carburetors employed one-to-one ratio throttle operation, a large-capacity Rio accelerator pump, and a centrally located pump shooter.

7. The pump cam(s) can be used when optimizing your calibration. Ideally, the number one hole provides a moderate fuel delivery rate initially with greater total delivered volume, while hole number two provides a greater initial delivery rate and less total volume.

3

4

from 2.5-10.5 ins. (Nos. 25 to 105) in increments of 1 in. of vacuum. Also, when selecting an opening value for your specific application, remember that the valve will be full open at the specified time, but will start to open about 1 in. sooner.

The type of power valve gasket used is important, too, since the valve must be seated correctly to operate effectively. Thus, a notched gasket should be used for valves with four or six holes, while the window type requires a round one. When new Holley valves are purchased the proper gaskets are included.

Secondary power system operation is not as critical as the primary valve function. Under typical driving conditions the only time the secondaries are open is during full throttle operation. Since the secondary power valve does not affect part throttle operation, it's possible to use a lower opening value, say between 2.5 and 4.5 ins. Hg. This will give full-power enrichment under full throttle, but will keep the secondary metering "lean" during any momentary partial load periods that may be encountered.

Removing either the primary or secondary power valve altogether (when used) is not recommended, except for racing applications where dual 4-bbl.'s are employed with simultaneous throttle opening. In fact, just removing the secondary valve—which requires a substantial increase in main jet size to compensate—can cause undue enrichment during braking, and can also cause "loading up" when driving under partial load. A good rule of thumb for recalibrating the secondary—if you *must* remove the power valve—is to increase the main jet *area* proportionate to the area of the power valve restriction. For example, suppose the standard main jet size is .060-in. and the power valve restriction is found to be .055-in. by select fitting wire drills into the restriction. Their areas are then .00283 and .00238 sq. ins., respectively, while their total area is .00521 sq. ins. This total area is proportionate to a main jet diameter of 0815-in.—or a No. 74 jet.

TWO-STAGE POWER VALVES

A more recent development from Holley is the two-stage power valve. Initial applications are intended for recreational vehicles in which a high weight-to-engine-size ratio is present,

5

6

7

HOLLEY

Holley's objective here was to gain economy and drivability. However, they don't guarantee better mileage when using these new valves, since individual driving habits can limit their effectiveness.

A few points to ponder before installing a two-stage power valve are: They work most effectively when the vehicle-weight-to-engine-displacement ratio is greater than 14:1. They should not be used in any machine which sees occasional drag strip·use, or in any carb with a power valve restriction greater than .060-in., since excessive leanness may result from the limited flow capacity of these valves. The two-stage valve will be most effective in RV's equipped with a 600-cfm emissions carb, or the new 4175 spread-bore, particularly when used in stop and go driving and in rolling or mountainous terrain. In addition, the two-stage valve should only be used when primary system calibrations are necessary.

Only two valves are available at the present time: Nos. 25BP-475A-12 and -25. The No. 12 valve is calibrated so as to affect a first-stage enrichment when manifold vacuum drops to 12 ins. Hg, while the second stage comes into action at 6 ins. Hg. The No. 25 operates similarly, but is intended for use when the vehicle will see frequent high-altitude driving (above 4000 ft.)—so the opening values are 10 and 5 ins. Hg for the first and second stages, respectively.

As a typical application let's outline the effect obtained with a 600-cfm R-6619 emissions carb. With No. 64 main jets (.064-in.) and the standard .055-in. power valve restrictions, this carb will deliver an air/fuel ratio of about 16:1 under cruise conditions, and 12.5:1 at full throttle and/or below 6.5 ins. of vacuum, when using the single-stage valve. With a two-stage valve the cruise (closed) and full power (stage two) mixtures are the same at 16:1 and 12.5:1, and are controlled by the main jets and power valve restrictions, respectively. However, the stage one feature provides a metering orifice inside the valve itself, which reduces the allowed enrichment, and gives an air/fuel ratio of 13.7:1 between 12 and 6 ins. Hg. Similarly, the No. 25 valve gives a leaner mixture between 10 and 5 ins. Hg, but since it is intended for higher altitudes its flow calibration is smaller—.021-in. compared to .028-in. for the No. 12 valve.

It might even be worth trying *both* valves if you have an extra-heavy vehicle—such as a four-wheel-drive rig—since the No. 25 valve might provide better economy for sea level driving when matched to a machine that normally has a high vacuum drop under·acceleration. But remember that the smaller calibration will give you a leaner mixture, which could cause *too* lean a condition for pulling long grades and such. With the 6619 the air/fuel ratio would be about 14.5:1. In any event, this does seem to be an area worth experimenting with, especially if you're looking to improve low-speed flexibility in your heavyweight. During emissions test cycles, Holley found that these·valves would allow an economy increase of up to 16% over a single-stage valve, while on-the-road comparisons went as high as 20-25%! However, Holley tried deliberately mismatching them to an engine in a light vehicle, and found that they *reduced* mileage, so they certainly aren't a cure-all.

ACCELERATOR PUMPS

The accelerator pump is probably your most important tuning tool for

2

3

optimizing a calibration for your street driven engine. Unlike most carburetors, the Holley employs a diaphragm-type pump assembly located at the bottom of the primary float bowl, or one for each bowl in the case of a double-pumper version. And though they are of the same basic design, two sizes are offered: the ''3cc'' and the ''5cc''—the latter being known as a ''Rio'' pump, since it was first introduced on that brand of *truck*.

Before attempting to tune the accelerator pump(s) it is advisable to rebuild your carburetor—unless you're working with a new unit. The reason for this is twofold: a rebuilt carb will give optimum metering, and any subsequent disassembly will vary the tolerances provided during tuning. You can also get a ''feel'' for how your stock carburetor performs in as-new condition, too—and it will be easier to evaluate the results when modifications are made. It's also advisable to keep a written record of changes made, to prevent any possible duplication of adjustments and/or procedures.

The accelerator pump's main purpose is to provide the proper momentary full-power air/fuel mixture necessary when the throttles are opened. Under both idle and cruise conditions the carburetor provides a more or

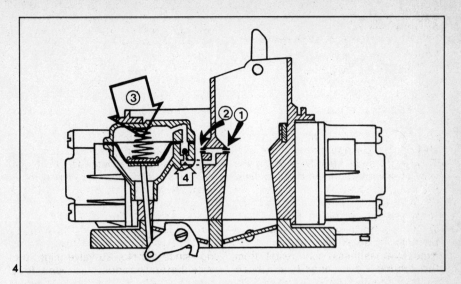

4

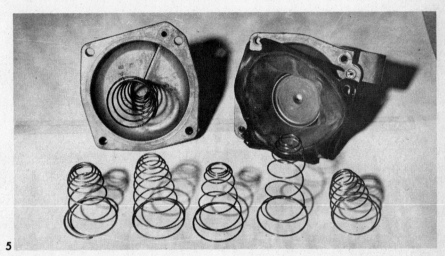

5

1. An engine's specific fuel consumption is calculated as the weight of fuel it will burn per hour for every horsepower. As can be seen, part throttle operation is a bit on the rich side, since the engine is not producing its maximum power.

2. Holley has also adopted a slightly revised secondary throttle linkage (right) on double-pumpers, for two reasons: to provide more positive throttle return, and to allow several different types of operating levers to be used without interference.

3. When large-plenum manifolds are used on tunnel ram manifolds in conjunction with center-pumper carburetors, it's possible to modify the opening point of the secondary throttles by grinding away a portion of the actuating cam (below). This provides better bottom-end performance out of the chute.

4. When air rushes through the primary venturi, the vacuum signal is read at restriction (1), which applies vacuum to the secondary diaphram, overcoming the throttle closing spring (3). As the secondary throttle opens, vacuum is added at restriction (2), opening the throttles faster, until the primary throttle is closed, stopping the vacuum signal and releasing the diaphragm vacuum via the check ball (4).

5. Holley supplies a secondary vacuum spring assortment that allows you to tailor your throttle opening to engine demands. Their tension is, in descending order: black; brown; plain (standard 3310); purple; yellow; and another, shorter yellow spring.

less constant flow of fuel, but when the throttle is cracked, such as during acceleration from a standstill or during a passing maneuver, there is a lag period during which fuel flow response cannot keep up with airflow. Thus, the accelerator pump provides the extra fuel needed to span this gap in flow time.

Holley's accelerator pump design is probably the most flexible in the industry, since it is adjustable for both delivery rate and volume. Variations in vehicle weight, gearing, transmission type, and carb size will affect both the amount of added fuel required and the rate at which it is delivered. Just applying the largest pump available won't work either, since performance can suffer if the engine receives too much fuel too soon—as much as if it received too little fuel too late!

Two components control the pump delivery: the pump cam and the discharge nozzle. The pump cam is located on the throttle shaft(s) in such a way as to contact the accelerator pump lever. As the throttle is opened the cam action lifts the spring-loaded operating lever, which in turn compresses the fuel in the pump dia-

phragm chamber, forcing it through the pump circuit to the discharge nozzles. The discharge nozzles are situated so as to aim the shot of fuel at the booster venturi, which is quite a big help in breaking the fuel up into smaller particles.

The pump cams have two operating positions. Generally, position No. 1 combines a moderate initial delivery with a greater total delivered volume, while location No. 2 provides a greater initial delivery with less final volume. The pump discharge nozzles, or shooters, are available in different sizes, and the nozzle diameter is identified by a number stamped on the side of the casting. Thus, a No. 31 shooter has .031-in. discharge nozzles. In effect, a smaller diameter shooter will lengthen the pump shot duration, while the reverse is true for the larger nozzles, which also deliver a greater initial volume of fuel. The former are recommended for vehicles with high power-to-weight ratios and numerically low axle ratios, while the latter should only be used where engine speed will build rapidly, such as in a light machine with 4-speed transmission and 4.11 + axle.

Although it is possible to purchase

HOLLEY

accelerator pump cams and shooters separately, we highly recommend Holley's "Trick Kits" for rebuilding a used carb. Not only do you get high-quality gaskets and replacement parts, but components such as needle/seat fittings and power valves are of the high-flow, performance type. Each kit also contains three pump cams and three pump shooters, plus very informative tuning instructions. Thus, you have all the components necessary to properly tune your accelerator pumps. We'll touch on these Trick Kits again in a moment.

Keeping records of the combinations used when tuning the pump(s) is very important in preventing duplication of effort, which could be time-consuming, to say the least. The simplest procedure is to switch the shooters until the smallest is found that still provides crisp throttle response. Then the pump cams may be juggled until crispness is improved further. Again, the shooters may be interchanged until the optimum response is attained. When the accelerator pump operation is optimized there should be no bogs or flat spots (indicating leanness) or black smoke (richness) when accelerating at wide open throttle from a standing start.

The best acceleration may be attained only when the pump delivers a "lean best power" air/fuel ratio to the engine; so if the shooter size required seems to be in between the sizes that you have at hand, the nozzles can be carefully hand drilled with a pin vise and a suitable drill bit.

With the introduction of the 4165 series spread bores a new pump shooter design was also released. Normally referred to as the "butter-fly" type, it is unusual in that the nozzles themselves are not exposed to the airstream in the carburetor, but are enclosed in small wings on each side of the casting. This configuration is intended to prevent fuel "pullover," a condition in which the fuel that is in the pump circuit is drawn into the venturi prematurely.

One other thought to keep in mind when tuning double-pumpers is secondary shot duration. The secondary pump should supply fuel for a sufficient length of time to allow the secondary main nozzles to start flowing. If not, a bog will result. Though Holley employs the larger "5cc" pump (50cc's per 10 shots) on all double-pumper secondaries, it is still possible to underrate them.

SECONDARY THROTTLE OPENING

The point at which the secondary throttle begins to open is important in attaining a smooth transition from standstill to high speed, or during long accelerations, such as when passing, or when climbing a freeway ramp. Double-pumper operation is pretty cut-and-dried, since the secondaries start to open at about half throttle and are fully open when the accelerator pedal is fully depressed. If this is not the case, then some adjustment must be made to the throttle cable or the actuating linkage to allow full throttle. Though it is possible to modify the secondary opening point of the double-pumper by re-shaping the operating cam-plate, it isn't recommended, since Holley has optimized the secondary opening time for each carb size. Also, the mechanical linkage double-pumper should not be used with an automatic transmission unless a high-stall-speed torque converter is used, as full throt-tle application will result in a bog when engine speed cannot keep up with throttle opening.

Vacuum-operated secondaries are another thing, since they're much more flexible from a tuning point of view. There are many misconceptions about the vacuum-operated system—and there have been many "tricks" devised to make the system operate more effectively; however, in *overall* performance it's pretty hard to beat the factory setup. It's been thought that opening the secondaries earlier will produce more horsepower, but this is seldom true. Some sources even recommend disconnecting the vacuum linkage altogether, and linking the primary and secondary throttles mechanically. And lastly, many think that they should "feel" the secondaries coming into operation.

Opening the secondaries earlier, or opening them mechanically, will usually *hurt* performance, for two reasons: (1) no secondary accelerator pump is provided for the needed momentary enrichment when the secondaries open, and (2) if Holley thought a mechanical linkage more efficient, they would have provided one. However, the greatest misconception of all is the "kick in the pants" you get when the secondaries open. What you're actually feeling is a flat spot or lean condition, which indicates that they are opening before there is sufficient airflow to bring the secondary main nozzles into action! In fact, Holley has found that a typical engine will produce more horsepower and torque when the secondaries open *later* rather than earlier.

Since the secondaries should not open until the engine requires additional air, two controls are provided: a restricted vacuum circuit, and a replaceable throttle diaphragm spring.

Under normal operation the vacuum diaphragm "reads" the signal from the primary venturi. When air speed is sufficient, the vacuum signal becomes great enough to overcome the tension of the diaphragm spring, and, as the secondary throttles gradually open, additional vacuum signal is provided from that venturi until they are completely open. This transition period starts at about 1500 to 2500 rpm, and the throttles are completely open between 5000 and 8000 rpm, depending on engine size and diaphragm spring tension. The diaphragm spring controls both the opening period and the rate of opening. Thus, a light spring will allow them to open sooner, a heavy spring later, while the former will be fully open at a lower engine speed than the latter. Holley supplies springs in kit form (eight different tensions), or three springs are provided in their Trick Kits when required. Generally, heavier vehicles require stiffer diaphragm springs to delay the secondary opening, and provide a more gradual opening rate. Even the air

1. *Another approach to modified secondary linkage with vacuum operation is to apply a lock screw to the secondary return link. If positioned properly, the effect is to allow full throttle acceleration for passing maneuvers by mechanically overriding the vacuum linkage, though heavy, part-throttle operation won't be affected.*

2. *Though not recommended for street use, it is possible to add an accessory link to a vacuum-secondary Holley, which will operate the secondary throttles mechanically. However, to cover up the subsequent flat spot caused by early opening secondaries, use of a Rio pump and a small pump shooter are required to extend the shot duration.*

3. *On Holley's side-hung bowls the only inlet filter used is a small fine-mesh wire screen, so use of an inline fuel filter is mandatory for trouble-free operation. Center-inlet bowls incorporate a sintered bronze element, which should be discarded, too, since it can limit fuel flow at high engine speeds.*

4. *Two types of float/inlet systems are used by Holley in their high-performance carbs. Though the center-pivot type (right) is most popular because of its ability to control fuel flow under hard cornering, the side-hung type (left) is more effective for acceleration and off-road performance.*

5. *This production-type bowl vent baffle leaves a bit to be desired in terms of fuel handling under adverse driving conditions. In fact, a small screen over the vent, in addition to this baffle, would be more effective.*

6. *Installation of the vent whistles to the metering block is relatively simple, but be certain that the vent is not squeezed closed when the lock pin is pressed into place. Usually, drilling the upper hole in the plastic vent slightly larger will prevent this.*

cleaner you're running can affect the secondary opening point, so be certain to install the air cleaner during your evaluations.

It should be impossible to open the secondaries by revving the engine free (no load); however, if the secondaries do open, you can expect them to open too early. When functioning properly they should only open when the engine is under substantial load, or at full throttle. And don't expect to clip a coil off the spring to make them open sooner, as, oddly enough, this will *increase* the spring rate and delay opening further!

INLET/FLOAT SYSTEM

It may seem that the inlet/float assemblies are the most unimportant, but this is far from the truth. A float level is specified for each carburetor, either in the O.E.M. specifications or in your carb rebuilding kit. The float level is not the same for all carburetors in a specific design category either, since the size of the inlet needle and seat fitting also controls the amount of fuel entering the bowl, and the float controls its opening and closing. There are also two types of fittings—the most popular among the high-performance carbs being an externally adjustable assembly.

The internally adjustable floats are set by bending the float arm until the

proper clearance between the top of the bowl and the float is obtained with the bowl assembly inverted. The externally adjustable floats are much easier to calibrate, as sight plugs are provided in the side of both primary and secondary bowls for optimizing the float level. Adjustment is accomplished by loosening the inlet seat lock screw. The seat assembly itself is threaded and may be turned either up or down in relation to the float until the fuel level at the sight plug is within 1/32-in. of the hole.

These procedures work well when the original components are used in the carburetor. However, some factory-installed carbs are equipped with low-flow capacity components. Typically, there are two types of adjustable inlet seat fittings, in which the flow passages from the fitting into the bowl are either hole- or window-shaped. The latter allows more total flow, even though the actual rate of flow is determined by the restriction in the needle seat. Seat sizes available are: hole type—.097-in., .101-in. and .110-in.; or window type—.110-in. and .120-in. in diameter. All but the last employ Viton tips for more dependable seating, while the "120" is a steel seat assembly for use with exotic fuel additives, such as alcohol, benzine or acetone. All of Holley's adjustable seats are identified by a

4   5

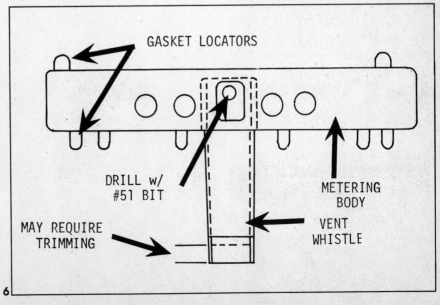

GASKET LOCATORS

DRILL w/ #51 BIT

MAY REQUIRE TRIMMING

METERING BODY

VENT WHISTLE

6

HOLLEY

number on the flat of their threads at the top of the fitting; this number corresponds to their flow orifice.

Generally, if a different than standard needle/seat fitting is installed, it will be necessary to readjust the float level accordingly. A smaller fitting will require a slightly higher setting, a larger fitting, slightly lower. For example: at a fuel pressure of 6 psi the window-type "110" flows about 7.3% more fuel than the "hole" type; and 31% more than a "97" needle seat. Steel needles for blended fuels can be applied as follows: .097-in. for small 4-bbl.'s, .110-in. for 700 to 750-cfm capacity and .120-in. for 780-cfm and larger versions.

Secondary float levels usually require a setting about 1/16 to ⅛-in. lower than the primary to prevent fuel "pullover" into the secondary main

nozzle on hard braking. In any event, try to set your float level to give optimum efficiency. A high float level will allow premature main nozzle start-up, which in turn increases fuel consumption and the tendency for the fuel in the bowl to "percolate," or turn to partial vapor before entering the fuel circuits. A low float level will delay main system start-up, causing holes or flat spots in the mixture transition from idle to main circuits—and the lower float level may uncover the main jets on hard cornering, thus starving the engine and causing "fade out." High fuel pressure will also raise the fuel level in the bowl about .020-in. per psi of increase, while low fuel pressure will do just the reverse.

Another factor to consider is the movement of the fuel in the bowl. Lateral movement can cause starvation when cornering, while rearward movement on acceleration can cause

two problems: starvation of the secondary jets as the fuel moves to the rear of the bowl, and flooding of the primaries as fuel finds its way into the primary bowl vent. Lateral starving can be alleviated considerably by use of the correct float bowl—namely the "center-pivot" type. Movement to the front of the bowl—or rear—such as in acceleration or braking, or in off-road maneuvers, can be minimized by using a side-hung float system.

When a metering block is used, a vent "whistle," or extension, can be pinned to the bowl vent passage to carry the vent to the front of the bowl (rear in secondary), while a small, angled brass baffle can be employed when only a metering plate is used in the secondary bowl. Also, when a secondary metering block is used, the main jets may be assured adequate fuel supply under acceleration, or when climbing hills, by the installation of "slosh tubes," which will allow the fuel to be picked up at the rear of the bowl. With these accessories, you should be able to cure any or all fuel-feed problems under adverse driving conditions.

TRICK KITS AND ADDENDUM

We mentioned the Trick Kits earlier, so we'll only describe their contents here. Just what components are included in your kit will depend on the model of your carburetor. Typically, you will get all of the required rebuilding gaskets and replacement valves, new pump diaphragm(s), suitable power valves (high performance), high flow-capacity inlet needle seats, vent whistles and baffles (as required), secondary slosh tubes (for 4150 and 4165), three accelerator pump shooters of various sizes, three pump cams per pump, and complete tuning instructions Of all the kits available, these have to be the most versatile for Holley carbs.

1

2

1. In some metering blocks it is necessary to peen the vent slightly to grip the vent whistle. This will prevent it from hanging down into the bowl and interfering with normal float operation.

2. This Trick Kit for the R-6210 spread-bore is a typical example of the completeness of the special tuning packages—and the added tuning components amount to only a few dollars more than Holley's regular-performance repair kits.

3. Though this chart is based on an average temperature of 59° at sea level, it will give you some idea of what effect the low air density can have on temperature and barometric pressures at various altitudes.

4. If you live at a higher than normal altitude, or you want to reject your carb for more efficient running when on skiing or camping trips, this cross-reference can be used as a guide.

The installation of your carburetor, and intake manifold, too—if you're installing a new one at the same time—is critical, and every effort should be made to prevent manifold vacuum leaks. Vacuum signal integrity is the lifeblood of the carburetor, and any faulty signals, regardless of their source, can upset most of the carb's calibrations. To insure against leaks, a gasket sealer of the silicon-base type (i.e., G.E. Silicon Seal) is highly recommended, particularly around the intake ports of the intake manifold, where vacuum leaks can materialize between the port and the valve lifter chamber. Such leaks are almost impossible to detect without removing the intake manifold. Generally, the carb need not be sealed to the intake manifold, since there is a generous surface area. However, do not try to tighten the carb flange down excessively in an attempt to stop a vacuum leak—use some sealer. Tightening the carb down too much has one distinct effect: warping of the carb flange—and it eventually results in either the primary or secondary throttles "hanging up." The main symptom of this condition is the engine's inability to return to idle speed after a hard acceleration run at wide open throttle.

A vacuum leak can usually be recognized by an off-idle hesitation in acceleration, since the carburetor is probably idling at a mixture ratio that "covers up" the vacuum leak. Opening the throttle leans the mixture when it can no longer compensate. Pre-emissions carbs had slightly richer idle mixtures, so you may only run across this problem in the newer-model carbs that are intended for emissions engines. Finally, if a vacuum lean condition persists, it will be necessary to remove the intake manifold, clean the mating surfaces, and reinstall the whole shebang with enough sealer to prevent a reoccurrence of the problem.

Another condition which sometimes gives similar running characteristics is fuel percolation. The high ambient under-hood temperatures associated with late-model emissions engines aggravate this problem, especially when standing at idle in traffic on a hot summer afternoon, or when driving off the road at a creeper pace. Under these conditions, the fuel temperature in the float bowl and accelerator pump passages can get as high as 200°. Thus, fuel percolation occurs in the fuel passages, which results in a rough, erratic idle, and a slight stumbling during moderate acceleration.

There are two effective methods of combating fuel percolation: routing cool outside air into the engine compartment and insulating the carburetor from the engine. When plumbing in cool air, try to aim it at the exterior of the carburetor. Insulating the carburetor from the engine can be done by employing special phenolic (plastic) heat barrier spacers between the carb and the manifold. Holley supplies a couple of different kinds for various applications, and they work quite well—but special care should be used when tightening down the carburetor, or the soft spacer will allow the carb base to warp. During the winter months the spacer should be removed, if you live in an area where the temperature may drop below 40°, since below this temperature carburetor icing may occur. Ice can form on either the throttle plates or in the venturis, which in both cases will reduce the airflow capacity of the carburetor. And icing is a particular hazard in warm climates where additives are not used in pump gasoline to prevent its occurrence.

Last but not least is the effect of altitude on carburetor mixtures. As altitude increases, air density decreases, so the carb will act as if it is larger than it really is. Thus, fuel is metered by the volume of air taken, not its weight. A quick-fix estimate for recalibrating for a higher altitude is to decrease the main jet size .001-in. for every 1000-ft. increase in altitude, or one "number" for every 2000-ft. increase. Thus, if you will be operating your vehicle constantly at, say, 6000 ft. at a ski resort, the main system should be leaned three numbers (about .006-in.). However, do not drive more than 2000 ft. below this altitude for any length of time, as the lean condition could seriously damage your engine! In fact, high engine loading, such as when climbing long grades or pulling a trailered load, can also cause high combustion temperatures in the upper altitudes with the leaner mixtures . . . so keep this in mind when recalibrating your carburetor for thinner air.

ALTITUDE feet	TEMP. °F	PRESS. in.Hg	PRESS. psi	DENSITY lbs/c.f.
-1000	55.6	30.98	15.23	.0787
s.1.	59.0	29.92	14.70	.0765
1000	55.4	28.86	14.17	.0743
2000	51.8	27.82	13.66	.0721
3000	48.3	26.81	13.17	.0700
4000	44.7	25.84	12.69	.0679
5000	41.2	24.89	12.22	.0659
6000	37.6	23.98	11.77	.0640
7000	34.0	23.09	11.34	.0620
8000	30.5	22.22	10.90	.0601
9000	26.9	21.38	10.50	.0583
10000	23.3	20.58	10.10	.0565
11000	19.8	19.79	9.72	.0547
12000	16.2	19.03	9.35	.0530

TEMP. °F	-1000'	SEA LEVEL	1000'	2000'	3000'	4000'	5000'
-20°	+.0062	+.0052	+.0042	+.0032	+.0022	+.0012	+.0002
-10°	+.0056	+.0046	+.0036	+.0026	+.0016	+.0006	-.0004
0°	+.0050	+.0040	+.0030	+.0020	+.0010	---	-.0010
10°	+.0044	+.0034	+.0024	+.0014	+.0004	-.0006	-.0016
20°	+.0039	+.0029	+.0019	+.0009	-.0002	-.0011	-.0021
30°	+.0033	+.0023	+.0013	+.0003	-.0007	-.0017	-.0027
40°	+.0027	+.0017	+.0007	-.0003	-.0013	-.0023	-.0033
50°	+.0021	+.0011	+.0001	-.0009	-.0019	-.0029	-.0039
60°	+.0016	+.0006	-.0004	-.0014	-.0024	-.0034	-.0044
70°	+.0010	---	-.0010	-.0020	-.0030	-.0040	-.0050
80°	+.0004	-.0006	-.0016	-.0026	-.0036	-.0046	-.0056
90°	-.0001	-.0011	-.0021	-.0031	-.0041	-.0051	-.0061
100°	-.0007	-.0017	-.0027	-.0037	-.0047	-.0057	-.0067
110°	-.0013	-.0023	-.0033	-.0043	-.0053	-.0063	-.0073
120°	-.0019	-.0029	-.0039	-.0049	-.0059	-.0069	-.0079

TEMP. °F	6000'	7000'	8000'	9000'	10000'	11000'	12000'
-20°	-.0008	-.0018	-.0028	-.0038	-.0048	-.0058	-.0068
-10°	-.0014	-.0024	-.0034	-.0044	-.0054	-.0064	-.0074
0°	-.0020	-.0030	-.0040	-.0050	-.0060	-.0070	-.0080
10°	-.0026	-.0036	-.0046	-.0056	-.0066	-.0076	-.0086
20°	-.0031	-.0041	-.0051	-.0061	-.0071	-.0081	-.0091
30°	-.0037	-.0047	-.0057	-.0067	-.0077	-.0087	-.0097
40°	-.0043	-.0053	-.0063	-.0073	-.0083	-.0093	-.0103
50°	-.0049	-.0059	-.0069	-.0079	-.0089	-.0099	-.0109
60°	-.0054	-.0064	-.0074	-.0084	-.0094	-.0104	-.0114
70°	-.0060	-.0070	-.0080	-.0090	-.0100	-.0110	-.0120
80°	-.0066	-.0076	-.0086	-.0096	-.0106	-.0116	-.0126
90°	-.0071	-.0081	-.0091	-.0101	-.0111	-.0121	-.0131
100°	-.0077	-.0087	-.0097	-.0107	-.0117	-.0127	-.0137
110°	-.0083	-.0093	-.0103	-.0113	-.0123	-.0133	-.0143
120°	-.0089	-.0099	-.0109	-.0119	-.0129	-.0139	-.0149

CARBURETOR SELECTION

For years, a common problem has been overcarbureting engines. Bigger is not necessarily better when it comes to carburetion. Another mistake is to arbitrarily select a carb identical to one that a friend is using, without regard to make of engine, displacement or whether any high-performance components are being used. Installing a carburetor that is not matched to a particular engine combination usually results in poor performance, lazy throttle response and so forth.

The accompanying chart, courtesy of Offenhauser Manifolds, is based on single carburetor applications (assuming 100 percent volumetric efficiency) for your particular cubic inches and engine rpm. To find the correct size carburetor, in cubic feet, to be used with most aftermarket manifolds, look down the "ENGINE C.I.D." (Cubic Inch Displacement) column and find the displacement nearest to that of your engine. Then look across the column marked "ENGINE RPM." Locate the maximum usable rpm capability of your engine. Where the C.I.D. and rpm columns intersect is the size carburetor, in cubic feet, that should

be used on your engine for street/strip applications.

As an example, a 350-cu.-in. engine capable of 6500 rpm would require a carb size of 658 cfm. Round this off to the nearest available size, and you find that a 650-cfm carb is the size you need.

CARBURETION GUIDE

ENGINE C.I.D.	ENGINE R.P.M.																
	1000	1500	2000	2500	3000	3500	4000	4500	5000	5500	6000	6500	7000	7500	8000	8500	9000
100	29	44	58	72	87	101	116	130	145	159	174	188	203	217	231	246	260
125	36	54	72	90	109	127	145	163	181	199	217	235	253	271	289	307	326
150	43	65	87	109	130	152	174	195	217	239	260	282	304	326	347	369	391
175	51	76	101	127	152	177	203	228	253	279	304	329	354	379	405	430	456
200	58	87	116	145	174	203	231	260	289	318	347	376	405	434	463	492	521
225	65	98	130	163	195	228	260	293	326	358	391	423	456	488	521	553	586
250	72	109	145	181	217	253	289	326	362	398	434	470	506	543	579	615	651
275	80	119	159	199	239	279	318	358	398	438	477	517	557	597	637	676	716
300	87	130	174	217	260	304	347	391	434	477	521	564	608	651	694	738	781
325	94	141	188	235	282	329	376	423	470	517	564	611	658	705	752	799	846
350	101	152	203	253	304	354	405	456	506	557	608	658	709	760	810	861	911
375	109	163	217	271	326	380	434	488	543	597	651	705	760	814	868	922	977
400	116	174	231	289	347	405	463	521	579	637	694	752	810	868	926	984	1042
425	123	184	246	307	369	430	492	553	615	676	738	799	861	922	984	1045	1107
450	130	195	260	326	391	456	521	586	651	716	781	846	911	977	1042	1107	1172
475	137	206	275	344	412	481	550	618	687	756	825	893	962	1031	1100	1168	1237
500	145	217	289	362	434	506	579	651	723	796	868	940	1013	1085	1157	1230	1302
525	152	228	304	380	456	532	608	684	760	836	911	987	1063	1139	1215	1291	1367
550	159	239	318	398	477	557	637	716	796	875	955	1034	1114	1194	1273	1353	1432
575	166	250	333	416	499	582	666	749	832	915	998	1081	1165	1248	1331	1414	1497
600	174	260	347	434	521	608	694	781	868	955	1042	1128	1215	1302	1389	1476	1563
625	181	271	362	452	543	633	723	814	904	995	1085	1175	1266	1356	1447	1537	1628
650	188	282	376	470	564	658	752	846	940	1034	1128	1223	1317	1411	1505	1599	1693
675	195	293	391	488	586	684	781	879	977	1074	1172	1270	1367	1465	1563	1660	1758
700	203	304	405	506	608	709	810	911	1013	1114	1215	1317	1418	1519	1620	1722	1823